Praise for *Engines of Liberty*

ONE OF THE *WASHINGTON POST*'S NOTABLE NONFICTION BOOKS OF 2016

"[Cole's] narratives weave a compelling portrait of advocacy-driven constitutional change. . . . Readable, accessible and . . . even gripping. . . . [A] deeply hopeful book."
—*Washington Post*

"Transforms one's understanding of the contributions of other forums—state legislatures, for example, and public opinion (at home and abroad)—in campaigns that eventually culminate in Supreme Court decisions."
—*New York Review of Books*

"A fresh and revelatory account of constitutional reform from the bottom up. The book carries a hopeful message: Despite the undue influence wielded by elite institutions, ordinary citizens can and do drive constitutional change."
—*Nation*

"[An] illuminating piece of opinion journalism."
—*American Scholar*

"[A] riveting book."
—*Dorf on Law*

"Cole's book is compelling, especially in today's climate of gridlock following the death of Supreme Court justice Antonin Scalia."
—*Kirkus Reviews*

"In *Engines of Liberty*, David Cole turns constitutional law on its head. With his characteristic intelligence and clarity, Cole demonstrates that the law changes from the bottom up, not the top down, and that it is citizens, not judges, who are the ultimate custodians of our nation's laws."
—JEFFREY TOOBIN, author of *The Oath* and *The Nine*

ENGINES
OF LIBERTY

Also by David Cole

The Torture Memos: Rationalizing the Unthinkable

*Justice at War: The Men and Ideas that
Shaped America's War on Terror*

*Less Safe, Less Free: Why America
Is Losing the War on Terror*

*Enemy Aliens: Double Standards and
Constitutional Freedoms in the War on Terrorism*

*Terrorism and the Constitution: Sacrificing
Civil Liberties in the Name of National Security*

*No Equal Justice: Race and Class in
the American Justice System*

ENGINES
OF LIBERTY

How Citizen Movements Succeed

For Lisa—
Thanks for your
commitment to civil
liberties.

Dal Cole

DAVID COLE

BASIC
BOOKS
New York

Basic Books
Hachette Book Group
1290 Avenue of the Americas, New York, NY 10104
www.basicbooks.com

Printed in the United States of America

Originally published in hardcover and ebook by Basic Books in March 2016
First Trade Paperback Edition: October 2017
Published by Basic Books, an imprint of Perseus Books, LLC, a subsidiary of Hachette Book Group, Inc.

The Hachette Speakers Bureau provides a wide range of authors for speaking events. To find out more, go to www.hachettespeakersbureau.com or call (866) 376-6591.

The publisher is not responsible for websites (or their content) that are not owned by the publisher.

Parts of the revised introduction were adapted from an essay initially published in a different form in the *New York Review of Books*: David Cole, "The Way to Stop Trump," *NYR Daily*, November 14, 2016.

Print book interior design by Linda Mark

The Library of Congress has cataloged the hardcover edition as follows:
Names: Cole, David, 1958– author.
Title: Engines of liberty : the power of citizen activists to make constitutional law / David Cole.
Description: New York : Basic Books, 2016. | Includes bibliographical references and index.
Identifiers: LCCN 2015036456| ISBN 9780465060900 (hardback) | ISBN 9780465098514 (ebook)
Subjects: LCSH: Law reform—United States—Citizen participation. | Justice, Administration of—United States—Citizen participation. | Constitutional law—United States. | Law reform—United States. | Political participation—United States. | BISAC: POLITICAL SCIENCE / Constitutions.
Classification: LCC KF384 .C65 2016 | DDC 342.73—dc23
LC record available at http://lccn.loc.gov/2015036456

ISBNs: 978-1-5416-1657-8 (paperback), 978-0-465-06090-0 (hardcover), 978-0-465-09851-4 (ebook)

LSC-C

10 9 8 7 6 5 4 3 2

*For Michael Ratner, who taught me
that the struggle for justice is always worthwhile,
even and especially where it appears most hopeless, and
that occasionally, justice prevails over hopelessness*

Contents

*Liberty lies in the hearts of men and women; when it
dies there, no constitution, no law, no court can save it;
no constitution, no law, no court can even do much to
help it. While it lies there it needs no constitution,
no law, no court to save it.*

—JUDGE LEARNED HAND

*Never underestimate the power of a small group
of committed people to change the world.
In fact, it is the only thing that ever has.*

—MARGARET MEAD

Introduction

NOTHING HAS UNDERSCORED THE IMPORTANCE OF CIVIL RIGHTS AND CIVIL LIBERTIES LIKE the election of Donald J. Trump. Trump shows little appreciation of, or respect for, constitutional rights. As a candidate, he threatened to "open up" libel laws, make abortion a crime, jail his opponent, ban Muslims from entering the country, and revive waterboarding of terror suspects and dragnet surveillance of Americans. As a president-elect, he said that citizens who burn the American flag should be jailed and stripped of their citizenship—apparently without any understanding that the Supreme Court had decades earlier declared flag burning a form of constitutionally protected political expression, and forbade the stripping of citizenship as punishment even for the most heinous crimes. And in just his first weeks in office, he issued an executive order that barred entry of immigrants from seven predominantly Muslim countries while containing an exception for "minority" faiths that he explained was designed to favor Christian over Muslim refugees—a textbook violation of the Establishment Clause. He dismissed the mainstream media as "the enemy of the people" and excluded from a press briefing representatives of media outlets that criticized him. He appointed as his attorney general Jeff Sessions, perhaps the most

1

conservative member of the Senate, who had long shown either blindness or outright hostility toward many of the rights he is now charged
with defending—including voting rights, women's rights, and LGBT
rights. Among Sessions's first acts were the rescinding of a guidance
letter forbidding schools from discriminating against transgender students, and the abandonment of a race discrimination challenge to a
Texas voting law.

The threat posed by President Trump is exacerbated by his party's control of so many levers of power. The Republicans have a solid
majority in the Senate and the House, and a majority of Republican-
appointed Supreme Court justices. Republicans hold the reins of
power in two-thirds of the state legislatures, too. So when I tell people I am the national legal director of the American Civil Liberties
Union (ACLU), and that I am confident that we can stop Trump's
abuses of civil liberties, many skeptically ask me how it can be done.
The answer, I reply, lies with all of us.

Whether Trump will succeed is as much in our hands as in his. If
Americans let him, Trump may well do all that he has promised—and
more. But if Americans now and in the coming years insist that Trump
honor our most fundamental values, including equality, human dignity, fair process, privacy, and the rule of law, and if we organize and
advocate in defense of those principles, he will be contained. It won't
happen overnight. There will be many protracted struggles. But if we
fight, we can prevail.

IF YOU THINK THIS is overly naive, consider the fate of George W. Bush's
"war on terror." In the immediate aftermath of the terrorist attacks of
September 11, 2001, Bush acted as if he were entirely unconstrained.
He had reason to think that he could get away with it. His popularity
soared to its highest level; he enjoyed approval ratings as high as 90
percent in the aftermath of the attacks. The Supreme Court had just
voted to put him in office in *Bush v. Gore*. And from the 2002 midterms
to 2007, he had a Republican majority in both Houses of Congress.

History was also on Bush's side; neither Congress, the Supreme Court, nor the American people had ever put up much if any resistance to a president in dealing with the "enemy" in a time of war. Presidents had jailed hundreds for merely speaking out against the war in World War I, and had interned 110,000 people on the basis of their Japanese ancestry during World War II. "Checks and balances" did nothing to stop those efforts. Presumably assuming he would have a similarly free hand, Bush authorized disappearances of terror suspects into secret CIA prisons, torture as an interrogation tactic, indefinite detention at Guantánamo without hearing or judicial review, "extraordinary rendition" of suspects to other countries so that they could torture them for us, and warrantless electronic surveillance of Americans. He insisted that he could ignore federal criminal statutes, that the Geneva Conventions did not apply to Al Qaeda detainees, and that Guantánamo was beyond the law.

At first, Bush did indeed get away with such tactics. But much to his dismay, Americans did not sit back and accept that the executive was above the law. As described in detail in Part Three of this book, they protested, recruited unlikely allies, filed lawsuits, wrote human rights reports, lobbied foreign audiences and governments to bring pressure to bear on the United States, leaked documents that revealed illegal programs, and broadly condemned the administration's actions as violations of constitutional and human rights. Human Rights First organized retired generals and admirals; the Center for Constitutional Rights (CCR) and Reprieve, aided by an army of pro bono lawyers and a robust investigative media, brought the plight of Guantánamo detainees to the world's attention; the Bill of Rights Defense Committee sparked a grassroots effort to adopt local referenda condemning the Patriot Act and other civil liberties abuses; and the ACLU used the Freedom of Information Act to dislodge thousands of documents detailing the CIA's torture program, which it and the PEN American Center then disseminated in accessible form.[1] The academy, the press, and the international community all joined in the condemnation of Bush's excesses.

As a result, the course of history changed. By the time Bush left office in 2009, he had released more than five hundred of the detainees from Guantánamo, emptied out the CIA's secret prisons, halted the CIA torture program, ended extraordinary renditions, and placed the NSA's surveillance program under judicial supervision. His claims of uncheckable executive power had been rejected, and his Defense Department had announced that the Geneva Conventions applied to all "enemy combatants."

Bush did not introduce these reforms because he came to realize the error of his ways. His memoir, like that of his vice president, Dick Cheney, is entirely unrepentant. But Bush was nonetheless checked— by American civil society, international criticism, and, for the first time in history during wartime, the Court and Congress. The Supreme Court established that any detainee held at Guantánamo has a right to judicial review (*Boumediene v. Bush*), that the Geneva Conventions apply to Al Qaeda detainees (*Hamdan v. Rumsfeld*), and that the president cannot hold US citizens as enemy combatants without affording them a meaningful opportunity to defend themselves (*Hamdi v. Rumsfeld*). In 2005, Congress, under Republican senator John McCain's leadership, and over the administration's strenuous objections, adopted the Detainee Treatment Act, a bipartisan prohibition on the use of cruel, inhuman, and degrading tactics against anyone in US custody—a measure designed to conclusively bar waterboarding and the other patently cruel interrogation tactics the CIA had been deploying.

If Bush could be stopped—despite widespread popular support, a large-scale attack on American soil leading to a war footing, and a history of judicial and congressional acquiescence in prior periods—Trump is also stoppable. Whereas Bush began, shortly after 9/11, with 90 percent approval ratings, Trump came to office having lost the popular vote, and with the lowest approval ratings of any president-elect in history. Taking office did not alter that reality, as he again set the record for the lowest approval ratings of any president in his first months in office. His initial effort to repeal and replace "Obamacare" failed despite a White House ultimatum. His travel bans were enjoined by the courts. He was under investigation for obstruction of justice. He may still succeed in implementing a number of his most damaging and threatening policies, at least initially, and his popularity may rise. But as the fate of the Bush administration's counterterror measures illustrates, even when the president seems most invincible, he can be checked. Doing so will take a persistent civil society, a vigilant media, brave insiders, and judges and other government officials who take seriously their responsibility to uphold the Constitution. But first and foremost, it will take an engaged citizenry.

THE CONSTITUTION WAS MADE to rein in people like Donald Trump. We live in a constitutional democracy, one that is expressly designed to check the impulses of dangerous leaders. But it will do that work if, and only if, we insist on it. The principal lesson of this book is that the ultimate protection of liberty is not the independent judiciary, the separation of powers, or federalism. It is the citizenry. As Learned Hand, a highly regarded federal appeals judge, told a large crowd of newly naturalized citizens in New York's Central Park in 1944, "Liberty lies in the hearts of men and women; when it dies there, no constitution, no law, no court can save it; no constitution, no law, no court can even do much to help it. While it lies there it needs no constitution, no law, no court to save it."[2]

Like many great quotes, Judge Hand's remark simultaneously captures an important truth and overstates the case. The liberty that "lies in the hearts of men and women" is indeed essential to a robust constitutional order, but the Court, Congress, and the Constitution play a more important part than Hand admitted. The Constitution embodies our most profound collective commitments, the laws are written in the shadow of constitutional limits, and judicial review both enforces the Constitution's commands and sparks further debate. But Hand is correct that if the people lose faith in constitutional liberties, the formal safeguards of law are unlikely to withstand popular or political pressures. In that sense, the fate of liberty under President Trump rests ultimately with us.

There are many reasons to be hopeful that citizens will not let liberty die. The fact that millions came out for the women's march the day after Trump's inauguration was only the first sign of a remarkably vibrant countermobilization. That march launched one hundred days of action, in which citizens came together in "huddles" in their homes to organize and inspire further collective responses to Trump's abuses as they arose. A group of former congressional staffers wrote an online guide to political resistance, "Indivisible," which was downloaded more than one million times in its first few months. The ACLU warned Trump that it would see him in court if he made good on his campaign promises, and hundreds of thousands of citizens were inspired to join and support the organization. The ACLU's membership, which stood at about 425,000 before Trump's election, soared to 1.6 million within three months of Trump taking office. The organization was flooded with offers to volunteer, and launched a new campaign to mobilize citizens in defense of liberty.

The reaction to Trump's executive order banning immigration from seven Muslim-majority countries illustrates both the extent of activism that Trump has aroused and the effectiveness of that engagement. The executive order was in some sense a tried-and-true tactic: it targeted foreigners, not citizens, and did so in the name of safeguarding national security. Such measures rarely spark much concern from citizens, as their rights are not directly imperiled. Yet this time was different. The first full day that the order was in effect, tens of thousands of Americans went out to airports across the country to protest the order and offer aid to those caught in its snares. Within hours of the order's issuance, the ACLU, with partners the National Immigration Law Center and a Yale Law School clinic, had filed the first court action against the order. General Michael Hayden, the head of the CIA and the NSA under George W. Bush, tweeted, "Imagine that. ACLU and I in the same corner." Dick Cheney and even John Yoo, who as a Bush administration lawyer wrote the memo approving the CIA's torture program, condemned the order, as did the presidents of America's leading universities, virtually all of Silicon Valley, and the nation's premier science organizations. Newspaper editorials condemned it. Several state attorneys general filed or joined suits challenging the order on behalf of their constituents. The acting attorney general for the United States, Sally

Yates, directed the Justice Department not to defend the law; Trump fired her for doing so.[3]

Buoyed by this unprecedented criticism, courts enjoined the Trump administration from enforcing the order—first in partial ways, but ultimately in a nationwide order issued by a district court judge in the state of Washington, an appointee of George W. Bush. Trump condemned the judge as a "so-called judge" and appealed, but his appeal was unanimously rejected by the US Court of Appeals for the Ninth Circuit, and Trump went back to the drawing board. A new order, issued in early March 2016, retained the anti-Muslim stance of the first order and prompted a fresh round of legal challenges, popular condemnations, and protests in the streets. Two district courts and two courts of appeals again enjoined the order.

This book argues that there is a direct link between the kind of public advocacy that greeted Trump's anti-Muslim executive orders and the reactions of the formal branches of government, including the courts. I wrote the book before Trump won the presidency, but its lessons have never been more urgent. Read in light of the current threat that President Trump poses to our core constitutional values, it offers both a prescription for action and a reason for hope. Indeed, Trump's election may mark a turning point in constitutional and democratic politics—but only if people continue to engage at the level that began on November 9, 2016, and has been building ever since.

How is constitutional liberty defended, and how does it evolve? These are crucial questions at any time, but never more so than today. Through three accounts of recent successful constitutional rights campaigns, this book shows that the defense of constitutional liberty is more democratic than we often admit, that ordinary citizens play a significant part, and that the forums for struggle extend far beyond the four walls of the United States Supreme Court. The stories recounted here show that if constitutional law were a sentence, the Supreme Court's decision would be the period at the end of the sentence—maybe sometimes an exclamation point—but the words of the sentence would reflect the work of citizens engaged in advocacy outside the Supreme Court altogether. And if that is true, it is more critical than ever that we all take on the responsibility of defending liberty in the forums accessible to us. It is in citizen engagement that our liberty lies.

To illustrate the point, *Engines of Liberty* considers the examples of Evan Wolfson, Marion Hammer, and Michael Ratner. Each had a major impact on constitutional law. And each did so only through the united acts of many fellow citizens.

When Evan Wolfson was a young student at Harvard Law School in the 1980s, there were no courses on sexual orientation and the law. It wasn't until two lawyers from the then-fledgling Lambda Legal Defense Fund, a gay rights public interest law firm, came to speak at the law school that it even dawned on Wolfson that one might devote a legal career to "gay rights." In his last year at Harvard, he decided to write an independent research paper exploring a gay rights issue. Harvard's constitutional law professors at the time viewed his proposed topic—whether the Constitution guarantees same-sex couples the right to marry—as so far-fetched that he could not find a supervisor. He finally persuaded a professor of trusts and estates, David Westfall, to take him on, even though constitutional law was not his field. Wolfson wrote a 141-page manifesto arguing that same-sex marriage should be constitutionally guaranteed. At the time, a handful of brave gay and lesbian couples across the nation had filed quixotic lawsuits claiming the right to marry, but all the suits had been dismissed, in some instances with outright derision. When the Minnesota Supreme Court heard one such case in 1970, for example, none of the justices asked the lawyer representing the gay couple a single question, and one justice is said to have turned his back on this unfortunate lawyer for the entire oral argument. The court cited the book of Genesis, an unusual source of constitutional law, in its decision unanimously rejecting the claim. When the couple sought review in the United States Supreme Court, the highest court in the land responded with a one-sentence dismissal of their appeal as presenting no serious legal question.[4]

Yet on June 26, 2015, the Supreme Court declared that same-sex couples have a constitutional right to marry. After the decision was announced, Evan Wolfson, who had gone on to become one of the country's leading advocates for marriage equality and had founded a major nonprofit advocacy group, Freedom to Marry, announced that the organization, having achieved its goal, would begin shutting down. The next day, he published an op-ed in the *New York Times* celebrating the victory, but at the same time insisting that "now we must get back to work." His new priority: "securing protections from discrimination for gay, lesbian, bisexual and transgender Americans."[5]

Marion Hammer's story is more likely to appeal to Trump's supporters than to his opponents, but we all would do well to examine and learn from it. As a little girl raised on a Florida farm in the 1940s and 1950s, Hammer was introduced to guns by her grandfather, who took her rabbit hunting. She loved shooting, but did not become politically active until 1968, when Congress passed the Gun Control Act in response to the assassinations of John F. Kennedy, Martin Luther King Jr., and Robert Kennedy. Hammer believed that she had a right to bear arms and that the new federal law was a first step toward the end of that right. She decided to fight back. Starting as a volunteer for United Sportsmen of Florida, she ultimately became the first female president of the National Rifle Association (NRA). Today, she is one of Florida's most effective lobbyists, and Florida is, largely because of her efforts, a bellwether state for protective gun rights laws. She has successfully pressed for state legislation to ensure that gun owners can not only keep weapons in their home but carry them on their person, and, through the controversial "Stand Your Ground" law, be assured of their right to use their guns in self-defense.[6]

In Hammer's view, and in the view of the NRA, the Second Amendment protects an individual right to bear arms. For most of her life, however, that was not the law. In 1939, the Supreme Court upheld a federal law banning interstate transportation of sawed-off shotguns and machine guns and suggested that the Second Amendment protected only the authority of states to raise militias, not the right of private individuals to bear arms. In 1990, then-retired Chief Justice Warren

Burger, a conservative Republican, dismissed the idea that the Second Amendment protects an individual right to bear arms as "one of the greatest pieces of fraud—I repeat the word 'fraud'—on the American public by special interest groups that I have ever seen in my lifetime." In 1996, conservative judge and scholar Robert Bork similarly contended that the Second Amendment protected only state rights, not individual rights. But in 2008, in *District of Columbia v. Heller*, the Supreme Court officially endorsed the right that Hammer and the NRA had been advocating for almost forty years, and ruled that the Second Amendment protects an individual's right to bear arms.[7]

Then there is Michael Ratner. In early 2002, when the then fifty-eight-year-old lawyer—who was with the New York–based Center for Constitutional Rights (CCR)—learned that President George W. Bush was holding prisoners in the "war on terror" at Guantánamo Bay Naval Base without hearings or access to attorneys, he resolved almost immediately to sue. Did he think he had any chance of success? "None whatsoever," he told me years later. So why did he do it? "We filed one hundred percent on principle." In Ratner's view, it was unconstitutional to lock up a human being without charges or any access to a court. As he put it, "Wasn't that what the Magna Carta was all about?" He hoped the lawsuit would bring attention to what he considered a grave human rights violation. But he had no illusions about the odds, either legally or politically. Fifty years earlier, the Supreme Court had ruled, in *Johnson v. Eisentrager*, that foreign prisoners of war held in Germany had no right to seek review in US courts. That decision, written by the widely respected Justice Robert Jackson, who himself had been a lead prosecutor in war crimes trials against Nazi leaders at Nuremberg, had never been overturned. So the law seemed dead set against Ratner. And as a political matter, why would Americans be concerned about the detention of foreign enemies their government told them were "the worst of the worst"? Guantánamo didn't threaten Americans' liberties. But Ratner, together with capital punishment defense attorney Joe Margulies and CCR, went ahead and sued anyway.[8]

They lost unanimously in the lower courts. But two years later, to the surprise of almost everyone, the Supreme Court agreed to hear the case and then ruled that Guantánamo prisoners had a right to sue the president in federal court. By the time he left office, President George Bush agreed, as did his secretaries of defense and state, that the prison at Guantánamo should be closed. The Bush administration released over five hundred of the people kept there. President Barack Obama took office promising to close the facility within a year. He confronted numerous obstacles, and did not succeed, but by the time he had left office, he had reduced the population at Guantánamo to forty-one detainees.[9]

WOLFSON, HAMMER, AND RATNER would have disagreed about many things. But they shared a deep-seated commitment to their respective constitutional visions and a willingness to work for many years to realize them. They shared a method, too. Each worked with civil society organizations that seek to preserve and protect particular fundamental values, through multiple forms of advocacy within and outside the courts. Wolfson was an attorney at Lambda Legal Defense Fund for many years, heading its Marriage Equality project, before branching off to start Freedom to Marry in 2002. Hammer worked with the NRA, probably the most effective individual rights organization in the country today. And Ratner's legal career was spent with CCR, a civil rights organization founded in the 1960s, where he litigated a wide range of seemingly impossible constitutional issues, many challenging US foreign policy. In turn, the work of each of these groups was supported by many others.

Freedom to Marry, the NRA, and CCR are examples of a particular kind of nonprofit group: one defined by and dedicated to constitutional values. There are many such groups in the United States, across the political spectrum. They include organizations dedicated to protecting the rights of the press, religious freedom, privacy, property, the freedom of contract, criminal defendants' rights, immigrants' rights, equality, the right to life of the unborn, and rights of sexual freedom and intimacy, among many others. The United States boasts a robust civil society, and the segment devoted to constitutional rights is particularly strong, almost certainly stronger than anywhere else in the world. Yet current accounts of constitutional law too often neglect the critical function of such groups in our constitutional order.[10]

The reality is that the formal mechanisms of constitutional law—the separation of powers, a Bill of Rights, federalism, and judicial review—are not enough to sustain liberty. Citizen engagement on the side of liberty is essential to the defense, and the evolution, of the nation's fundamental values. Absent a constitutional amendment, only the courts can actually change constitutional doctrine. Groups committed to the protection of constitutional rights must therefore ultimately turn to the federal courts, as did the groups in each of the three stories recounted in this book. But in each instance, the vast majority of the work necessary to transform constitutional law took place outside the federal courts altogether.[11]

There is a simple reason for this. When existing federal law does not reflect your views, you cannot simply file a lawsuit to change it; the most likely result will be a prompt dismissal. Instead, you must look for other, more sympathetic forums—which, in the stories recounted here, include state legislatures, state courts, the media, the academy, the public at large, Congress, the executive branch, and even foreign and international opinion. When groups represented by Wolfson, Hammer, and Ratner did succeed in federal court, it was generally because they had helped to change public opinion and the views of legal experts through work outside the federal courts. And often these groups won constitutional victories without any formal judicial intervention at all.

To focus on federal judges and courtroom lawyers is therefore to miss much of the story—and probably the most important part. Look behind any significant judicial development of constitutional law and you will nearly always find sustained advocacy by multiple groups of citizens, usually over many years and in a wide array of venues. Whether it is the NAACP Legal Defense Fund and civil rights, the ACLU Women's Rights Project and gender equality, or the NRA and the right to bear arms, behind almost every important constitutional transformation in the modern era have stood groups of politically engaged citizens united by their devotion to a particular constitutional vision.[12]

Lawyers sometimes speak of the "living Constitution" to underscore that constitutional law is not static, but evolving. But as this book shows, the Constitution is "living" in another sense, too. It "lives" in each of us—and especially in the groups we form to safeguard and advance foundational values. These groups are, in an important sense, living embodiments of our most basic commitments. They carry the torch of constitutionalism, and it is their work that ultimately shapes the directions in which the living Constitution—in the first sense—grows.[13]

As the political diversity of the groups featured here illustrates, citizens' associations do not necessarily lead constitutional law in a more liberal direction. As the NAACP Legal Defense Fund, gay rights groups, and the ACLU have successfully pressed for liberal understandings of constitutional ideals, so right-to-life groups, the Institute for Justice, the NRA, and the Chamber of Commerce have advanced conservative understandings. My purpose here is not to opine on the validity of particular constitutional claims, but rather to examine a more fundamental matter: how citizen movements succeed.

"What can I do?" This is the most frequent question I've received from citizens in the wake of Donald Trump's election. This book provides answers, gleaned from the history of three successful campaigns for constitutional liberty, in the hope that readers will be inspired to adapt those lessons to their own purposes. The lessons are summarized in the Conclusion. The first and broadest should already be clear: the defense of liberty depends as much or more on citizens engaging collectively to fight for the values they believe in than it does on the courts and the lawyers who appear before them. The preservation of liberty through a written constitution was a major innovation in modern democracy. But it has survived more than two centuries not because the job was assigned to courts, but because "we the people" have consistently taken up the charge to define, defend, and develop liberty in our own image, so that it reflects *our* deepest commitments, not just those of a privileged elite who do not represent us.

In the age of Donald Trump, the necessity for engagement is greater than ever. Fortunately, the appetite for activism also appears to be greater than ever. These phenomena are not unrelated. As one former NRA president told me when I asked him why NRA members were so reliably responsive to the organization's requests for political action, "You've got to have the threat." For NRA members, he explained, the threat that inspires them to act is that the government will confiscate their weapons. For those who believe in a country that respects liberty, dignity, and equality for all human beings, Donald Trump is the ultimate threat. He has sparked citizen engagement like no president in living memory, and that activism has the potential not just to check President Trump's efforts to violate our civil rights and liberties but also to strengthen liberty's safeguards.

The activism necessary to preserve liberty is not a one-march or one-day or one-week enterprise. It requires commitment over the long haul. It also requires organization and coordination. That's why the right of association is so critical to preserving all our constitutional freedoms. Associations of citizens dedicated to constitutional ideals help ensure that "liberty lies in the hearts of men and women." They alone can do the sustained work necessary to defend and change constitutional law. If the "spirit of liberty" lies in the people's hearts, it is these civil society groups that nourish it, fuel it, and ensure that liberty's fires remain lit.

PART ONE

MARRIAGE EQUALITY

THE PATH TO MARRIAGE EQUALITY DID NOT BEGIN, OF COURSE, WITH EVAN WOLFSON'S Harvard Law School paper. The very fact that Wolfson could conceive of such a paper was itself testament to the efforts of countless gay and lesbian advocates before him, operating in far more difficult circumstances.

A good place to start in assessing the prehistory of the marriage equality movement is the Mattachine Society, one of the first gay organizations in the United States. Founded in Los Angeles in 1950, the Mattachine Society ultimately included chapters around the country, and in the 1950s and 1960s was the nation's leading gay organization. It took its name from masked critics of ruling monarchs in medieval France. At its inception, the very idea of a gay organization was so radical that the group met only in secret.[1]

The Mattachine Society's most illustrious member was Frank Kameny, a Harvard-educated astronomer who was fired by the US Army Map Office in 1957 when an FBI investigation revealed that he was gay. Kameny appealed his firing all the way to the Supreme

Court, without success. But the experience prompted him to become one of the nation's first openly gay activists. He founded the Washington, DC, chapter of the Mattachine Society in 1960, and also launched a systematic attack on the federal government's discrimination against gay and lesbian employees. Notwithstanding his lack of legal training, Kameny operated as a "lawyer without portfolio," assisting hundreds of employees in administrative appeals of their dismissals and shepherding their cases through the courts. With the support of the ACLU, he won his first victory in 1965, when the US Court of Appeals for the DC Circuit reversed the Civil Service Commission's disqualification of Bruce Scott from the civil service on grounds of "immoral conduct." In 1975, after many more battles with Kameny, the Civil Service Commission reversed its policy of categorically disqualifying gay and lesbian applicants. Kameny also took on the Defense Department for denying security clearances to gays and lesbians, and in 1975 it, too, abandoned that practice.[2]

The first challenge Kameny and the Mattachine Society faced was simply to be free to associate as gay men. Sodomy statutes made intimate relations between same-sex couples a crime. Psychiatrists considered homosexuality a mental illness. Admitting publicly that one was gay or lesbian could result in ridicule, harassment, assault, isolation from one's family, the loss of a job, or worse. Most gays and lesbians understandably chose to keep their sexual orientation hidden.

The invisibility of the "closet" made mobilizing for lesbian and gay rights all but impossible. Thus, the first strategic step toward achieving equality was, as gay rights scholar and advocate Bill Eskridge has called it, a "politics of protection." The aim was to create space for gays and lesbians to come together without fear of official harassment. Gay and lesbian community centers, bars, and bathhouses all served this function. The Stonewall riots of 1969, in which gay patrons at a Greenwich Village bar turned on police and collectively asserted their right to be out, gay, and together in a public place, were the most dramatic and historic manifestation of this initial phase.[3]

The next step was to make it safe—or at least, less costly—to "come out" by publicly identifying oneself as lesbian or gay. Gay rights groups fought for legal protections that would make it more likely that gay men and lesbians might feel sufficiently comfortable to identify themselves publicly. The ACLU Lesbian and Gay Rights Project, for example, invoked the First Amendment to protect the rights of students to form gay and lesbian student associations, first in colleges and later in high schools. And gay rights advocates argued for expanding anti-discrimination laws to prohibit discrimination on the basis of sexual orientation in employment, housing, and other fields.[4]

In the 1980s, the AIDS crisis transformed the gay community. Many men were in effect outed by the disease itself as it afflicted them or their lovers. The life-or-death necessity for research and treatment spawned the creation of new advocacy organizations, such as Gay Men's Health Crisis and ACT UP, as gay men and lesbians increasingly recognized the pressing need for nondiscriminatory health services, and came to understand that only through political organizing could they convince the government to invest sufficient resources in developing effective treatments. In a tragic but real sense, gay rights came out and of age during the AIDS crisis, as growing numbers of gays and lesbians proclaimed their sexual orientation publicly, joined political associations, and engaged in collective action to demand equal care and respect.[5]

The AIDS crisis also set the stage for the fight for marriage equality. It urgently revealed the many problems that gay couples confronted when the states did not recognize their relationships. Gay employees whose partners were sick and dying could not get health insurance for them through their work. Gay men were denied visitation with their partners at hospitals because they had no officially sanctioned relationship with the patient. They often were not authorized to make end-of-life decisions for their partners. They faced difficulties dealing with funerals, estates, and the like, again because their relationships, even if longstanding, lacked formal status. The importance of "relationship recognition" became painfully evident, and the press ran many stories about the obstacles gay men faced as they navigated the ends of their partners' lives.[6]

When advocates began to address the myriad problems gay couples faced in dealing with AIDS, they did not at first demand marriage, still an unthinkable option. Instead, they requested lesser forms of domestic partnership recognition and benefits. They began by approaching sympathetic private corporations, universities, and cities. Over time the concept of same-sex domestic partnerships took hold in a wide range of private and public settings. The same pattern is evident with respect to legal protection from discrimination.[7]

These developments, vitally important on their own terms, also contributed to making a marriage equality campaign possible. The care and support offered, and devastating losses suffered, by surviving partners became familiar to many straight Americans. As discrimination on the basis of sexual orientation was more widely prohibited, gay men and lesbians were more free to come out. It became increasingly common for straight people to learn that a family member, friend, colleague, or acquaintance was gay or lesbian—and deeply human and vulnerable. That knowledge in turn made it less likely that straight people would demonize, and more likely that they would empathize with, gay men and lesbians.

Some of the most important early gay rights advocacy focused not on legal and political change but on cultural transformation. In the midst of the AIDS crisis, gay activists founded Gay and Lesbian Alliance Against Defamation, now known simply as GLAAD. Their mission was to promote accurate and positive portrayals of gay men and lesbians in the news and entertainment media. Among other accomplishments, GLAAD helped persuade CBS's *60 Minutes* to suspend commentator Andy Rooney for three months without pay when he made homophobic remarks on air. It blocked a planned television show to be hosted by Dr. Laura Schlesinger, a radio talk show host who had described homosexuality as a "biological mistake." GLAAD also encouraged comedian Ellen DeGeneres to have the character she played on her television show, *Ellen*, come out as lesbian, and helped to convince the news media to shift their terminology from "homosexual" to "gay and lesbian," and from "sexual preference" to "sexual orientation."[8]

There is no precise way to measure the effects of these wide-ranging efforts. But nearly all of the advocates, lawyers, and activists with whom I spoke agreed that each of the developments summarized here provided an important foundation for the marriage equality campaign. They helped make it possible for Evan Wolfson to write his law school paper, and for the many initiatives that would be necessary, inside and outside of courts, before the right to marriage equality that Wolfson envisioned could be realized.

1

The Vision

As THE NATION AWAITED THE SUPREME COURT'S LANDMARK DECISION IN *OBERGEFELL v. Hodges* in the summer of 2015, it seemed virtually inevitable that the Court would rule in favor of marriage equality. The majority of Americans favored recognition of same-sex marriage. Two years earlier, the Supreme Court had struck down a law denying federal benefits to married gay and lesbian couples. And in the interim, the overwhelming majority of lower federal courts had ruled that the Constitution required states to recognize same-sex marriage on equal terms with opposite-sex marriage.

But it was not always so. Some thirty years earlier, when Evan Wolfson was still in law school, a few isolated same-sex couples had already sued, asserting a right to marry, but their suits had been uniformly rejected. Same-sex sodomy was still a crime in many states. In its 1986 *Bowers v. Hardwick* decision, the Supreme Court ruled it constitutionally permissible for states to make gay sodomy a crime. If states could make it a crime for a same-sex couple to have sex, surely such couples could not claim a constitutional right to marry.[1]

Wolfson's career is emblematic of the path of the marriage equality campaign more generally. His student paper, "Samesex Marriage and Morality: The Human Rights Vision of the Constitution," was academic in both senses of the word: it was scholarly and thought provoking but seemingly insulated from the real world. Wolfson drew on philosophy, liberal political theory, and constitutional and human rights principles to argue that the Constitution should protect the right of same-sex couples to marry. The paper anticipated many of the arguments that the courts would confront when, more than a decade later, they first began to take seriously the claim for marriage equality. Wolfson rejected, for example, the extension of "quasi-marital status" or other sorts of partnership benefits as at best "separate but equal," just as the Massachusetts and California Supreme Courts did more than two decades later when they each found that domestic partnerships and civil unions were insufficient to satisfy the mandate of equality. Discussing a 1976 Supreme Court decision that declined to invalidate Virginia's sodomy law, Wolfson wrote that the dissenters, Justices William Brennan, Thurgood Marshall, and John Paul Stevens, "hit the critical constitutional points: free choice, intimate values, absence of harm, no legitimate state interest in regulation, and, finally, the inadmissibility of government promotion of 'morality.'" These would eventually become the "critical constitutional points" in the marriage debate as well.[2]

Wolfson's paper also articulated what would become the most important principle in the constitutional recognition of gay rights generally: namely, that "majority distaste or discomfort is no basis for the abridgment of protected human rights." Many laws discriminating against gay men and lesbians have been founded on such moral disapproval, so rejection of that interest as an insufficient justification for differential treatment was a critical step. In 1987, dissenting in *Bowers v. Hardwick*, Justice Stevens made the same point: "the fact that the governing majority in a State has traditionally viewed a particular practice as immoral is not a sufficient reason for upholding a law prohibiting the practice." In 2003, in *Lawrence v. Texas*, the Supreme Court reversed *Bowers*, and Justice Anthony Kennedy, writing for the majority, quoted Stevens's words with approval, making his dissent part of governing constitutional doctrine. That conclusion precluded states from successfully relying on moral opprobrium to justify their refusals to recognize same-sex marriage; and without moral disapproval, the states had great difficulty articulating a reason to deny same-sex couples the right to marry.[3]

Wolfson was not the first to make these arguments; many of them had been advanced in one form or other in the various unsuccessful lawsuits seeking recognition of same-sex marriage. What is most notable, in retrospect, is his paper's nearly exclusive focus on formal legal arguments. The paper contained no discussion of what it might take politically, strategically, or culturally to advance this cause, an ironic absence given Wolfson's eventual role as one of the marriage equality campaign's lead strategists and organizers. As a law student, Wolfson saw constitutional law, as it had no doubt been taught to him, as a series of theoretical and normative propositions. As an activist lawyer, however, Wolfson soon learned that constitutional change required much more than a well-footnoted argument.

WOLFSON'S FIRST LEGAL JOB was as a prosecutor for the Manhattan district attorney's office, but his heart wasn't in it. The first openly gay prosecutor in the office, Wolfson obtained approval—extremely unusual for a prosecutor—to do volunteer work in his free time on gay rights cases. He worked in this capacity for Lambda Legal Defense Fund, the organization that had first made him realize that one could be a gay rights lawyer. In 1989, Lambda hired Wolfson as a full-time staff lawyer.

From his earliest days at Lambda, Wolfson urged the organization to press for equal marriage rights for same-sex couples. As he recalled, "my push on marriage defined me in the eyes of my colleagues, for better or worse." His colleagues, like the rest of the gay rights movement, were sharply divided on the issue. A minority agreed that marriage equality was a worthwhile focus of their work. Many had seen the absence of marital status unnecessarily complicate the already tragic efforts of gay men to care for their partners dying of AIDS. And some agreed with Wolfson that the denial of marriage to same-sex couples was central to anti-gay discrimination because it reflected a rejection of the legitimacy of their love.

The majority of those in the gay rights movement, however, were opposed to fighting for marriage. When the National Gay and Lesbian Task Force polled its members in 1991 on the leading gay rights issues of the day, for example, it did not even list marriage as an option. Some opposed seeking marriage on ideological grounds. Many viewed it as an assimilationist project and preferred to forge and defend a distinct lesbian and gay identity and culture. They saw marriage as a fundamentally compromised institution, fraught with gender stereotypes, central both to women's subordinate status and to the treatment of heterosexuality as compulsory. The divide often tracked gender lines, with lesbians more skeptical of marriage than gay men because of marriage's role in patriarchal culture.[4]

Still other gay rights activists objected to pressing for marriage on strategic grounds. They believed the time wasn't right, and gay rights groups would be better served prioritizing efforts to combat other forms of discrimination, police harassment, anti-gay violence, and sodomy prohibitions. Because it might provoke particularly intense opposition, some felt that seeking marriage could jeopardize efforts for equality in other areas. According to Wolfson, marriage was "the number one question that we fought about within the gay rights community." In 1989, Lambda's legal director, Tom Stoddard, and its lead lawyer, Paula Ettelbrick, took opposite sides in a much-publicized debate on same-sex marriage. Stoddard defended the struggle for marriage, while Ettelbrick expressed strong reservations. As Ettelbrick argued, "Justice for gay men and lesbians will be achieved only when we are accepted and supported in this society *despite* our differences from the dominant culture and the choices we make regarding our relationships. . . . I do not want to be known as 'Mrs. Attached-to-Somebody-Else,' Nor do I want to give the state the power to regulate my primary relationship."[5]

Despite siding with Wolfson on the desirability of seeking same-sex marriage, Stoddard quashed Wolfson's first attempt to bring a lawsuit for marriage equality. The opportunity arose in 1991, two years after Wolfson began full-time at Lambda. Three couples in Hawaii asked

Wolfson to represent them in a state court challenge to Hawaii's refusal to recognize same-sex marriage. Wolfson was eager to take up the fight and thought Hawaii a favorable place to do so. It was a liberal state, and had been an early proponent of both interracial marriage and women's rights. But Stoddard declined Wolfson's request to take the case, deeming it premature as a strategic matter. The ACLU also turned the case down, for the same reason. Indeed, at that time, according to Stoddard, "no gay rights organization of any size, local or national, [had] yet declared the right to marry as one of its goals." Undeterred, the Hawaiian couples turned to a local civil rights attorney, Dan Foley. Perhaps reflecting his own internal ambivalence, Stoddard allowed Wolfson to work on the case as long as he remained behind the scenes, and Wolfson consulted closely with Foley as the case proceeded.[6]

Foley's complaint was limited to claims that the refusal to recognize same-sex marriage violated Hawaii's constitution. He did not assert that Hawaii's practice violated the US Constitution, even though, as Wolfson had shown in his Harvard paper, one could certainly fashion such an argument. Lawyers generally do not forgo arguments that might support their cause; in fact, they are taught to take the opposite tack, advancing every alternative argument they can think of, even ones that are barely plausible. Foley (and Wolfson behind the scenes) resisted making federal constitutional arguments for a very particular reason: to keep their case out of federal court and therefore away from the US Supreme Court. The federal courts and the Supreme Court have the power to review federal legal issues decided by state courts, and defendants alleged to have violated federal law who are sued in state court have the right to transfer the case to federal court. But if a lawsuit filed in state court makes only state law claims, the federal courts have no power to interfere. By limiting their claims to state law, the Hawaiian couples avoided federal court, where they knew they had no chance of prevailing.

When Ninia Baehr and her partner, Genora Dancel, filed suit in 1991, the US Supreme Court was by no means ready to rule that states must recognize same-sex marriage. The Court had dismissed the issue as posing no substantial federal question in 1972. It had upheld a law making same-sex sodomy a crime in 1986. As of 1991, no state in the Union, and no jurisdiction in the world, recognized same-sex marriage, and the Supreme Court was not about to impose such recognition on the nation.

The odds, while still very long, were better under state law. For one thing, a victory in Hawaii would have direct implications only for Hawaii, and so was a more modest request. State constitutions may extend protections to individuals that are not recognized by US constitutional law. Advocates could strategically choose the most sympathetic states to pursue their clams. And a loss in state court under Hawaiian law would similarly be limited in its effects to Hawaii, whereas a loss on a federal claim would have nationwide implications. For these reasons, until 2009, nearly all of the marriage equality lawsuits limited their claims to state law and were filed only in the most hospitable state courts.[7]

In the Hawaii trial court, the *Baehr* couples initially received the same treatment that every suit before theirs had received: dismissal of all claims. When Baehr appealed to the Hawaii Supreme Court, however, that court reversed. The court's decision, issued May 5, 1993, was the first in the nation to suggest that the denial of marriage to same-sex couples might be unconstitutional. The court reasoned, somewhat counterintuitively, that Hawaii's law constituted sex discrimination, not sexual orientation discrimination, noting that the only reason Baehr could not marry her partner was her gender. But the law treated men and women equally in this respect—the reason a man could not marry his partner was *his* gender, after all. The real aim of the law was not to treat men and women differently, but to treat gay and lesbian couples differently from straight couples. However, the court's reasoning was less important than the fact that it had taken the claim seriously and suggested that laws denying same-sex marriage might be unconstitutional. The Hawaii Supreme Court sent the case back to the trial court to give the state an opportunity to advance its interests for restricting marriage to opposite-sex couples. A formal ruling requiring recognition of Baehr's marriage would await the result of the trial on remand. But the state's burden would be substantial; under Hawaii's constitution, marriage could be limited to opposite-sex couples only if the state had a "compelling state interest" for doing so.[8]

At the time, Wolfson called the Hawaii Supreme Court decision "a tidal wave out of Hawaii that will reach every corner of the country and affect every gay issue." He was right, but at least in the short term, not in the way he meant. The decision sparked a powerful backlash not only in Hawaii but across the country. Hawaii's governor and Speaker of the House, both Democrats, condemned the decision. Legislators criticized the court for judicial activism and passed a bill reaffirming that marriage is limited to opposite-sex couples.[9]

Several states on the mainland reacted similarly. Utah and South Dakota immediately passed laws making clear that marriage in their states was limited to straight couples, and that they would not recognize same-sex marriages performed in other states. In 1996, three years after the *Baehr* decision, thirteen states adopted similar laws; the following year another nine followed suit. Also in 1996, Congress overwhelmingly passed, and President Bill Clinton signed, the Defense of Marriage Act (DOMA), which both affirmed the rights of states to refuse to recognize same-sex marriages performed elsewhere and denied over one thousand federal marital benefits to couples married in states that did recognize same-sex marriage. By 2001, thirty-five states had passed laws limiting marriage to a union of one man and one woman. And all this transpired before a single state had permitted same-sex marriage. The sweeping reaction was almost entirely sparked by the Hawaii court's preliminary decision in *Baehr*, which merely suggested that same-sex marriage might eventually be recognized in a single state.[10]

Meanwhile, the trial court in Hawaii that had initially dismissed the *Baehr* suit was compelled to consider the case again. Lambda realized, in Wolfson's words, that "the world had changed," and it authorized him to join the case as co-counsel. In a ten-day hearing in 1996, the trial court conducted the first-ever evidentiary hearing on marriage equality. Hawaii asserted that it limited marriage to opposite-sex couples to encourage procreation to take place in traditional marriages and to protect children, who it claimed were best raised by heterosexual couples. Plaintiffs' witnesses refuted both contentions. In December 1996, the trial court ruled that the state's justifications were insufficient. As for procreation, the court found that people marry for a variety of reasons beyond procreation, and that Hawaii had not shown that recognizing same-sex marriage would have any adverse effect on straight couples' inclinations to marry. With respect to children, the court concluded that "gay and lesbian parents and same-sex couples can be as fit and loving parents as non-gay men and women and different-sex couples." Accordingly, it required Hawaii to recognize same-sex marriage on equal terms with opposite-sex marriage, but allowed the status quo to continue pending appeal.[11]

The plaintiffs, their lawyers, and the gay community at large celebrated the Hawaii trial court decision, the first in the country to declare a right to marriage for same-sex couples. But they knew this was not the end of the battle. The state appealed. And in April 1997, Hawaii's legislature passed a proposed constitutional amendment, subject to popular approval in a statewide referendum, that would overrule the trial court by specifically authorizing the legislature to limit marriage to unions between a man and a woman. At the same time, to increase prospects for the amendment's passage, the legislature extended to same-sex couples most of the "reciprocal benefits" associated with marriage. Hawaiians overwhelmingly approved the amendment by 69 percent to 31 percent, and the Hawaii Supreme Court then vacated the trial court decision. In the end, no gay couples were married as a result of the *Baehr* litigation.[12]

A replay of sorts followed shortly thereafter in Alaska, when a gay couple filed a parallel suit claiming the right to be married. A trial court ruled for the couple, finding that the state's law constituted sex discrimination. In short order, however, as in Hawaii, the Alaska legislature and the state's voters responded by amending the state constitution to limit marriage to a union between a man and a woman, erasing the short-lived judicial victory.[13]

EVEN WHERE RECOGNITION OF same-sex marriage was temporarily won in court in these cases, it was soon lost in the democratic arena through state constitutional amendments. In some ways the movement was worse off afterwards, as the *Baehr* decision had inspired adverse legislation across the country. It was plainly not enough to make powerful legal arguments in court. Same-sex marriage would have to be won outside the court as well as inside. It required a political as well as a legal campaign.

Wolfson's own trajectory reflects this lesson. He left Lambda Legal Defense Fund in 2002, and in 2003 he founded Freedom to Marry, a national organization devoted exclusively to realizing the right to marriage equality. By 2014, it had a $9 million annual budget. Tellingly, apart from an occasional "friend-of-the-court" brief, Freedom to Marry did no litigation. It was not opposed to lawsuits. But it concentrated on all the other work that it believed necessary to achieve its goal. It advised on where it made sense to sue, and where it made sense to seek legislative reform. It offered templates for ballot initiative campaigns, social media strategies, and targeted fundraising, and it worked with local gay rights groups. It engaged the media to mold public opinion in its favor. Its considerable resources were directed almost entirely to work outside the courts: educating the public, recruiting and training volunteers, managing websites, consulting on referendum campaigns, and lobbying legislators—in short, laying the ground for change and working to defend gains from those who would reverse them. Wolfson's own writing abandoned the legal theory that suffused his law school paper in favor of articles and a book directed to the general public, and strategy pieces aimed at activists about how to make progress and respond to defeats. As he shifted his focus from courtroom advocacy to everything else involved in the campaign for marriage equality, Wolfson became one of the campaign's lead strategists.[14]

Wolfson and his allies in the marriage equality campaign drew inspiration from several prior struggles. They noted that while the first court decision striking down a law barring interracial marriage came in 1948, from the California Supreme Court, in *Perez v. Sharp*, it wasn't until 1967 that the US Supreme Court, in *Loving v. Virginia*, declared anti-miscegenation laws unconstitutional under the federal Constitution. The states led the way: the US Supreme Court did not follow until thirty-four states had already permitted interracial marriage. The women's suffrage movement likewise conducted a successful state-by-state campaign, even as it advocated for a federal constitutional amendment. By the time the Nineteenth Amendment to the US Constitution was ratified in 1920, guaranteeing women the right to vote, fifteen states had already granted women the right to vote generally, and another twelve had granted them the right to vote for president. Progressive legislation to protect workers' rights similarly began in the states, and was extended to the nation as a matter of federal law only during the New Deal. And advocates of a woman's right to abortion won their initial battles in state legislatures in the late 1960s and 1970s, and only then sought and obtained protection under the US Constitution in *Roe v. Wade*. In these and other campaigns, the road to changing federal constitution law wended its way through the states.[15]

The reaction to *Baehr* made clear that, even where it could be won in the state courts, the battle for marriage equality would have to be fought on multiple fronts. The next sites of contest were Vermont and Massachusetts, about as far from Hawaii as one can go within the United States. These were the first states in which marriage cases were filed by gay rights organizations, rather than against their advice. Taking advantage of lessons learned from Hawaii, marriage equality proponents in both states were more successful. But there, too, the court victories were only a small part of the overall effort.

2

A Marathon, Not a Sprint

VERMONT

LATE ON A NOVEMBER NIGHT IN 1996, SUSAN MURRAY AND BETH ROBINSON, ATTORNEYS with a family law and litigation practice in Middlebury, Vermont, were making the three-hour drive from Brattleboro back to Middlebury. They had been to Brattleboro to meet with a small group interested in extending marriage to same-sex couples. The group, pulled together by Bari Shamas, a mother of two, included a rabbi, several local ministers, a couple of Quakers, and gay and lesbian activists. The meeting had gone well, but as they drove back late into the night, the two lawyers began listing all the things they still had to do if they were to succeed in achieving same-sex marriage in Vermont. As the list grew longer, Susan reminded Beth: "Remember, it's a marathon, not a sprint." It would be another thirteen years before Vermont became the first state to extend marriage to same-sex couples through legislation and without a court order. No one is more responsible for that achievement than Robinson and Murray.[1]

Murray, one of Vermont's leading family law attorneys, first became interested in the issue in 1989, while representing Susan Bellemare, a woman whose partner, Susan Hamilton, had been killed in a car accident. Hamilton and Bellemare had been together for a dozen years, shared ownership of a home, and had jointly raised Hamilton's biological son, Collin. Shortly before Collin was born, Hamilton had written a will specifying that, in the event of her death, her children should be raised by Bellemare. But Collin's grandparents were not at all happy with this, and felt that they should raise the child, notwithstanding the will. Murray represented Bellemare through two years of litigation, winning in the courts until the grandparents eventually agreed to let Bellemare retain full custody and parenting of Collin. As Murray explained when I interviewed her in 2014 in her law firm's offices, "I realized that had it not been for the will, Bellemare might well have lost custody of her son. She was without the protections that automatically flow from a marriage."

The Bellemare case generated widespread publicity in Vermont, and gay and lesbian couples increasingly sought Murray's assistance. She litigated one of the first cases in Vermont to allow a lesbian partner to adopt her partner's biological child—known as "second-parent adoption." As Murray says, "at that point we had obtained legal recognition of the relationship between the parents and their child, two sides of the triangle, but there was no legal recognition for the relationship between the parents themselves—the third side of the triangle." And there were many other rights and benefits that Murray could not obtain for gay and lesbian couples absent the legal status of marriage itself.

In July 1994, Murray received a call from a woman named Pasha who said that she wanted to marry her partner, Penny. Pasha and Penny had managed to obtain a marriage license, issued in error by the town clerk. When he recognized his mistake, the clerk asked Pasha to return the license, but she refused. Pasha and Penny went ahead with a wedding ceremony, but the clerk declined to register the marriage. Pasha had heard about the Hawaii Supreme Court decision in *Baehr*, and she thought that she, too, should have the right to marry. She wanted to sue, and she asked Murray to represent her.

Murray thought Pasha and Penny had a strong argument under the Vermont Constitution's "Common Benefits Clause," which requires that the state government be instituted "for the common benefit . . . of the people . . . and not for the particular emolument or advantage of any single person, family, or set of persons." She consulted with her young associate, Beth Robinson, who had graduated from University of Chicago Law School, served in a prestigious clerkship on the US Court of Appeals for the DC Circuit, and worked at the corporate law firm of Skadden Arps before moving to Vermont to join Murray's practice. They agreed that the legal claim was strong, but concluded, in light of the legislative backlash against *Baehr*, that the issue could not be won in the courts alone. They convinced Pasha and Penny not to sue, and instead began to build popular and political support for the idea of marriage equality in the state. In order to obtain and hold onto a court victory, they believed, they would first need the full support of the gay and lesbian community, other allies, and enough legislators to defeat a constitutional amendment. [2]

They turned to Vermont's only statewide gay and lesbian organization, the Vermont Coalition for Lesbian and Gay Rights (VCLGR). At first, the group and Vermont's gay and lesbian community more generally were divided on the question of marriage, for the same reasons Wolfson confronted at Lambda. At a statewide "queer town meeting" sponsored by VCLGR in November 1993, Lambda's Paula Ettelbrick had reprised her debate with Tom Stoddard (although this time she faced off against David Chambers, a University of Michigan professor). Despite the historic victory in the Hawaii Supreme Court earlier that year, the audience was split. A year later, the VCLGR town meeting offered a workshop on marriage equality, but only a handful of people showed up, and this group, too, was divided on the question.

In 1995, a leading Vermont state senator, Leon Graves, announced that he believed the legislature should bar gay and lesbian partners' second-parent adoptions—a measure that would have reversed Murray's earlier court victory. Graves's announcement sparked a major lobbying effort by gay and lesbian activists, the first of its kind in the state. Over the course of much of that year, Murray helped organize gay and lesbian Vermonters to write letters, meet with their representatives, and testify at multiple public hearings.

The campaign was a huge success. When the legislature reconvened in January 1996, Graves, who had since retired, wrote his former colleagues saying that he had changed his mind and urging them to support second-parent adoptions after all. In the end, the legislature's family law bill preserved gay and lesbian adoption rights in full. [3]

The fight to preserve second-parent adoptions affected the gay and lesbian community's views on marriage. In November 1995, in the midst of that struggle, VCLGR held its third annual "queer town meeting." This time, a standing-room-only crowd of seventy-five to eighty people attended a marriage equality workshop run by Murray and Robinson. The ambivalence was gone; everyone wanted to move forward. [4]

Murray surmised that the battle over second-parent adoptions, which had consumed much of the community's energy in 1995, tipped the balance. The threat that second-parent adoption might be repealed illustrated the tenuous hold that gay families had on legal protections. And the lobbying and education effort to sustain second-parent adoptions had involved an intensive public discussion of gay and lesbian families. As Murray put it, "the overwhelming grassroots work done that year . . . helped to give us our voice, and helped show us that we could, as a community, fight the marriage fight."

OUTSIDE VERMONT, THE MARRIAGE equality movement was simultaneously reeling from the backlash to *Baehr* and inspired by the short-lived court victory there to seek marriage elsewhere. Gay rights advocates were guided in part by an influential 1994 article by Kees Waaldijk, a Dutch scholar. In a comparative review of the path to same-sex marriage in Scandinavia and Europe, Waaldijk found that marriage recognition was often the capstone of a series of incremental gay rights reforms. Recognition of same-sex marriage, he argued, tended to follow a "standard sequence," in which states first repealed criminal sodomy laws, then added sexual orientation to anti-discrimination and hate crimes laws, and then began to recognize the validity of same-sex relationships in partial or indirect ways, such as through extending domestic partnership benefits, or reforming family law to acknowledge gay and lesbian parents' rights to adopt, foster, and raise children.[5]

Waaldijk's findings confirmed what Murray and Robinson and many other gay rights advocates had realized; namely, that they should proceed cautiously, pressing for marriage recognition only after initial steps had been taken in a given state. Since receptiveness was uneven at best across the fifty states, the key was to seek marriage recognition in states that had already come furthest in their accommodation of gay rights. Holding that course, however, was easier said than done. Gay couples throughout the country had heard about the Hawaii case. Many sought the protection of marriage and wanted to sue. Advocates from all the leading gay rights groups devoted substantial effort in those early years to dissuading gay and lesbian couples from filing marriage suits, just as Murray had done with Pasha and Penny. Hawaii had demonstrated the risks of suing for marriage prematurely.

In the mid-1990s, Vermont was as hospitable to gay rights as any state. In 1990, six years before the legislature expressly codified second-parent adoptions, it added anti-gay bias to the forms of animus covered by the state hate crimes law. In 1992, it prohibited discrimination on the basis of sexual orientation in employment, housing, and public accommodations. In 1993, the Vermont Supreme Court approved of second-parent adoptions. In 1994, Vermont became the first state to offer health insurance benefits to same-sex partners of its state employees.[6]

The Hawaii experience had illustrated that another consideration was also important: how easy was it to amend the state's constitution? State constitutions vary significantly in this regard. Here, too, Vermont's rules were favorable, as they made a backlash constitutional amendment difficult. A proposed amendment to the Vermont constitution could not be presented to the voters unless it first was approved by two successively elected legislatures. Legislative approval required not only a majority of the state's House of Representatives, but two-thirds of its Senate. Vermont has thirty state senators, so eleven senators can block a constitutional amendment. A victory in the Vermont courts would therefore be difficult to overturn. And knowing that its decision was less vulnerable to popular override might give the state supreme court more courage in ruling in favor of marriage in the first place.[7]

Still, Robinson and Murray were reluctant to file suit until they had done more preparatory political work. After the standing-room-only marriage equality session at the November 1995 VCLGR "queer town meeting," they organized a follow-up meeting to create a working group specifically focused on same-sex marriage. Only twelve people attended the first meeting, held in a church basement in the state capital. The working group became the Vermont Freedom to Marry Task Force. It had no office, and no paid staff until 1999, when the group hired, part-time, a woman who had a photocopier in her living room.

The Task Force's most important contribution to the marriage equality effort was its message that same-sex couples were just like other couples in their desires for stable, committed, and loving relationships. It trained advocates in how to talk about marriage, and developed a set of "speaking points" that informed many subsequent efforts in other states. It taught gay and lesbian couples how to tell their own stories effectively. In one such training session, Robinson recalls advising Lois Farnham and Holly Puterbaugh, a lesbian couple in their fifties: "Nobody should ever hear the two of you speak without learning up front that you've been together for twenty-three years and that Lois is a seventh-generation Vermonter."

After studying a video made by opponents of same-sex marriage, the Task Force realized the critical need to undermine stereotypes about gays and lesbians as licentious and libertine. So they made their own video featuring ordinary Vermonters—both gay and lesbian couples and heterosexuals—explaining why recognition of same-sex marriage was important to them. As befits Vermont, the video was nothing fancy, but with simple, plainspoken testimonials it effectively defused fears about gay and lesbian couples being frighteningly different from straight couples.

The Task Force also lobbied their representatives. Vermont is a small state, so a relatively small group can reach a critical mass of legislators. The Task Force did not ask legislators to enact a same-sex marriage law; that would have been wholly unprecedented. Instead, the

Task Force asked the legislators merely to let a future judicial process run its course, and to oppose a constitutional amendment should the case succeed. Many legislators were, according to Robinson and Murray, visibly relieved when they learned that they were being asked only to play defense. By the time Robinson and Murray filed suit in 1997, they had obtained assurances from enough legislators to be confident that if they won in the courts, they could defeat a constitutional amendment initiative. Indeed, when Robinson argued the case in the Vermont Supreme Court in 1998, twenty senators had committed to opposing a constitutional amendment, almost twice the number needed.[8]

ONLY AFTER ALL THIS groundwork did Robinson and Murray file suit. By 1997, Robinson explains, "we had gotten as far as we could in organizing in the absence of a case. It's hard to call a Rotary Club and ask for an event without a case." The plaintiffs in *Baker v. State* were three carefully selected couples who had been denied licenses to marry: Stan Baker and Peter Harrington, Nina Beck and Stacy Jolles, and Lois Farnham and Holly Puterbaugh. They had good jobs and solid, long-standing relationships. Two of the three couples were raising or had raised children. Their stories contradicted stereotypes about gay and lesbian "lifestyles." Murray and Robinson were joined as co-counsel by Mary Bonauto, from Gay & Lesbian Advocates & Defenders (GLAD), which had been collaborating with Murray and Robinson for years. Bonauto, who went on to argue and win both the first state case and the first US Supreme Court case to recognize a right to marry (*Goodridge*, in Massachusetts in 2004, and *Obergefell* in the Supreme Court in 2015), was already one of the nation's leading gay rights lawyers. But all agreed that Robinson and Murray should be the primary public faces on the case. It was important that the case be brought by and for Vermonters.

I interviewed Bonauto in her hometown of Portland, Maine, in 2013. A soft-spoken, serious woman, she speaks quickly and decisively. Even though our conversation took place some fifteen years after the events in question, Bonauto recalled them with precision: "The Vermont Supreme Court heard oral argument on November 18, 1998. It was two weeks after Hawaii and Alaska had amended their constitutions in response to marriage cases there. The justices asked about that at the oral argument." The court was well aware that its decision might not be the last word.[9]

Robinson argued the case, and by all accounts did a terrific job. The video of her argument was broadcast on Vermont public television repeatedly thereafter. On December 20, 1999, the Vermont Supreme Court unanimously ruled that denying same-sex couples the benefits associated with marriage violated the Vermont Constitution's "Common Benefits Clause." But perhaps with an eye to what had happened in Hawaii, the court did not require the state to issue marriage licenses to the plaintiffs. It quoted Harvard law professor Cass Sunstein on the value of taking small steps in adjudicating controversial disputes: "Courts do best by proceeding in a way that is catalytic rather than preclusive, and that is closely attuned to the fact that courts are participants in the system of democratic deliberation." Rather than imposing a specific remedy, the court referred the matter to the state legislature, to provide the same "state benefits, protections, and security" available to straight married couples. In effect, it suggested two options: extend marriage to same-sex couples, or create a new status for same-sex couples with all the legal rights and benefits afforded to married couples.[10]

The court's decision, the first from a state supreme court declaring unconstitutional a law denying marriage benefits to same-sex couples, was controversial despite its soft touch regarding the remedy. A poll taken shortly afterwards found that 52 percent of Vermonters opposed the decision, while only 38 percent supported it. In the legislature, reactions broke largely along party lines. Republicans generally opposed both options the court had suggested. Democrats supported the second alternative. Almost immediately after the *Baker* decision issued, Vermont Governor Howard Dean proposed that route. As Murray recalled, "we hadn't finished reading the opinion before Governor Dean announced he wouldn't push for marriage." The Democratic leader of the House polled his colleagues and concluded that they, too, supported such an approach. The parallel structure, which the legislature called "civil unions," permitted politicians to offer a measure of equal treatment to gay and lesbian couples, while softening the blow to voters who objected to changing the definition of marriage. Polls consistently found more support for civil unions (and other forms of domestic partnership recognition) than for same-sex marriage. But at this stage, even civil unions were a hard sell. In March 2000, on Vermont "Town Meeting Day," fifty community meetings took votes on the issue. Not a single meeting supported same-sex marriage. Thirty-eight voted to reject both marriage and civil unions.[11]

Thomas Little, the chair of the Vermont House Judiciary Committee, held a series of hearings on the matter. Robinson, Murray, and Bonauto worked intensively on the hearings, identifying and preparing witnesses and speaking to the media. The hearings attracted the largest crowds for a legislative hearing in anyone's memory, even though the first one took place in the middle of a blizzard. Murray and Robinson felt it especially important to have the legislators hear the voices of ordinary Vermonters. The strategy worked. As one Republican legislator explained, "somehow when you listen to the compelling stories of gay and lesbian people, it demystifies who they are, what they stand for, and how valuable they are for our communities." After several hearings, the judiciary committee held a straw vote. Eight committee members voted for the parallel track, and three voted for marriage. The legislature followed the committee's lead, and established "civil unions," a new legal status that, for the first time anywhere in the United States, afforded same-sex couples all the rights, benefits, and obligations of marriage.[12]

Murray and Robinson believed only marriage could provide true equality. But they were under pressure from many of their allies in the legislature and the governor's office to support a parallel structure, and, after the committee's straw vote in favor of civil unions, they, their clients, and the Task Force felt they had no alternative but to do just that. They helped the legislature draft the civil unions bill, and chose not to challenge that outcome in court. Yet they insisted that civil unions represented only a temporary step toward full marriage equality. They recognized the dangers of a "separate but equal" status. But as Vermont's only openly gay legislator said, "Marriage, someday. But it does not feel hollow. It feels like a tremendous victory."[13]

The Task Force's work was by no means done. A group opposed to the decision, Take Back Vermont, targeted legislators who had supported civil unions in the 2000 elections. The Task Force campaigned for those same legislators. Though many supporters of civil unions won reelection, including US Senator James Jeffords, the governor, lieutenant governor, secretary of state, and state auditor, sixteen pro-civil-union legislators lost their seats, and the Republicans took control of the House.

When, four years later, the Massachusetts Supreme Court required recognition of same-sex marriage under its state constitution, and expressly rejected civil unions as an inadequate remedy, Vermont's civil union law began to look less appealing to gay rights advocates. In 2007, Peter Shumlin, the president of the Vermont Senate, set up a commission to study the issue of civil unions and same-sex marriage, and held hearings across the state, often in districts opposed to the advance of gay rights. Robinson and the Task Force again took charge of identifying and preparing witnesses and handling media outreach, and again overwhelmed the opposition. The commission's report concluded that civil unions were insufficient to provide true equality.[14]

In 2009, the Task Force pressed for full marriage rights, but this time through the legislature, which passed a same-sex marriage bill on April 6 of that year. Governor Jim Douglas vetoed it. The vote on the override was the very next night. The Task Force knew they had enough votes in the Senate, but feared they did not in the House. That night, Robinson drafted a speech stressing the need to keep moving forward despite the defeat. But to everyone's surprise, marriage equality proponents eked out a two-thirds majority in the House by a single vote. As a result, fifteen years after Pasha and Penny had approached Murray about wanting to marry, Vermont became the first state to recognize full marriage equality for gays and lesbians without a court order requiring it to do so.

THE RESPECTIVE TRAJECTORIES OF the Vermont and Hawaii cases illustrate the benefits of patient incrementalism. In both states, courts found the state's denial of same-sex marriage unconstitutional as a matter of state law. While neither state immediately recognized same-sex marriage, both were impelled by the litigation to extend more generous benefits to gay and lesbian couples than any state had before them. But where the Hawaiian court ordered marriage in one very big step, only to have its ruling overturned by the people, the process was more incremental in Vermont.

By proceeding more cautiously, and against a carefully prepared backdrop, the Vermont court's decision did not spark the same kind of backlash as the Hawaii decisions did. Traditionalists in Vermont and elsewhere certainly objected to the state supreme court's decision, and Take Back Vermont mounted an impassioned campaign to overturn the decision. But whereas 52 percent of Vermonters disapproved of the decision when it was issued, just six months later, 52 percent approved of the new law. Efforts to amend Vermont's constitution to override the court's decision failed.

The Vermont case also triggered a smaller backlash outside the state than did *Baehr*, although six more states banned same-sex marriage between 2000 and 2003. The civil union approach appealed to some same-sex marriage opponents because it preserved "traditional marriage." And it appealed to some who favored same-sex marriage as a step—at that point, the biggest thus far—toward the ultimate goal. As a compromise solution, civil unions garnered more support and provoked less resistance.

Mary Bonauto told me that in the *Baker* case the plaintiffs and their attorneys did not so much choose the "civil union" strategy as have it thrust upon them. In her words, "we didn't see incrementalism as an option here, because before the case, the notion of civil unions didn't really exist." Once the court suggested a parallel structure, however, and it became clear that the legislature strongly preferred that route, the plaintiffs made a strategic choice to accept the victory, even if it was incomplete. Still, as with most compromises, it was not without some regret. Shortly after civil unions were established, Bonauto attended a national meeting of gay rights litigators, fully expecting to have to apologize for the compromise. "Are you kidding? This is great!" her national colleagues responded. Murray had a similar reaction, explaining that the full significance of the victory only dawned on her when she attended the gay and lesbian March on Washington in 2000, where the Vermont contingent was treated "like royalty."[15]

As the Vermont experience illustrates, when attempting to establish a new constitutional right, incrementalism is often essential. The Dutch scholar Waaldijk's work suggests that each of the measures of progress on gay rights that preceded *Baker v. State* was likely critical to making that decision possible. The more modest opposition prompted by *Baker* than by *Baehr* underscores the point.

Many gay rights advocates made principled objections to civil unions on the grounds that they fell short of equality. Some also worried that accepting civil unions might slow the momentum for same-sex marriage, entrenching gay and lesbian couples in a second-class status. In hindsight, however, it's clear that civil unions were more a temporary way station than a final destination. Both Vermont and Hawaii ultimately adopted same-sex marriage laws. (The Hawaii legislature established civil unions in 2011, and marriage equality in 2013.) In both states domestic partnerships and civil unions were important stepping stones along the path to marriage equality.

The progression from the Stonewall riots to AIDS activism to corporate domestic partnership benefits and local nondiscrimination ordinances to Hawaii's "reciprocal benefits" and Vermont's civil unions was a series of small but cumulative steps. If Hawaii demonstrated that taking too large a step could have substantial negative repercussions, Vermont showed that progress could be made more gradually without provoking such a strong reaction. Change will always be resisted, especially change that questions established traditions. But the Vermont story illustrates that civil society can achieve lasting constitutional change by patiently but persistently pursuing small steps toward their ultimate goals.

3

One Step Forward,
How Many Back?

MASSACHUSETTS

DESPITE HER COLLEAGUES' ASSURANCES THAT WINNING CIVIL UNIONS IN VERMONT WAS a major victory, Mary Bonauto and her colleagues at GLAD were not satisfied. Even if a civil union came with all the tangible rights, benefits, and obligations that marriage provided under a state's laws, it was not marriage. Indeed, that was the entire point—to avoid extending marriage to same-sex couples and thereby appease the opposition and reduce resistance. But a claim to equal treatment, Bonauto believed, must ultimately demand true equality.

With the Vermont fight over, at least for the time being, Bonauto turned her sights on GLAD's home state of Massachusetts. For years, Bonauto had dissuaded gay and lesbian couples from filing marriage lawsuits there, concerned that the time was not yet right. As in Vermont, she believed it was essential to do substantial political groundwork before bringing a suit.

By 2000, she and GLAD decided that it was time to file. Like Vermont, Massachusetts had already taken a series of steps recognizing the equal status of gay men and lesbians, and to a degree, their family relationships. In 1989, Massachusetts had become the second state in the country to add sexual orientation to its statewide non-discrimination law. (Some Massachusetts towns had begun doing so as early as 1976.) In 1991, sexual orientation was added to the state's hate crimes law. In 1993, the state supreme court ruled that a lesbian parent could jointly adopt her partner's child. The same year, Governor William Weld extended same-sex domestic partnership benefits to state employees. The legislature passed a "safe schools" measure aimed at protecting gay and lesbian students in 1993. And in 1999, the state supreme court recognized that a child of a lesbian couple who were separating had rights of access to both parents.

Massachusetts was also an attractive venue because, like Vermont, the process for amending the state constitution is cumbersome, making a political override of a judicial victory less likely. If a legislator proposes a constitutional amendment, it cannot go to a ballot for popular approval until it has first been approved by a majority of the legislators, acting in a "constitutional convention" called specifically for that purpose, in two successively elected legislatures. Citizens can initiate an amendment, but that requires a petition signed by at least 3 percent of the total number of voters in the preceding gubernatorial election, and then approval by 25 percent of the legislature in two successively elected sessions. Elections are every two years, so at a minimum the process takes several years.

Bonauto felt that if she could win in court, time was on her side. She believed that a significant part of the opposition to same-sex marriage was a fear of the unknown. If gay and lesbian couples began to marry, she was confident, people would see for themselves that there were no negative effects on families, local communities, or society more broadly, and the fear and opposition would dissipate. What was needed, in her view, was for same-sex marriage to "come out." Gay and lesbian couples had long been living in long-term, committed, loving relationships. Public acknowledgement of that fact, through the ritual and recognition of marriage, could only help the cause. As in Vermont, so in Massachusetts, a key aspect of the strategy was to demonstrate that gay and lesbian couples were, with respect to marriage, no different from straight couples.

Another factor in Bonauto's and GLAD's decision to file was a desire to seize the initiative from the opposition. GLAD learned that an organization opposed to same-sex marriage, Massachusetts Citizens Alliance (later Massachusetts Citizens for Marriage), intended to put a law defining marriage as a union between a man and a woman on the ballot in 2002, and planned to press for a constitutional amendment to the same effect in 2004. The issue of marriage equality was soon going to come to a head, whatever GLAD did. Based on her experience in Vermont, Bonauto thought that winning an affirmative suit for marriage would put marriage equality advocates in a better position than reacting to an agenda set by their opponents. As she later put it, "I saw the senators struggle with the principles that had been announced in the Vermont Supreme Court decision. They explored their convictions and consciences knowing that voting for an amendment would be voting against equality principles." The state court decision, she felt, helped cast the terms of debate in Vermont in her side's favor. And if her lawsuit failed, that result would likely take the steam out of her adversaries' plans for a constitutional amendment.[1]

In framing the Massachusetts lawsuit, Bonauto and her colleagues at GLAD considered not only the best legal arguments to advance in court, but also the political fight that was sure to follow. To that end, Bonauto believed it was important to file on behalf of couples from across the state who were in stable, committed relationships; who were involved in their communities and in many cases raising children; and who had stories that ordinary citizens could relate to. As she put it, "You try to do it in a way that makes it most palatable and focused on what you have in common—these are your neighbors." By selecting couples from different parts of the state, they would increase local press interest in Massachusetts's multiple media markets, offering the opportunity to use the case—and the couples' personal circumstances—to educate the broader public about the issues at stake. GLAD filed suit in April 2001 on behalf of seven couples. Hillary and Julie Goodridge were the first plaintiffs listed, and the case bore their name: *Goodridge v. Massachusetts Department of Public Health.* As in Hawaii and Vermont, the suit asserted only state law claims to ensure that it would escape review in the federal courts.

DESPITE ITS REPUTATION AS a liberal state, and despite having an attorney general who had expressed support for marriage equality during his campaign, Massachusetts offered a full-throated defense of its restriction of marriage to opposite-sex couples. It argued that doing so facilitated responsible procreation and childrearing, and conserved government resources. But in a landmark ruling issued on November 18, 2003, the Massachusetts Supreme Judicial Court ruled for Hillary Goodridge. By a 4–3 margin, the court held that, because the state could advance no rational reason for its disparate treatment of straight and gay couples, denying marriage to same-sex couples violated the state constitution.[2]

Chief Justice Margaret H. Marshall, writing for the majority, acknowledged that the state's asserted interests were legitimate in a general sense, but found no reason to believe they would be furthered by denying marriage to same-sex couples. Same-sex couples can and do procreate, and opposite-sex couples often do not; and the state had never required an intent or ability to procreate as a condition for getting married. Massachusetts law and policy actively facilitated the rearing of children by unmarried as well as married couples, and by gay as well as straight parents, and there was no reason to believe that recognizing a same-sex couple as married would harm their children; on the contrary, denying these children the benefits of having married parents would disserve the children's interests. The court also saw no basis for believing that recognizing same-sex marriage would in any way reduce straight couples' inclinations to marry and raise children. Finally, denying marriage to same-sex couples might well conserve resources, by reducing the cost of the benefits the state afforded to married couples, but the court found no justification for conserving resources by selectively denying them to same-sex couples.

Following Vermont's lead, the Massachusetts Supreme Court stayed its ruling "to permit the Legislature to take such action as it may deem appropriate in light of this opinion." Some construed this to leave open the possibility of civil unions as a remedy, as in Vermont. But when the legislature formally asked the court for an "advisory opinion" on whether civil unions would cure the constitutional violation, the court emphatically foreclosed that option. In no uncertain terms, it concluded that nothing short of extending marriage would provide equality. On May 17, 2004, the judicial stay expired, and Massachusetts became the first state in the nation, and only the sixth jurisdiction in the world, to recognize same-sex marriage.[3]

The fight was not over. As in Hawaii, Alaska, and Vermont, critics of the decision, including Massachusetts Governor Mitt Romney, proposed amending the state constitution. The state legislature sat as a "constitutional convention" in 2004, 2005, and 2007 to consider such proposals. Each convention generated extensive local and national media coverage, and drew large crowds of demonstrators on both sides. In 2004, the convention voted by a bare majority (105 of 200 legislators) to approve a proposed amendment that would have established civil unions for same-sex couples and reserved marriage for opposite-sex couples. To qualify for the ballot, however, the proposal had to be approved by a subsequently elected legislature. In intervening special elections and the general election, MassEquality, a coalition of groups favoring same-sex marriage, spent hundreds of thousands of dollars and mobilized hundreds of volunteers to campaign for candidates who supported marriage equality and against their adversaries. Legislators who had supported same-sex marriage all won reelection, and several who opposed it lost. The second time around, in the newly elected legislature, the proposed amendment was defeated by a surprisingly lopsided vote, 157 to 39.[4]

Still, opponents of same-sex marriage did not give up. They pursued a citizens' initiative to amend the constitution, which required them to gather over 66,000 signatures, and garner the votes of at least

25 percent (50 votes) of two successively elected legislatures. The Massachusetts Family Initiative collected twice as many signatures as needed by December 2005, and the measure then received 62 votes from the 2006 legislature, more than sufficient. In the subsequently elected legislature, however, in 2007, the measure mustered only 45 votes, and died. By that time, about 56 percent of Massachusetts respondents approved of same-sex marriage. So despite sustained efforts by its critics, *Goodridge* withstood the test of the amendment process, and remains the law to this day.[5]

MUCH LIKE THE HAWAII *Baehr* decision, the *Goodridge* decision in Massachusetts touched off a series of negative reactions around the country. Two prominent law professors, Gerald Rosenberg of the University of Chicago and Michael Klarman of Harvard, both of whom are sympathetic to the underlying cause of marriage equality, have argued that *Goodridge* did more harm than good. Rosenberg has written that "*Goodridge*, perhaps more than any other modern case, highlights the folly of Progressives turning to litigation in the face of legislative hostility." In his view, the nationwide backlash that *Goodridge* sparked was "nothing short of disastrous for the right to same-sex marriage." Before *Goodridge*, only three states—Alaska, Nebraska, and Nevada— had constitutional amendments banning same-sex marriage. In 2004 alone, thirteen states enacted constitutional amendments against same-sex marriage. By the end of the 2006 elections, twenty-seven states banned same-sex marriage by constitutional amendment, and forty-five states prohibited it by statute, constitutional amendment, or both. In view of these results, gay rights activist John D'Emilio in 2006 pronounced the campaign for same-sex marriage "an unmitigated disaster."[6]

There is no question that *Goodridge* provoked a significant negative response across the nation, and if one looked only at the short- and medium-term aftermath of that case, one might question the decision to file suit in the first place. Indeed, a good argument can be made that by 2006, marriage equality proponents were considerably worse off, nationwide, than they were before the *Baehr*, *Baker*, and *Goodridge* cases were filed, as they faced more legal and political obstacles in many states than before *Goodridge*.[7]

From the standpoint of 2015, however, these criticisms look short-sighted. The benefits of filing *Baehr*, *Baker*, and *Goodridge* are evident from a longer view. As Evan Wolfson has said, "wins trump losses." When one seeks to establish a right that is not recognized in existing constitutional law, setbacks should be expected. Court decisions granting rights not supported by the majority will prompt negative political reactions, as *Baehr* and *Goodridge* did. But the critical question is: compared to what? What alternatives did Ninia Baehr and Hillary Goodridge really have?

Had they petitioned their respective legislatures for laws extending marriage to same-sex couples, their requests would have gone nowhere. Legislators are not required to entertain any particular proposal from citizens, and the easiest way of dealing with a request that is unlikely to command majority (or powerful interest group) support is simply to ignore it. No legislature in the United States recognized same-sex marriage until 2009, only after several courts had done so. The first legislature to succeed in doing so was Vermont's after *Baker*. Proceeding through the political branches on behalf of a claim that lacks majority support is generally not a viable alternative.

Courts cannot ignore individuals who claim to have been denied an asserted constitutional right in some tangible way. Unlike executive officials or legislatures, courts must address the merits of the argument. Constitutional rights claims, moreover, by definition arise because a particular right has not received protection through the political process. For advocates seeking recognition of same-sex marriage at that time, courts were the only realistic alternative.[8]

Goodridge had a galvanizing effect, moreover not only on opponents of marriage equality, but on gay and lesbian couples across the nation. For the first time, they saw a state's highest court declare that they were entitled to marry as a matter of fundamental principles of equality. And this led to increased demands for recognition of same-sex relationships more generally. Before 1993, no state legislature had extended domestic partnership benefits of any kind to same-sex couples; between 1997 and 2008, legislatures in twelve states voted to extend domestic partnership benefits to gay and lesbian couples—often while marriage litigation was pending.[9]

In addition, backlash can be productive. The response to *Baehr* and *Goodridge* arguably gave same-sex marriage more visibility than gay rights advocates could have given it themselves. In Evan Wolfson's view, the opposition in turn sparked a critically important counter-response, as more people within the gay community and outside it began to see the issue as legitimate and vital, and to lend their support, financial or otherwise, to the struggle.[10]

In short, state court litigation played a crucial part in the marriage equality campaign, taking marriage claims seriously long before they could have had a favorable reception in the political process. By winning the right to marry in Massachusetts, advocates could show the nation that allowing gay and lesbian couples to marry had no negative consequences. By carefully selecting sympathetic states, gay rights advocates had a chance to develop and test arguments that could then be exported to other venues. And because most state constitutions share basic features with the federal Constitution, in particular in their safeguards for equality, due process, and privacy, state courts were a fertile ground for developing the arguments that would later be advanced in federal court.

IN 2004, HOWEVER, THE backlash to *Goodridge* posed a challenge for the campaign. Funders of gay rights groups worried about the wave of state constitutional amendments that *Goodridge* had triggered. The Gill Foundation, the largest funder of marriage equality efforts, convened a national strategy meeting in Denver of the principal organizations, activists, and lawyers involved in the marriage equality campaign. Everyone sensed that the campaign for marriage equality was at a critical juncture, but it was unclear which way things would go. Although they

had won a few important court victories, they had consistently lost ballot initiatives, usually by substantial margins, and same-sex marriage
was now constitutionally barred in many states. Division had broken
out within the gay rights community.

The 2004 meeting authorized a small task force to devise a working
plan. The task force included many of the campaign's leading advocates.
Matt Coles of the ACLU Lesbian and Gay Rights Project took the lead
in drafting the plan. At fifty-three, he had been a gay rights lawyer since
graduating in 1977 from University of California's Hastings College of
Law, and that made him an elder statesman in this nascent movement.
In June 2005, the group approved a fifteen-page document, "Winning
Marriage: What We Need to Do," that laid out a strategy for attain-
ing marriage equality in fifteen to twenty-five years, by 2020 or 2030.
Notably, the document contained no legal analysis; the challenge was
not formulating arguments to make in court, but identifying the work
outside the federal courts that might make the legal argument plausible
in the Supreme Court. The memo assumed that the Court does not so
much lead as reflect social change. It reaffirmed the incremental strategy deployed in Vermont and Massachusetts. And it confirmed that the
road to federal constitutional change required what might be called
a "federalist" strategy: working in the states to establish a legal norm
that would then help to shape the understanding of similar provisions
in the federal Constitution. The memo advised that before presenting
a case to the Supreme Court, advocates should first win recognition
of marriage, civil unions, or some other form of same-sex partnership
recognition in a critical mass of states. These state-level successes, the
memo predicted, would prompt a "tipping point," after which full marriage equality could be attained at the federal level.[11]

The memo also called for more coordinated strategizing at the national level. It recommended the creation of an umbrella organization
to perform such a coordinating role; a public education campaign, to
be carried out at local, state, and national levels; and development
of a significantly strengthened "field" program capable of mobilizing
volunteers and experts on gay rights issues in every state. Shortly thereafter, the Gill Foundation and other funders created the Civil Marriage

Collaborative, an umbrella entity devoted to funding marriage equality battles, and Evan Wolfson expanded Freedom to Marry, which, in collaboration with the existing gay rights groups, provided strategic and tactical assistance in many of the campaign's battles nationwide.

These strategic, structural, and organizational details are as crucial to the marriage equality story as the arguments made in court. Changing the Constitution to encompass same-sex marriage required a vision of the end goal, a strategy for how to make that vision a reality, a plan for coordination at the national and local levels, and financial and organizational commitment for the long haul. At the time of Coles's memo, civil society organizations on the opposing side had mobilized against same-sex marriage, and were consistently winning in their preferred venue: state ballot initiatives. The "Winning Marriage" memo united the marriage equality movement behind a common plan, coordinated at the national level but still very much focused on the states. The backlash had compelled the participants to come together and to transform what had been a largely decentralized campaign into a more unified national struggle. Over time, these efforts paid off. But it took one more major setback to turn the marriage equality campaign into one that could win in the US Supreme Court.

4

A Victory Lost— and Regained

CALIFORNIA

ALIFORNIA WAS NOT SUPPOSED TO GO THIS WAY. IN THE LATE 1990S AND EARLY 2000s, the nation's leading gay rights groups collectively decided not to seek same-sex marriage through the courts in California—at least not yet. As in Vermont and Massachusetts, gay rights advocates in California had campaigned for years, and had made substantial progress, at both the municipal and statewide levels, on nondiscrimination protection, hate crimes laws, and increasingly robust versions of domestic partnership recognition. They did not doubt that they had a good chance of prevailing in the California Supreme Court. But in California, it was all too easy to place a constitutional amendment on the ballot. As in Hawaii, a favorable decision by the state's highest court could prompt a ballot initiative that they would likely lose. As Jennifer Pizer of Lambda Legal put it, the central question was, "If we were to win in the supreme court, what would we need to do to hold on to it?"[1]

They chose another route, pursuing an incremental approach through the legislature. They started small. In the 1980s and 1990s, Matt Coles worked on some of the first campaigns to get municipalities to recognize domestic partnerships. Berkeley became the first city in the country to do so, in 1984. In 1996, San Francisco passed a domestic partnership ordinance that applied not only to public workers, but to any private company that did business with the city. In 1999, California passed a statewide domestic partnership law. By design, the bill provided only minimal benefits in order to make it harder to oppose.[2]

Over time, California gradually expanded the rights and benefits associated with domestic partnerships. In 2000, the legislature added the right of same-sex partners to secure senior housing together. In 2001, the legislature expanded the benefits to include a range of family rights, including the right of gay couples to adopt and to make medical decisions for one another. The following year, domestic partners gained inheritance rights. Finally, in 2003, the legislature passed a comprehensive domestic partnership law, giving partners "the same rights, protections, and benefits, and . . . the same responsibilities, obligations, and duties under law . . . as are granted to and imposed upon spouses." At each step along the way, advocates created a legislative record showing that same-sex couples were similarly situated to married couples—resulting in findings that proved useful when a state constitutional challenge was eventually filed in court.[3]

In 2003, the Williams Institute at UCLA School of Law hosted a roundtable of the nation's leading gay rights advocates and scholars to consider next steps on marriage in California. In a memo written in preparation for the meeting, Lambda Legal's Jon Davidson warned that "any decision to file a marriage case in California . . . needs to include [consideration of] whether the political, donor and public support for allowing same-sex couples to marry has increased sufficiently that [an anti-marriage-equality] initiative could be defeated at the polls." The group decided that the time was still not right for litigation, because "it would be too difficult to defeat a subsequent initiative" if they won in court. But as in Massachusetts, circumstances would force same-sex marriage advocates' hand.[4]

IN A ROUNDABOUT WAY, *Goodridge* set the California litigation in motion. In January 2004, the newly elected mayor of San Francisco, Gavin Newsom, attended President George W. Bush's State of the Union address, in which Bush condemned the recent decision in *Goodridge*. Newsom was so enraged by Bush's remarks that he decided to authorize San Francisco's City Hall to issue marriage licenses to same-sex couples. When Kate Kendell, a lawyer with the National Center for Lesbian Rights, heard of the mayor's decision from Newsom's chief of staff, Steve Kawa, the Friday before the public announcement, she immediately expressed concern. She worried that Newsom might unleash a backlash. Kawa politely listened to her concerns, and replied, "I hear you, Kate, but the mayor is going ahead and I wanted you to know." She was being notified, not consulted. The mayor had made up his mind before consulting anyone in the gay rights movement.[5]

Mayor Newsom's initiative, which began February 12, 2004, was greeted with unbounded enthusiasm by many in the gay and lesbian community. Thousands of couples began making their way to City Hall to get married. Gay rights groups made sure that the first couple to marry was Phyllis Lyon and Del Martin, longtime feminist activists who had been together for fifty-one years. But beyond that, they had little control. Every day, couples stood in long lines outside the doors of City Hall waiting their turn. About four thousand couples were married in a single month. The event was transformative, a bold and dramatic public action, vividly demonstrating to the nation the desires of thousands of gay and lesbian couples to wed.

Molly McKay, founder of Marriage Equality California, a statewide grassroots organization, described the dramatic impact of Newsom's action in this way:

> Newsom put same-sex couples on the radar screen of the nongay world in a way those couples had never been before. He allowed an opportunity to see real-live couples being impacted in a way that no paid-for advertising campaign or national gay and lesbian spokesperson could ever do. It was so real, and to have all of these couples wrapping around the block, standing out in the elements. . . . Here

you had people in their fifties and sixties waiting in line for hours in the cold and pouring rain. But they were willing to do it to make history. . . . It changed the nature of the debate. It wasn't something theoretical anymore. It became real. . . . There were all these lesbian and gay couples in long-term, committed relationships, with their children, with their parents, with family there celebrating, and who'd been together at least as long as most nongay couples. And the sky didn't fall, and the world didn't end, and we didn't see a spike in the divorce rates of heterosexual couples.[6]

But as a legal matter it wasn't so simple. By issuing licenses to same-sex couples when state law authorized only opposite-sex marriage, the mayor was disregarding California law. The California attorney general sued, maintaining that the mayor lacked such authority. Proponents of traditional marriage also sued. Mayor Newsom argued that the denial of marriage to same-sex couples violated the California Constitution, and therefore he was acting in line with his constitutional duties. On March 11, the California Supreme Court preliminarily ordered the mayor to stop issuing marriage licenses, pending its ruling on the legality of his action. But the court also stressed that its ruling did "not preclude the filing of a separate action in superior court raising a substantive constitutional challenge to the current marriage statutes." That very afternoon—again without consulting the gay rights groups—the city filed a separate lawsuit challenging the constitutionality of denying marriage to same-sex couples.[7]

Gay rights advocates filed their own state constitutional challenge the following day. As Jennifer Pizer of Lambda Legal explained, they really had no choice: "There was no question that we would accept [the invitation] and file that case. . . . This is a state with a great many lawyers and LGBT people who wanted marriage. [The court's invitation] would receive a response, if not by us, then by others."[8]

In August 2004, the California Supreme Court held that Mayor Newsom's marriages were invalid: the mayor lacked authority to override a state law simply because he believed it was unconstitutional. Four years later, however, ruling on the constitutional challenge it had invited, the same court declared that the legislature's refusal to recognize same-sex marriages violated the state constitution's guarantees of equal protection and due process. It reasoned that the right to marry was fundamental, that treating same-sex couples differently because of their sexual orientation was suspect, and that the state had no compelling justification for the differential treatment. Notably, the court's constitutional reasoning turned in large measure on the gains that gay rights advocates had previously won. The court found that in light of state laws recognizing gay and lesbian couples' family law rights (such as adoption, inheritance, and medical decision making), there was no good reason not to let such couples marry. And it further found that because the state legislature had extended to gay couples all the tangible benefits of marriage through its domestic partnership law, it had no justification (other than discrimination) for denying them the status of marriage. The incremental gains that preceded the litigation not only made marriage equality more thinkable as a political matter, but actually undermined the state's arguments for denying marriage to gays and lesbians.[9]

There ensued the most hard-fought, expensive, and closely watched marriage ballot campaign in US history. Even before the California Supreme Court's decision was handed down, opponents of marriage equality had begun gathering signatures to put a state constitutional amendment on the ballot limiting marriage to unions of one man and one woman. Less than a month after the court's decision, they had collected enough signatures for what became "Proposition 8," to be voted on during the 2008 elections. In the months that followed, each side spent approximately $40 million trying to rally support.

Early polls suggested that marriage equality had the upper hand. But as election day neared, the marriage equality campaign's internal polls suggested that they were losing. In the campaign's closing weeks, Proposition 8 proponents aired a television advertisement featuring a young child telling her parents that she had learned in school that men could marry men, and women could marry women. By most accounts, the advertisement was extraordinarily effective, preying on fears that parents would lose control of the values their children were taught. In the end, on the same day that Californians helped the nation elect its first black president, they also approved Proposition 8 by a 52–48 percent margin.[10]

The defeat was the marriage equality movement's most devastating loss. As Dave Fleischer, a political consultant working with the LA Gay and Lesbian Community Center, put it to me, "if marriage equality could not prevail at the ballot box in one of the most progressive states in the nation, with millions of dollars spent to advance it, and where the law already extended to same-sex couples all the rights, benefits and obligations associated with marriage, where could it succeed?" The loss sparked second-guessing and recriminations, as supporters attempted to figure out what had gone wrong and disappointed advocates began to assign blame.

In retrospect, however, like *Goodridge*, the Proposition 8 loss was the catalyst that pushed marriage equality down the road to what not long afterward seemed like inevitable success. In a long-term constitutional campaign, losses can have a silver lining if they motivate supporters to commit even more time and effort to the cause. Proposition 8 had just that effect. It triggered massive popular protests, directed at the Mormon and Catholic churches, the principal funders of the Proposition 8 campaign. And it prompted gay and lesbian advocates to reconsider their approach, develop a newly united advocacy strategy, and redouble their efforts.

IMMEDIATELY AFTER THE VOTE, Proposition 8 gave rise to the first federal court challenge to a state same-sex marriage law since the modern marriage equality movement began. The case, initially called *Perry v. Schwarzenegger*, received national attention. Its backers, a newly minted gay rights organization, American Foundation for Equal Rights (AFER), backed by Hollywood film director Rob Reiner, hoped to establish a federal constitutional right to marry nationwide. They recruited the unlikely legal team of David Boies and Ted Olson, two of the nation's top lawyers, one a Democrat, the other a Republican and former solicitor general to President George W. Bush. Boies and Olson had famously squared off against each other in *Bush v. Gore*, but they came together to challenge Proposition 8.

The lawyers who had been working for marriage equality for nearly two decades before Boies, Olson, and AFER came along adamantly opposed the suit's filing. They warned Boies and Olson, privately and publicly, that it was premature to ask the Supreme Court to declare a right to marriage equality. Doing so, they believed, risked a loss that could set the movement back decades. Marriage equality proponents had been carefully pursuing an incremental state-by-state strategy, intentionally avoiding federal claims in order to keep the issue out of federal court. In their view, the Supreme Court was unlikely to impose same-sex marriage on every state in the Union until a critical mass of states had recognized same-sex marriage, civil unions, or domestic partnerships. And in May 2009, when Boies and Olson filed their suit, only four states had recognized same-sex marriage—Massachusetts, Vermont, Iowa, and Connecticut—and over forty had explicit laws against it. By contrast, when the Supreme Court declared anti-miscegenation laws unconstitutional in 1967, thirty-four states already permitted interracial marriage. When the Court established a constitutional right to assistance of counsel for indigent defendants in 1963, all but fifteen states already provided such assistance as a matter of state law. And by the time the Supreme Court invalidated Texas's gay sodomy law in *Lawrence v. Texas* in 2003, only four states still singled out homosexual sodomy as a crime.[11]

Boies and Olson rejected the gay rights groups' advice. Their most persuasive response was that someone would surely challenge Proposition 8 in federal court, and it was better that their highly skilled and heavily resourced team take it on than someone less capable. Ironically, gay rights groups had made similar arguments to justify their own filing of a state constitutional challenge after the California Supreme Court's invitation in March 2004. But then, the court had all but asked for a suit, San Francisco had already filed its own suit, and another suit was already pending. No other federal suits were pending when Boies and Olson filed theirs. And while they could not guarantee that no one else would file, Wolfson, Bonauto, Coles, Davidson, and many others had repeatedly talked couples and lawyers out of filing when the time or place was not right. They felt that they could continue to do so. But they couldn't dissuade Boies and Olson.

Boies and Olson were a formidable team, and the mere fact that they had united behind the cause sent a powerful signal about the importance and broad appeal of the claim. But they were not acting alone. Even though the gay rights groups opposed the *Perry* suit's filing, they had already contributed as much as or more than Boies and Olson to its success. The extensive groundwork they had done in California meant that significant political forces in the state were allied with their cause. As a result, both California Governor Arnold Schwarzenegger, a Republican, and Attorney General Jerry Brown, a Democrat, took the extraordinary step of declining to defend Proposition 8. And as it turned out, these decisions not to defend the law would determine the result when the case reached the Supreme Court.

In the absence of any state government lawyers authorized to defend the law, the district court allowed the organization that had successfully petitioned for Proposition 8—ProtectMarriage.com, led by California Senator Dennis Hollingsworth—to intervene and present a defense. In August 2010, after an extensive hearing that reprised the one Evan Wolfson and Dan Foley had conducted in Hawaii's *Baehr* case fifteen years earlier, the district court struck down Proposition 8, marking the first time a federal court had ruled a state's refusal to recognize same-sex marriage unconstitutional under federal law. While the decision did not expressly cite them, its analysis largely tracked the state court decisions from Vermont, Massachusetts, Iowa, Connecticut, and California that had previously declared same-sex marriage bans inconsistent with their state constitutions.[12]

In the state marriage cases, as we have seen, the courts had found unconvincing state interests in promoting procreation, protecting the interests of children, preserving tradition, and conserving resources. The state courts had reasoned that states did not require opposite-sex couples to procreate or raise children, and same-sex couples were fully capable of doing so. Children could be raised healthily by same-sex and opposite-sex couples alike, and the former were already permitted to adopt. Tradition and saving resources were insufficient justifications for discrimination. The state courts had also found no evidence that allowing same-sex couples to marry would undermine straight marriages. The federal district court in *Perry* reached the same conclusions. In many respects, the district court in *Perry* simply adopted arguments that had first succeeded in the state courts. The gay rights groups' strategy of building a case for marriage equality at the state level in order to influence federal constitutional law had worked.[13]

On appeal, the US Court of Appeals for the Ninth Circuit upheld the district court decision, but on peculiar reasoning that appears to have been driven more by a desire to avoid Supreme Court review than by its persuasive force. The appeals court concluded that Proposition 8 was invalid because it had taken away a right that gay and lesbian couples had, albeit briefly, enjoyed after the California Supreme Court's decision in their favor. The appeals court reasoned that the state bears a higher burden of justification when it takes away a right than when it declines to grant it in the first place—even if, as had happened, the right was extended only because of a temporary court victory overturned promptly by the people. By limiting its rationale to states that took away marriage rights from same-sex couples, the court of appeals' reasoning applied only to California, as no other state had granted a constitutional right to marry before reversing course.[14]

If the court of appeals' strained reasoning was an attempt to evade Supreme Court review, it did not work. The proponents of Proposition 8 asked for Supreme Court review and the Court granted it. Yet the Supreme Court ultimately avoided deciding the merits altogether. It ruled instead that State Senator Hollingsworth and ProtectMarriage.com lacked "standing" to appeal. "Standing" doctrine requires that a party appealing a judgment be concretely harmed by the judgment in a particularized way. The state could have appealed, but the Proposition 8 proponents did not speak for the state. And in their own right, the senator and organization were not affected by the decision in a sufficiently specific and concrete way. Boies and Olson had barely objected to the Proposition 8 proponents' standing; they wanted a ruling on the merits. But the standing issue was prominently raised by a friend-of-the-court brief filed by Georgetown Supreme Court Institute director

Irving Gornstein on behalf of former US acting solicitor general Walter Dellinger, and the Court accepted this way out.[15]

Because it found a lack of standing to appeal, the Court's ruling left in place the district court decision declaring Proposition 8 unconstitutional. As a result, same-sex couples in California were afforded the right to marry. But the Court left for another day the ultimate question of whether states were constitutionally compelled to recognize same-sex marriage. The hesitancy of the gay rights advocates at the outset of the *Perry* litigation had been warranted, after all. By issuing a narrow procedural decision, the Court avoided confronting a question it apparently did not feel ready to answer.

The *Perry* litigation thus ended in something of a whimper rather than a bang. It did restore same-sex marriage to Californians, a major victory. But the issue that drew Boies and Olson to the case—the constitutionality of state laws limiting marriage to opposite-sex couples—was left unaddressed at the Supreme Court, and even the intermediate appellate, levels. The most critical move in the litigation, it turned out, was the decision by Governor Schwarzenegger and Attorney General Brown not to defend the law. That decision left the Proposition 8 proponents as the only defenders of the law, and they turned out to lack the requisite concrete interests to appeal.

Highly attentive to public relations, Boies and Olson gave unusual inside access to a *New York Times* reporter, Jo Becker, to chronicle their efforts in *Perry*. Her book on the case opens breathlessly: "This is how a revolution begins." Boies and Olson titled their own book about the case *Redeeming the Dream.*[16] Yet *Perry* was neither the beginning nor the end of any revolution. Nor did it "redeem the dream." As we have seen, the revolution began—in mostly small, unheralded steps—long before Boies and Olson even considered filing a lawsuit, and long before AFER existed. Their success, moreover, was made possible only by the many years of advocacy that preceded the suit. And *Perry* itself achieved far less than its protagonists hoped, as the Supreme Court declined to address the merits of the marriage issue. Its procedural ruling did nothing to disturb existing marriage laws nationwide. In the end, *Perry* was just another step along the way.

5

Losing Forward

MAINE

T HE BEST PLACE TO LOOK TO UNDERSTAND THE BROADER SIGNIFICANCE OF PROPOSITION 8 is not the *Perry* suit filed in its wake in California, but a referendum campaign in Maine. Four years after Proposition 8 amended California's constitution to reserve marriage for heterosexual couples, Maine voters made history by approving a pro-marriage-equality ballot measure. Before that moment, marriage equality proponents had consistently lost same-sex marriage ballot initiatives. Popular referenda are less susceptible to reasoned deliberation than either litigation or legislation, and more vulnerable to fear-mongering and demagoguery. Traditional marriage defenders had obtained constitutional amendments by referenda in thirty states.[1]

Yet on November 6, 2012, the traditionalists' winning streak came to an abrupt halt. Marriage equality proponents won ballot initiatives that day not only in Maine, but in Maryland, Washington, and Minnesota as well—every state where the issue was on the ballot. What made the outcome in Maine all the more remarkable was that just three years earlier, Maine voters had reached the opposite result. In a 2009 ballot initiative, Mainers voted, 53 to 47 percent, to overturn the legislature's recognition of same-sex marriage.

In an important sense, the loss on Proposition 8 four years earlier made possible the win in Maine. The most significant outgrowth of Proposition 8 were the lessons marriage equality proponents learned about how best to argue their cause to the public. Studying what had gone wrong in California, advocates changed both the content and delivery of their message. They began emphasizing marriage as an expression of love and commitment rather than as a measure of equal rights and important tangible benefits. They used straight people as their messengers. And they adopted a new approach to canvassing, one that attempted to persuade voters through open-ended conversations rather than merely identifying supporters and moving on. In Maine, marriage equality proponents tested the new tactics in a real-time campaign. The test was a rousing success. Understanding why requires consideration both of the history of the Maine gay rights movement and of the specific lessons derived from the Proposition 8 defeat. Maine demonstrated that the marriage equality movement could prevail not only in the courts and legislatures, but at the ballot box. And that lesson in turn laid critical ground for eventual recognition of a constitutional right.

BETSY SMITH IS A true Mainer. She grew up on a farm in rural Maine, and gained her first political experience campaigning door to door for her father, who was both a farmer and a state legislator. Politics is in her blood; her great-grandfather and grandfather were Maine legislators, too. Betsy, however, initially followed a different path. She began her career as a high school math teacher. When her employer's discovery of her lesbian relationship forced her to leave her teaching position, she moved to Colorado and briefly became a ski bum. Soon thereafter, she enrolled in Colorado State University to get a master's degree in education. She joined a nascent gay and lesbian student group, and when a dispute arose over whether the group should receive funding from the student council, she spoke out at a campus meeting in support of the group's right to equal treatment. The next day, her picture appeared in the local newspaper and she realized that she had publicly come out. As she put it to me in 2013 during an interview at an inn in Portland, Maine, it was her "Harvey Milk moment."

Smith returned to Maine to teach in 1992 and soon found herself volunteering with the Maine Lesbian and Gay Political Alliance to fight a ballot initiative intended to roll back a Portland ordinance that barred discrimination on the basis of sexual orientation. The Alliance, founded in 1984 after three high school students beat and killed a young gay man in Bangor, was all-volunteer at the time. Its members donated their time after work and on weekends, meeting in and working from one another's homes. The group was well into its second decade before it hired its first paid staff. Today, the group, now named EqualityMaine, is still the state's principal gay and lesbian rights organization. Smith was elected its president in 1996 and, after a brief hiatus, became president again in 2002. She served in that role through 2014.

Smith led the fight for gay and lesbian equality in Maine for more than a decade. The protections she and her organization sought were, in their view, constitutional rights. But they did not file lawsuits in state or federal court. Instead, they advocated for equal treatment in the legislature and at the ballot box. They knew they were unlikely to win gay rights victories under federal constitutional law, which as yet did not recognize such rights. And under state law, their victories had to come through the political process, both because the courts were unlikely to rule in their favor without broad support from Maine's residents, and because even if they prevailed in court, ballot initiatives were relatively easy to institute in Maine, and could erase any court victory. Their opponents had repeatedly launched statewide ballot measures to overturn gains won through gay-friendly local ordinances and state legislation. They knew that any court decision would almost certainly trigger the same response. The battle for equality had to be waged and won politically.

The campaign for marriage equality in Maine was preceded by a twenty-eight-year effort to pass a state law prohibiting discrimination on the basis of sexual orientation in employment, public accommodations, housing, credit, and education. The nondiscrimination campaign began in 1977, before the Maine Lesbian and Gay Political Alliance even existed. After the Alliance was founded, its members made that campaign their primary goal. In 1993, the Alliance managed to convince the Maine legislature to include sexual orientation in the state nondiscrimination law, but the governor vetoed the bill. In 1995, opponents initiated a ballot measure that would have barred Maine towns and counties from covering sexual orientation in local antidiscrimination ordinances. The Alliance won that battle, although as Smith noted ruefully, "we didn't get anything out of it but the status quo." Still, Smith cites that victory as the beginning of a robust gay and lesbian rights advocacy community in Maine. In 1997, the Maine legislature once again passed a nondiscrimination law encompassing sexual orientation, and this time the new governor, Angus King, signed it. But the opposition succeeded in overturning the law by ballot initiative in a 1998 special election.

The legislature yet again passed a nondiscrimination law in 1999, and this time took the initiative to put the issue on the ballot themselves. Again, gay and lesbian rights advocates lost at the ballot box, although by only about 1 percent. Five years later, in 2005, the Alliance, known by then as EqualityMaine, tried again, and the legislature again passed a law prohibiting discrimination on the basis of sexual orientation. This time, the voters rejected the inevitable ballot initiative from opponents. Twenty-eight years after the issue first arose, the gay and lesbian community had finally prevailed. According to Smith, the protracted struggle for a nondiscrimination law taught her and her fellow activists that the fight for equality might be long, with repeated setbacks, but it could be won.

Almost as soon as the celebrations concluded, EqualityMaine and its allies began strategizing about marriage. In 2003, they had won a statewide domestic partnership law, but in 2005 they concluded that it was too early to pursue marriage itself; at the time, Massachusetts was the only state in the country that recognized same-sex marriage. Instead, they laid out a strategy for achieving marriage in three to five years. They would build support in a number of ways—through public advocacy, campaigning for pro-equality legislators, identifying favorable voters so that they could be mobilized when the time came, and establishing a religious coalition in support of marriage equality. They set various benchmarks, and by 2008, they had achieved all but one—they had initially planned on not seeking marriage equality unless Proposition 8 was defeated in California. But Maine had a Democratic legislature and governor, and EqualityMaine believed it had a sufficient number of voters on its side, so it decided to proceed.

In January 2008, the Maine legislature introduced a marriage equality bill; by May, it had been passed into law. But the very next day, Stand for Marriage Maine filed the paperwork to launch a campaign for a ballot initiative to repeal the marriage law. By September the Maine secretary of state certified that the repeal initiative had gathered the requisite signatures to qualify for the November 2009 ballot.

Frank Schubert, the architect of the successful Proposition 8 campaign, designed the marriage equality opponents' campaign in Maine as well. As in California, he invoked the specter of young schoolchildren being taught that same-sex marriages were normal. As in California, Maine's marriage equality proponents did not have an effective response. They ran an ad featuring Maine's attorney general explaining that schools would not be required to teach about same-sex marriage, but as Smith noted, that response appealed "to the head, not the heart." When the results came in, marriage equality proponents had lost yet another referendum.

As in California, the defeat in Maine was disappointing but not disabling. After all, the Maine gay and lesbian community had seen defeat many times before on nondiscrimination. EqualityMaine, GLAD, and allied organizations immediately undertook an investigation of what went wrong. They decided to try again, but this time on their own terms and timing. In the past, they had let their opponents choose when to put marriage on the ballot. They knew that in order to prevail, they had to win at the ballot box, and that their odds were greatest in a high-turnout election, when young people, who disproportionately favor marriage equality, would be likely to vote in larger numbers. So they decided to propose a ballot measure themselves, scheduled to co-incide with the presidential election of 2012.

They also adjusted their approach to voters, employing a new kind of door-to-door canvassing known as "long-form persuasion." After Proposition 8 passed, Dave Fleischer of the LA Gay and Lesbian Center sent out volunteers to learn why people had voted for the initiative. From these interactions, Fleischer proposed that marriage equality advocates conduct a new kind of canvassing. Traditionally, political canvassing seeks merely to identify allies, in order to know who to mobilize on election day. Canvassers are trained to spend no more than a minute or two per interaction, enough time to record preferences and to deliver a brief message, but not enough time to try to persuade.[2]

Fleischer argued that conflicted voters could be persuaded to support marriage equality through more in-depth conversations, in which the canvasser asked open-ended questions designed to invite home-owners to share their experiences. If the cause of marriage equality was to prevail, Fleischer felt, it was important to engage people's concerns directly, and to attempt through extended discussion to persuade them to support marriage equality.

Sarah Reece, an organizer and trainer at the National LGBTQ Task Force who oversaw the Proposition 8 field campaign, agrees that one of the most important lessons she and other advocates learned from that loss was the importance of trying to persuade voters, not just to identify potential supporters. As Reece put it, "early research showed that there is a correlation between knowing someone gay, lesbian, bisexual, or transgender, and supporting marriage equality. But what we now know is that the stronger correlation is when people both know someone gay, lesbian, bisexual, or transgender, and have had a conversation with that person about what marriage means to them." In a related initiative, marriage equality advocates encouraged gay men and lesbians to, in a sense, "come out" on the issue of marriage with their family and friends, by having similar open-ended discussions with them.[3]

Advocates in Maine took the lesson of Proposition 8 to heart. Through EqualityMaine and Mainers United for Marriage, a separate campaign organization created specifically for the 2012 referendum, and with help from the Task Force, GLAD, Freedom to Marry and others, volunteers and paid staff had more than two hundred thousand extended conversations with Maine voters. By their count, about 12,500 voters changed their minds on marriage as a result. They also hoped that the conversations would solidify support among their more ambivalent allies, so that people would in fact turn out for them on election day. And in the end, they did.[4]

IT WAS NOT ENOUGH, however, to change the process by which advocates built support for their cause; they also needed to recast the content of their message. The campaign for marriage equality was, at bottom, a rights campaign; it was a battle for recognition of an equal right to get married. But another lesson of the unsuccessful Proposition 8 campaign was that sometimes it's better to talk about a right in terms other than rights.

Battered by the loss on Proposition 8, advocates undertook several initiatives to diagnose what went wrong. Thalia Zepatos, director of public engagement at Freedom to Marry and a veteran of many marriage battles, launched an effort to devise a new message, enlisting pollster Lisa Grove and the center-left think tank Third Way. They examined more than eighty-five studies from six states on marriage equality struggles. A coalition of thirty gay rights groups conducted a collectively designed survey. And the Courage Campaign, an online organizing group in California, hired a distinct team consisting of pollsters Amy Simon and David Binder, applied psychologist Phyllis Watts, former deputy director of the 2008 Obama campaign Steve Hildebrand, and retired union director Dean Tipps. This team conducted twenty-six separate focus groups and ten roundtables in California in 2009.[5]

The focus groups were divided by race, sex, religion and class to assess how particular audiences responded to the issue. The roundtables brought together a wide range of community leaders from different parts of the state, including Christian ministers; labor union representatives; African American, Asian, and Pacific Islander leaders; parents; teachers; and school administrators. The discussions were anonymous and confidential. All of the participants were straight. As a researcher, Amy Simon felt that the latter restriction was essential because it was more likely to elicit candid responses from the straight people who, at this point, marriage equality proponents needed to persuade.

Simon and her colleagues tried to assess how emotions motivated people's reactions to same-sex marriage. As Phyllis Watts explained, "You have to pay attention to what is going on emotionally. You are unlikely to change anyone's mind with a purely rational argument. You need to understand what triggers their concerns, and the triggers are often more emotional than rational." They found that many people were not merely undecided, but deeply conflicted; they had strong impulses in both directions. On the one hand, as Watts and Simon both noted, people wanted to see themselves as non-judgmental, open-minded, and fair to others. On the other hand, many worried that same-sex marriage might upset the status quo in unpredictable ways. Others experienced same-sex marriage as incompatible with their Christian beliefs and identities. Sometimes anxieties about the pace and nature of social change were expressed in surprising ways. In several focus groups, different men independently worried that recognizing same-sex marriage would raise their taxes; another said that it would be "like the mortgage meltdown." Simon explained: "For these men, taxes and the economic crisis were a sort of stand-in for their general anxiety that somehow this societal change would be imposed on them against their will, and be personally costly."

Hiring outsiders like Simon proved critical. Movement activists are often too convinced of the justice of their cause to understand what might be shaping the views of those not already with them. Some of the ads that had run against Proposition 8 reflected this blindness. One ad portrayed a young and hip pro-marriage-equality character, with a middle-aged, old-fashioned, and decidedly uncool opponent of marriage equality—not an ad that was likely to speak to those on the fence, many of whom might very well have empathized with the uncool opponent. Other ads characterized marriage as a "civil right" and linked the fight for marriage equality to the battles against segregation and race-based internment of Japanese-Americans in World War II—thereby implicitly likening those who questioned same-sex marriage to racial bigots. Such messages are unlikely to appeal to those who are genuinely conflicted about supporting marriage equality. In Simon's view their worries needed to be addressed empathically, not dismissed, mocked, or compared to racism.[6]

Simon believed that many advocates erred by demanding voters to fully embrace their point of view. "They wanted voters to not just allow same-sex marriage but to celebrate it. They wanted people to go from zero to sixty, but human beings aren't wired that way, they can't go that far that fast. This is a step-by-step process, and we only need people to go so far to win on Election Day." In Simon's view, to win, the request could and should be more narrow: "In a single ballot initiative, we're not going to be able to help people move past all of the internal discomfort they may feel about gay people. But if you can make this election be about allowing marriage, not approving, not anything else, you can get people there." In effect, Simon advocated the kind of incrementalism in referendum messaging that the gay rights groups had long understood necessary in their legislative and litigation strategy. But it took an outsider to draw that lesson from the Proposition 8 campaign.

Drawing on social psychologist Jonathan Haidt's analysis of the moral foundations of politics, Simon believes that one of the most powerful factors in moral decision making is loyalty to one's "in-group." If people identify with those affected by a particular choice, they are more likely to care for them, to want to be fair to them, and to support their rights. History supports Simon's view. Many of the nation's most repressive measures were initially targeted at "the other"—whether foreigners, slaves, or minorities. It is easier, for example, to sacrifice liberties for security if they are someone else's liberties, and many of the most extreme counterterrorism measures adopted after 9/11—such as torture, renditions, and disappearances into secret prisons—were limited to foreign nationals. Similarly, it is easier to disregard the human costs of mass incarceration or aggressive stop-and-frisk policing if most of those affected are seen as fundamentally different. A successful campaign for marriage equality, therefore, needed to encourage people to see those affected as in some basic way like them—as members of their "in-group." This intuition is confirmed by polls showing that people who have a gay family member or friend are more likely to support marriage equality than those who do not. And that's why the more that gay men and lesbians came out to their friends, colleagues, and families, the more persuasive their claims to equal treatment were with the public. The marriage equality campaign's messaging needed to evoke those emotions.[7]

Ironically, given that the ultimate goal was to establish a constitutional right to marry, Simon and Watts also found that arguments phrased in the language of "rights" were not particularly effective. "People do not think of marriage as a bundle of rights," according to Watts. "They think of it as an expression of love and commitment." It is better, they found, to stress the importance of expressing and solemnizing one's commitment to another than to treat marriage as a "bundle of rights" (even though it is assuredly both). Or as Freedom to Marry's Thalia Zepatos and Third Way's Lanae Erickson Hatalsky put it in a 2015 op-ed, "talking about 'rights' in the context of marriage reinforced a negative notion that gay couples didn't really understand what marriage was about in the first place. Americans in the middle needed to hear that gay couples wanted to get married for the same reason anyone else does: to make a lifetime commitment."[8]

The "love and commitment" theme, it should be said, was not discovered in 2009. These themes had long been a part of the arguments for marriage equality. Gay rights scholar and advocate Bill Eskridge's 1996 book, *The Case for Same-Sex Marriage*, begins: "Americans are romantics. We fantasize about finding our 'one true love.' For most of us, that fantasy culminates in a proposal of marriage . . . sharing mutual love, perhaps creating a larger family, and parting only at death." Wolfson's 2004 book, *Why Marriage Matters*, argues in its opening pages that "marriage is now the vocabulary we use to talk of love, family, dedication, self-sacrifice, and stages of life. Marriage is a language of love, equality, and inclusion." Wolfson had long maintained that the denial of marriage was central to anti-gay discrimination precisely because it rejected gay people's love for one another. But marriage as an expression of a generous kind of love and commitment had been drowned out by the language of "equal rights" and the "benefits" and "protections" that marriage afforded. The research conducted by Simon and her colleagues revealed that the claim was more likely to appeal to conflicted voters if expressed in terms of love and commitment.[9]

As a result, the tenor of the successful 2012 referendum campaigns in Maine, Washington, Minnesota, and Maryland differed markedly from the Proposition 8 campaign. Simon consulted closely with the communications teams that crafted the ads for Maine and Washington, bringing to bear the lessons she had learned in her research. All of the 2012 Maine ads, for example, featured, not political activists or actors, but genuine Mainers, speaking personally about their own views on marriage equality. In one ad, a ninety-year-old World War II veteran is seated at his dining room table with four generations of his family, including his lesbian granddaughter and her partner. The veteran, Harlan Gardner, explains that he flew "in the last battle of World War II," and then says of his granddaughter, "it takes a great deal of bravery to be a lesbian. I'm so proud of Katie and Alex." His wife of fifty-nine years then says, "I would in my lifetime really like to be able to see Katie and Alex get married, legally." Gardner closes the ad by saying, "This isn't about politics. It's about family and how we as people treat one another."[10]

Almost every speaker in the 2012 Maine ads was straight. They included elderly and middle-aged couples whose child or grandchild was gay or lesbian; the straight son of two moms; a religious minister; a Republican legislator; and a squad of volunteer firefighters, one of whose members was gay. In their own words, the speakers often acknowledged their initial doubts about same-sex marriage, and then explained what led them to change their mind—usually by referring to some person in their family or community who was gay or lesbian. Those who were married spoke about what they valued in their own marriages before saying that they had come to believe that their gay son, granddaughter, or friend should have the same opportunity that they had enjoyed. Where the California ads derided opponents and spoke of civil rights, the Maine ads expressed sympathy with the internal conflict that people on the fence might have, showed how they might overcome their concerns through care for others, and stressed love and commitment. They spoke in an entirely different register. And with this improved messaging and new messengers, marriage equality advocates for the first time prevailed in referendum campaigns. They had now shown that they could win at the state level in the courts, in the legislature, and at the ballot box.

IN A LONG-TERM CAMPAIGN for constitutional reform, losses can be as productive as victories. And the marriage equality campaign had its fair share of losses. The short-lived *Baehr* victory in Hawaii was overturned by constitutional amendment, and sparked a long run of legislation and ballot initiatives elsewhere defining marriage as a union between one man and one woman, including at the federal level in the 1996 Defense of Marriage Act (DOMA). Proposition 8 was in some sense the culmination of that string of losses. But the campaign turned the loss on Proposition 8 to its advantage by coming together, carefully examining what went wrong, and altering its tactics in important ways. Similarly, Professors Michael Dorf and Sidney Tarrow have argued that the initial round of legislative losses after the Hawaii Supreme Court decision in *Baehr* may have advanced the marriage equality movement by bringing more attention to the issue than the advocates themselves could have, and by inspiring the gay rights community to make marriage equality a priority.[11]

Evan Wolfson, no stranger to losing, agrees. He likes to talk about "losing forward." As his movement lost a seemingly endless series of ballot battles in the first two decades of the marriage equality campaign, Wolfson repeatedly insisted that the movement could and should use its losses to advance the ultimate cause by mobilizing more supporters and learning from past mistakes. The Proposition 8 defeat led marriage equality proponents to change the very terms by which they pleaded their cause. Instead of emphasizing division, a natural frame for legal disputes, the campaign emphasized what gay and straight couples shared—a desire to express their love and commitment in a deep, abiding, and socially valued form.

These efforts to understand how best to persuade the public about the legitimacy of same-sex marriage are as much a part of the work of constitutionalism as the briefs filed and arguments made in *Baker*, *Goodridge*, *Perry*, and *Obergefell*. The forums were not courts. Indeed, they were not official venues of any kind. The conversations occurred at people's front doorsteps or kitchen tables; the messages were conveyed by television and radio and the print media. Taken together, they constituted an intensive and extended public and private dialogue about the importance of offering marriage on equal terms to gay and lesbian couples. The conversations and advertisements almost certainly never cited Supreme Court case law, the Framers, or even a provision of the Constitution. They appealed to empathy and emotion as much as reason. But they were a critical part of the nation's path to the recognition of a fundamental right. These conversations and messages helped transform Maine in three short years from a state that voted to reject recognition of same-sex marriage into one that voted to authorize it. Along with similar results in Washington, Michigan, and Maryland, the marriage equality campaign had demonstrated that it could win on its opponents' chosen battlefield, the popular referendum. The tide was very definitely turning.

6

The End Game

WINDSOR AND OBERGEFELL

A FTER THE HANDFUL OF WATERSHED MARRIAGE EQUALITY REFERENDUM VICTORIES IN November 2012, the pace of change quickened dramatically. In June 2013, even as it declined to rule on the merits of the challenge to Proposition 8, the Supreme Court struck down a central provision of the federal Defense of Marriage Act (DOMA), the 1996 law that denied more than one thousand federal benefits to same-sex couples whose states recognized their marriages. The Court's decision in *United States v. Windsor*, written by Justice Anthony Kennedy, rested in large part on the unusual character of the federal law's intrusion into family law, a domain traditionally reserved to the states. It was carefully written so as not to predetermine the outcome of a challenge to state laws limiting marriage to unions between one man and one woman. Chief Justice Roberts wrote a separate opinion expressly for the purpose of underscoring that the decision left open the validity of traditional state marriage laws. Justice Antonin Scalia, however, warned that a constitutional right to marry was just around the corner.[1]

Gay and lesbian couples across the country, and their lawyers, took their cues from Scalia, and filed more than eighty lawsuits building on *Windsor* to argue that state laws denying marriage to same-sex couples were invalid. Nearly all of the federal courts that heard such cases ruled for the lesbian and gay couples. When a federal court of appeals in Ohio in 2014 ruled against marriage equality the Supreme Court agreed to hear the case. In April 2015, the case was argued, fittingly, by GLAD's Mary Bonauto, who had won *Goodridge* in Massachusetts in 2004, had been co-counsel in the Vermont civil unions case, and had been the principal architect of the challenge to DOMA.

On June 26, 2015, the Supreme Court recognized a constitutional right to marry—some five to fifteen years earlier than the target dates advocates had set in the 2005 national strategy memo drafted by Matt Coles. Justice Anthony Kennedy announced the Court's decision in *Obergefell v. Hodges*, as celebrations (and protests) erupted on the courthouse steps and around the nation. Evan Wolfson responded: "I always believed we would win, but I didn't expect to cry." Two days later, large and ebullient crowds joined in conveniently timed annual Gay Pride marches in New York City and San Francisco, formally honoring the memory of the Stonewall riots of June 28, 1969, but more immediately celebrating the historic Supreme Court victory earlier that week.

Many commentators remarked that the constitutional right to same-sex marriage had developed with blinding speed. In fact, as we have seen, the campaign took more than twenty years, and built on progress made on other gay rights issues over more than half a century before that. Still, constitutional law tends to move at a glacial pace, and especially at the end, the progress on marriage equality was anything but glacial.

In 2009, at the same time that gay rights advocates were warning David Boies and Ted Olson not to file a federal constitutional challenge to Proposition 8, Mary Bonauto and GLAD were preparing to file a federal lawsuit challenging the constitutionality of DOMA for denying federal benefits to same-sex marriages. By defining marriage for purposes of all federal laws as a marriage between a man and a woman, DOMA precluded same-sex married couples from a raft of federal marriage benefits, including tax, health care, and survivors' benefits. GLAD's lawsuit on behalf of Nancy Gill and her partner, Marcelle Letourneau, captioned *Gill v. Office of Personnel Management*, advanced claims that were, at least on the surface, strikingly similar to those that Olson and Boies were pressing in the Proposition 8 case: same-sex marriage was constitutionally protected by the equal protection clause and due process, and therefore the government could not refuse to recognize it. Why, then, did Bonauto and GLAD feel that it was appropriate to challenge DOMA in federal court, but not Proposition 8?

In fact, gay rights advocates were divided about whether Bonauto's suit was a good idea. Many lawyers, including James Esseks, director of the ACLU LGBT Rights Project, opposed filing, for some of the same reasons they were skeptical about challenging Proposition 8. Esseks and others worried that both cases risked a federal constitutional loss regarding same-sex marriage. A federal court loss would be much worse than a state court loss on an issue of state law. There are fifty states, with fifty different state constitutions. A setback in one state is not insurmountable and does not necessarily foretell a loss in another. But a loss at the federal level under the US Constitution would be much harder to reverse, and would affect the country as a whole. The gay rights community had seen that happen before. In 1986, in *Bowers v. Hardwick*, the US Supreme Court upheld a Georgia sodomy law against a challenge by a gay man arrested for having consensual sexual relations with another man in his own bedroom. That loss took seventeen years to reverse—a remarkably quick Supreme Court constitutional about-face, but painfully long in daily human experience. Many advocates thought it better to delay pursuing federal constitutional claims until they could be more confident about prevailing. And as long as the marriage equality campaign was making progress at the state level, why involve the federal courts?[2]

Despite the doubts voiced by some of her peers, Bonauto and GLAD pressed ahead with their case. One of their considerations was that, given the number of states that had constitutional amendments defining marriage as a union between one man and one woman, the opportunities for further progress in the states were limited. In such states, the only way to prevail would be by constitutional amendment—not as challenging in most states as at the federal level, but still a tall order. But the more important factor in her decision was her view that the DOMA challenge was considerably less risky than the Proposition 8 lawsuit. Bonauto saw a DOMA case as important both in itself and as the next incremental step in the campaign for marriage equality, and by 2009 she felt it was time to pursue it.

As she saw it, the federal courts could strike down DOMA without confronting whether states must allow same-sex couples to marry, and therefore it was a more modest "ask." In most instances, declaring a federal law unconstitutional is a more serious step than declaring a state law unconstitutional. But in this circumstance, the potential consequences of the Proposition 8 case, which challenged California's failure to recognize same-sex marriage, were actually much more sweeping than the challenge to DOMA. Marriage and family law have long been the province of the states, and the federal government has generally had a very limited role in these matters. A decision declaring DOMA unconstitutional for failing to honor lesbian and gay marriages where states recognized them did not challenge the longstanding primacy of states to define marriage as they deemed fit. The question of state authority to define marriage restrictively could be left for another day.

Bonauto and GLAD were careful to stress from the outset that their suit did not challenge the distinct authority of states to define marriage. The organization's initial press materials, for example, stated that "this case has no bearing on any state's marriage licensing or recognition laws. . . . This is not a case seeking a federal constitutional right to marry that would override any state's marriage laws or amendments." Bonauto's suit claimed only that where states already recognized gay and lesbian marriages, those unions should be treated by the federal government like other marriages. The suit maintained that Congress had discriminated, in other words, not against all gay and lesbian couples, but only against certain state-authorized marriages. So framed, it was almost as much about states' rights as gay rights.[3]

Because Congress generally does not regulate marriage or family relations, Bonauto thought that Congress would have a difficult time justifying its irregular foray into the subject. States have the authority to recognize and license marriages, and therefore they must necessarily draw some line specifying who may (and may not) get married. The states have long done just that. Before DOMA, by contrast, the federal government had not drawn lines of its own with respect to the definition or validity of certain kinds of marriage, but had simply deferred to the states to determine who was married and therefore entitled to federal marriage benefits. Because it had no traditional role in this area, the federal government would have difficulty explaining why, suddenly in 1996, it needed to start distinguishing between different kinds of state-sanctioned marriages.

In addition, Bonauto and the GLAD team predicted that the dynamics of federal versus state power that DOMA presented might appeal to Justice Kennedy, the Court's likely swing vote. In the past, Kennedy had been sympathetic to both gay rights claims and the prerogatives of states. A case directly challenging a state's decision not to allow same-sex marriage, like the Proposition 8 challenge, would force Kennedy to choose between gay rights and state power. In the DOMA case, by contrast, he could side with both gay rights and the states' family-law prerogatives by ruling against the federal government.

Supreme Court precedent authored by Kennedy also appeared to offer strong support. In the Court's first pro-gay-rights decision ever, *Romer v. Evans*, decided in 1996 (the same year Congress passed DOMA), the Court invalidated a Colorado ballot initiative that had amended the state constitution to preclude any current or future state or municipal anti-discrimination laws from prohibiting discrimination on the basis of sexual orientation. Writing for a five-justice majority, Kennedy pointed to the highly unusual character of the law, and its extraordinary breadth in disabling the people and their representatives from maintaining or creating any anti-discrimination protections for gays and lesbians, as evidence that it was impermissibly motivated by homophobic animus, and therefore denied equal protection. Shortly after *Romer* was decided, Evan Wolfson, then at Lambda, wrote a legal memo arguing that DOMA was similarly unusual and sweeping, and that *Romer* was therefore strong precedent for challenging DOMA.[4]

Finally, the evidence that DOMA was enacted out of animus against gay men and lesbians was patently clear. The House Report that accompanied the law stated that it was designed to express "moral disapproval of homosexuality, and a moral conviction that heterosexuality better comports with traditional (especially Judeo-Christian) morality."[5] (That legislators in 1996 felt free to express such sentiment in the official legislative record illustrates how much the nation has changed in the intervening years.) In *Lawrence v. Texas*, the 2003 decision striking down a Texas law criminalizing homosexual sodomy, the Court specifically declared that moral disapproval alone could not justify a law that intruded into the "personal and private life of the individual" by regulating sexual intimacy between consenting adults. Thus, the explicitly stated purpose of DOMA was suspect under Supreme Court precedent.[6]

Although DOMA became law in 1996, it had no immediate concrete effect on anyone, as no states then recognized same-sex marriage. That changed in 2004 when Massachusetts became, with *Goodridge*, the first state to do so. Now same-sex couples married in Massachusetts were married for state law purposes but not for federal law purposes. As a result, they could not, for example, file joint federal income tax returns, obtain health insurance for their spouses from federal employers, or receive Social Security survivors' benefits.

After she won *Goodridge* in the Massachusetts Supreme Judicial Court, Bonauto started hearing from gay married couples in the state who were confronting difficulties brought on by DOMA. At first, she discouraged legal challenges. She and GLAD were still fighting to hold on to the victory in *Goodridge*. In their view, it would have been premature to seek federal benefits based on state-recognized gay marriages while the status of those state marriages was itself still in doubt. Once the efforts to reverse *Goodridge* via state constitutional amendment failed and the Massachusetts victory was secure, however, she and GLAD began to develop a DOMA challenge.

They constructed their DOMA suit carefully. They selected plaintiffs who had been denied basic federal benefits that everyone could understand, such as Social Security and health care. They emphasized the detrimental effects of the law on children raised in gay families. They characterized the discrimination not as directed against gay and lesbian couples, but against one class of "state-recognized marriages." And they persuaded the Massachusetts attorney general to file a companion case on behalf of the state, dramatically underscoring the extent to which the case pitted state power against federal interference in an area traditionally reserved to the states.

Despite having written a memo arguing that DOMA was unconstitutional when it was first passed, Evan Wolfson had long been ambivalent about challenging it in court. Like Bonauto, he recognized that there were good reasons to proceed. But he was more concerned about the risks, and for some time advised advocates to stick to the state-by-state approach and stay out of federal court, even if that meant leaving DOMA on the books for the time being. For him, the calculus changed with the election of Barack Obama. Obama had been strongly supported by the gay community, and as a candidate he had advocated DOMA's repeal. If a DOMA suit were filed after Obama's inauguration, he would have to decide whether to defend a statute that he had publicly committed to repealing. And if Obama declined to defend the law in court, the odds of a victory would improve significantly. Wolfson urged his contacts in the new administration to press the president to decline to defend DOMA if it were challenged. And he was not alone; this issue was high on the agendas of many of the new president's gay and lesbian supporters.

At first, the Justice Department defended the law. There is a strong presumption that the president will defend federal laws when challenged in the courts even if he disagrees with them. Bonauto and other gay rights lawyers met repeatedly with Justice Department lawyers, maintaining that this was an extraordinary case in which the ordinary presumption was rebutted because the law plainly rested on anti-gay animus. They asked the administration not merely to decline to defend DOMA, but to take the legal position that because the law overtly discriminated against gay and lesbian couples, the courts should subject it to "heightened scrutiny."

Under the Supreme Court's equal protection doctrine, "heightened scrutiny" has traditionally been reserved for laws that discriminate on the basis of race, sex, or national origin. Laws subjected to heightened scrutiny are in effect presumptively invalid, and will be upheld only if a court finds that the law serves an important or compelling interest, and is closely tailored to advance that purpose. Laws that discriminate on the basis of other factors, by contrast, such as age, trigger only deferential scrutiny, and are valid as long as the court can think of any rational justification for the classification. The Supreme Court has not yet addressed what level of scrutiny should apply to discrimination against gays and lesbians. But a strong case can be made that all the factors that guide the application of heightened scrutiny support its application to sexual orientation discrimination: gay men and lesbians, like racial minorities and women, have historically been the victims of discrimination and prejudice; sexual orientation, like race and sex, has no relevance to actual ability to participate in society; sexual orientation, like race and sex, is generally immutable; and gay men and lesbians, like African Americans or Latinos, constitute a discrete minority unlikely to be protected as equals by the democratic process.

Justice Department lawyers defending the *Gill* case told Bonauto that their hands were tied because the US Court of Appeals for the First Circuit, whose decisions are binding in federal courts in Massachusetts, had previously ruled that discrimination on the basis of sexual orientation triggered only deferential scrutiny. So Bonauto and other gay rights groups looked for an opportunity to raise the issue in a federal circuit that had not already resolved the issue of the level of scrutiny. In 2010, Bonauto filed a second DOMA challenge, this time in

Connecticut. The same day, James Esseks of the ACLU LGBT Rights Project and Roberta Kaplan, a partner with the Paul, Weiss law firm, filed a similar case on behalf of Edith Windsor in New York—*Windsor v. United States*. Both states are in the Second Circuit, whose court of appeals had not yet decided what standard of review to apply to discrimination on the basis of sexual orientation. Now the Obama administration had to confront the issue squarely.

Meanwhile, the broader gay community seized the issue when, in June 2009, the Justice Department filed a motion to dismiss yet another case challenging DOMA that had been filed in California. A gay blogger, John Aravosis, obtained a copy of the government's brief and uploaded a post that called it "gratuitously homophobic." He pointed to, among other things, the brief's citations to cases upholding states' rights not to recognize marriages between first cousins and involving a sixteen-year-old. The brief had cited the cases only for the generic proposition that states have long had the authority to decline to recognize marriages entered into in other states if they violate their public policy. But Aravosis characterized the brief as comparing gay marriages to incest and marriages of children. In his words, "Holy cow, Obama invoked incest and people marrying children." The charge got picked up by ABC News, and the following day, Joe Solmonese, president of Human Rights Campaign, wrote President Obama, saying, "I cannot overstate the pain that we feel as human beings and as families when we read an argument, presented in federal court, implying that our own marriages have no more constitutional standing than incestuous ones." The *New York Times* followed up four days later with an editorial condemning the administration for its defense of DOMA.[7]

This was more than enough to put the DOMA litigation on the White House's radar. After much internal wrangling, the administration did what Bonauto, Wolfson, and many others had asked: it took the position that heightened scrutiny should apply to DOMA, and that it could not defend the law under such scrutiny. It informed the courts and Congress of the decision. The leadership of the House of Representatives, controlled at the time by Republicans, then intervened to take up the defense of the statute in the Justice Department's stead.

Thus, by the time DOMA reached the Supreme Court, the executive branch was no longer defending the statute.

The First and Second Circuits each declared DOMA unconstitutional, finding no legitimate reason for the federal government to treat same-sex married couples differently from opposite-sex couples where states had recognized both as properly married under state law. The House leadership and the Obama administration requested Supreme Court review in both cases. (The administration argued that the law was unconstitutional, agreeing with the courts of appeals, but supported Supreme Court review to secure a final resolution of the issue.) The Court granted review in *United States v. Windsor*, the Second Circuit case filed in New York by the ACLU. It probably chose *Windsor* over *Gill* because Justice Elena Kagan was recused from *Gill*, having worked on it when she was solicitor general, and the Court prefers having a full bench. That meant that Roberta Kaplan and the ACLU were lead counsel in the Supreme Court, not Bonauto and GLAD, who nonetheless assisted by coordinating the "friend of the court" briefs.[8]

In June 2013, the Court declared DOMA unconstitutional. Justice Kennedy cast the deciding vote and wrote the opinion for the Court's 5–4 majority. Even though Bonauto did not argue the case, one can draw a straight line from her initial framing of the issue in *Gill* (also advanced by the plaintiffs in *Windsor*) to Justice Kennedy's opinion. Like Bonauto, Kennedy emphasized that the law discriminates against a class of marriages recognized by the states. Like Bonauto, Kennedy cited the harms inflicted on the children of same-sex couples. Like Bonauto, Kennedy noted that marriage is the traditional province of the states, and that DOMA marked an unusual federal intrusion into the state's province. Like Bonauto, Kennedy concluded that the unusual character and sweeping breadth of DOMA suggested that the law was ultimately motivated by animus against gay and lesbian couples, an impermissible purpose. And like Bonauto, Kennedy was careful to stress that the case involved couples whose marriages states had chosen to recognize, and not whether states could be compelled to recognize such marriages in the first place.[9]

Notwithstanding the care Kennedy took to leave undecided the question of state marriage authority, a flood of litigation ensued, as same-sex couples in virtually every state in the Union that did not already recognize same-sex marriage filed suit, arguing that the US Constitution required the states to recognize same-sex marriage on the same terms and conditions as traditional marriage. In the two years following *Windsor*, virtually all the federal courts ruled that equal protection, due process, or both, indeed required states to treat same-sex couples equally by permitting them to marry. By the time the Supreme Court accepted review in *Obergefell* in January 2015, more than sixty courts, including four federal courts of appeals, had ruled that the Constitution requires equal recognition of same-sex marriages. Only four courts, including one court of appeals, had ruled the other way.[10]

The landslide of federal court decisions that preceded the Supreme Court decision in *Obergefell* cannot be explained by *Windsor* alone. Nothing in that decision compelled lower courts to strike down state laws barring same-sex marriage. The question remained an open one— and evidently by design. But an incensed Justice Scalia, in his dissent in *Windsor*, had predicted that the majority's reasoning would lead to the invalidation of state marriage laws as well. He turned out to have been right. By 2013 and 2014, recognition of same-sex marriage had come to seem inevitable.

In 2014, five states whose marriage laws had been declared unconstitutional by lower courts—Virginia, Indiana, Wisconsin, Oklahoma, and Utah—filed five separate petitions for Supreme Court review. Most commentators expected the Court to take up one or more of those cases. The Court nearly always grants review where a lower federal court has declared a state law unconstitutional, and in all but one of those cases the laws declared invalid were not just ordinary laws but state constitutional provisions. In October 2014, however, the Court denied review in all five cases, apparently preferring to let matters develop further before taking up the question for national resolution.[11]

The Court could not put off the inevitable for long. The very next month, in November 2014, the US Court of Appeals for the Sixth

Circuit, by a 2–1 vote, upheld four state laws limiting marriage to straight couples. The opinion, written by Judge Jeffrey Sutton, a highly respected and relatively young conservative judge, maintained that the question of whether marriage should be extended to same-sex couples was properly left to the democratic process, as neither due process nor equal protection required states to change their long-standing definitions of marriage as limited to a union of one man and one woman. Now there was a clear disagreement among the federal courts of appeals. The losing parties petitioned for Supreme Court review, and this time the Court agreed to hear the matter.[12]

The lead case arose from Ohio. James Obergefell and his partner, John Arthur, Ohio residents, traveled to Maryland to get married, and then sued Ohio for failing to recognize their marriage upon their return. John was terminally ill with amyotrophic lateral sclerosis, commonly known as Lou Gehrig's disease, or ALS, and they wanted to be able to list James as the surviving spouse on John's death certificate. When Ohio refused, they sued.

The Supreme Court argument in the case, held on April 28, 2015, focused on whether the Court should allow the issue of same-sex marriage to continue to develop at the state level by declining to find a constitutional right, or should, by recognizing such a right, require every state to license same-sex marriages. Justice Kennedy expressed concern about intervening precipitately, observing that "the word that keeps coming back to me in this case is 'millennia.' . . . This definition [of marriage] has been with us for millennia. And it's very difficult for the Court to say, oh, well, we know better." Justice Scalia voiced a similar worry: "The issue, of course, is not whether there should be same-sex marriage, but who should decide the point. . . . And you're asking us to decide it for this society when no other society until 2001 ever had it." Chief Justice Roberts noted that, given the pace of change, the issue might be better resolved through the democratic process than by a constitutional decision imposed by the Court. At the same time, neither Kennedy nor the liberal justices seemed persuaded by the arguments advanced by the states to defend differential treatment of straight and gay marriages.

Solicitor General Don Verrilli, representing the Obama administration, argued that the state laws were unconstitutional. He closed his
argument with a powerful call for recognizing same-sex marriage now,
and not leaving the issue to the states:

> What the Respondents are ultimately saying to the Court is that with
> respect to marriage, they are not ready yet. And yes, gay and lesbian
> couples can live openly in society, and yes, they can raise children.
> Yes, they can participate fully as members of their community. Mar-
> riage, though, not yet. Leave that to be worked out later. . . . But what
> these gay and lesbian couples are doing is laying claim to the promise
> of the Fourteenth Amendment now. And it is emphatically the duty
> of this Court, in this case . . . to decide what the Fourteenth Amend-
> ment requires.
>
> And what I would suggest is that in a world in which gay and
> lesbian couples live openly as our neighbors, they raise their children
> side by side with the rest of us, they contribute fully as members of
> the community, that it is simply untenable, untenable, to suggest that
> they can be denied the right of equal participation in an institution
> of marriage, or that they can be required to wait until the majority
> decides that it is ready to treat gay and lesbian people as equals. Gay
> and lesbian people are equal. They deserve equal protection of the
> laws, and they deserve it now.[13]

On June 26, 2015, the Court announced its decision. Justice Kennedy again wrote the opinion, just as he had in all three prior gay
rights victories at the Supreme Court. Joined by Justices Ruth Bader
Ginsburg, Stephen Breyer, Sonia Sotomayor, and Elena Kagan, Justice Kennedy declared that the Constitution's "right to marry" applies
without distinction to same-sex and opposite-sex couples. He relied
principally on the Constitution's proviso that "liberty" shall not be de-
prived without "due process of law." That safeguard had long been read
not only to mandate procedural fairness, but also to protect certain
fundamental rights central to private life, including the rights to marry,
to choose how to educate one's children, to engage in sexual intimacy

with a consenting adult, to use contraception, and to terminate an un-wanted pregnancy. The Court had previously ruled that states could not deny the right to marry to couples of different races, to prisoners, or to fathers who had failed to make their child custody payments. Of course, each of those cases involved marriage between a man and a woman, a definition, as Kennedy had noted at oral argument, that had existed for millennia.[14]

To answer whether same-sex couples should have the right to marry, Kennedy asked why the Court has protected the right to marry, and whether there was any basis, given those reasons, for treating gay and straight couples differently. He identified four reasons the right to marry was constitutionally protected: (1) freedom to choose with whom to share one's life is a fundamental aspect of individual autonomy; (2) marriage furthers the right to intimate association; (3) marriage safe-guards children; and (4) marriage is a "keystone of the Nation's social order" and therefore is supported through a wide array of official ben-efits. Each of these principles, Kennedy reasoned, applies with equal force to opposite-sex and same-sex couples, and therefore there is no legitimate basis for denying the right to the latter.[15]

Kennedy also relied on the equal protection clause, although, as in his prior gay rights decisions, he avoided specifying whether dis-crimination against gays and lesbians warrants heightened scrutiny. He simply noted that in this instance the principles of equal protection and liberty reinforce each other to require equal recognition of same-sex marriage.

ALL FOUR DISSENTING JUSTICES in *Obergefell* wrote separately to decry the result, and their dissents offer a window on the ongoing debate over the true meaning of constitutionalism in America. Scalia, by far the most vituperative, condemned the majority opinion as "pretentious," "egotistic," and filled with "hubris" and the "mystical aphorisms of the fortune cookie." "Today's decree," he warned, "says that my Ruler, and the Ruler of 320 million Americans coast-to-coast, is a majority of the

nine lawyers on the Supreme Court." Justice Thomas went further, arguing not only that the majority was wrong, but that all prior decisions protecting personal liberty with respect to education, sexual intimacy, marriage, contraception, and abortion were wrong, because the Framers intended the "liberty" referred to in the due process clause to protect only freedom from physical restraint. And Chief Justice Roberts spoke directly to those who would celebrate the result, cautioning, "do not celebrate the Constitution. It had nothing to do with it."[16]

Chief Justice Roberts's dissent asked why, under Kennedy's analysis, there would not also be a constitutional right to polygamous marriages. Parroting Kennedy's reasoning, Roberts noted that recognition of polygamous marriages could also be said to further the dignity of those who choose such marriages, and might well further the interests of children raised by such families. But Roberts's question fails to take into account what actually brought constitutional recognition of same-sex marriage. It was not a particular doctrinal analysis, but a long campaign of constitutional advocacy, that transformed the nation's views on same-sex marriage.

Roberts's dismissive analogy springs from the same fallacy advanced by professors who teach constitutional law exclusively as a series of technical legal arguments. If polygamous marriage were ever to receive constitutional protection, it would not be because five justices found Roberts's parallels analytically inescapable. It would be because a mass of people cared enough to create a set of civil society institutions that worked to legitimate the idea of polygamous marriage over an extended period of time, all the while responding to and assuaging public concerns about it. The answer to Roberts is that constitutional law develops not by slippery-slope arguments made in the abstract, but through public debate about fundamental principles and values, pressed by people with powerful commitments willing to make sustained efforts in multiple arenas—local, state, and federal, public and private, at home and at work. Gay rights advocates had pursued just such a debate over many decades, and it was their work and their commitment, not an abstract legal rationale, that was the foundation of their victory.[17]

It should be evident from the Supreme Court's closely divided vote that, as a pure matter of constitutional interpretation, the Court in *Obergefell* could have gone either way. Kennedy's attempt to derive general principles from the established "right to marry" in order to discern its scope and apply it to new facts is what judges have always done when considering how precedent should cover a new situation. But at the same time, the dissenters have a point that this newfound right—one not recognized by any American jurisdiction before 2004, and by any jurisdiction anywhere in the world before the Netherlands did so in 2001—is not self-evidently supported by the Constitution. As the Court's one-line dismissal of a marriage equality claim in 1972 illustrates, not long ago no justice even believed that the claim presented a "substantial federal question."[18]

That's why Chief Justice Roberts objected that the Constitution "had nothing to do with it." True, the result was dictated not by doctrinal argumentation as much as by a transformation in Americans' fundamental values. But in a more important sense Roberts was wrong. The Constitution is designed to reflect the nation's deepest commitments. Those commitments have evolved over time, and will continue to evolve. Constitutional law has changed to reflect those developments, and will continue to do so. As Justice Kennedy wrote, "the right to marry is fundamental as a matter of history and tradition, but rights come not from ancient sources alone. They rise, too, from a better informed understanding of how constitutional imperatives define a liberty that remains urgent in our own era." The same is true with respect to equal protection, he added, where "new insights and societal understandings can reveal unjustified inequality within our most fundamental institutions that once passed unnoticed and unchallenged."[19]

In *Obergefell* the Court did not so much rewrite constitutional law as recognize that it had been rewritten. This was not a case of five justices imposing their personal values on the American people, but of recognizing, in the act of constitutional interpretation, a shortcoming in existing protections pointed out and vividly decried over several decades. The decision is correct not because it comports with liberal values, but because it reflects an extended transformation in how America's fundamental values apply to lesbians and gays. When American values develop in ways that promote conservative views, constitutional law similarly reflects those changes (as the next section on the right to bear arms illustrates). In the case of marriage equality, that development occurred not because federal judges imposed their own views, but through understandings forged over time in local governments, private businesses, state courts and legislatures, ballot initiatives, the media, and personal conversations. By the time the Supreme Court decided *Windsor*, marriage equality advocates had won numerous state court victories, had convinced several legislatures to pass laws extending marriage, and had won all four ballot initiatives in the 2012 presidential election. Public opinion polls consistently showed that a majority of Americans favored recognition of same-sex marriages. Countless gay and lesbian couples had married, with no identifiable negative effect on "traditional" marriage. Tens of thousands of children were being raised by married gay and lesbian parents. President Obama himself had publicly endorsed same-sex marriage, as had many other politicians, Republicans as well as Democrats. The country was ready for marriage equality, and arguments that allowing same-sex couples to marry would harm anyone appeared increasingly far-fetched. Properly understood, constitutionalism encompasses all of this, and not just what happens in the federal courts. In this sense, and contrary to Chief Justice Roberts's assertion, the Constitution had everything to do with the result in *Obergefell*.

As did civil society. *Obergefell* is unimaginable absent the decades of advocacy of small groups of committed individuals—including the Mattachine Society, ACT UP, the ACLU LGBT Project, GLAD, Lambda Legal, Freedom to Marry, the National Center for Lesbian Rights, the Equality Federation, GLAAD, Human Rights Campaign, the National LGBTQ Task Force, and countless state-based groups—and their visionary leaders, including Evan Wolfson, Mary Bonauto, Frank Kameny, and Matt Coles. These organizations and individuals, working in conjunction with countless others, were the engines that propelled constitutional law's recognition of marriage equality.

PART TWO

RIGHT TO BEAR ARMS

THE SECOND AMENDMENT, ADOPTED IN 1791 WITH THE REST OF THE BILL OF RIGHTS, remained a dead letter as a matter of formal constitutional law until 217 years later, on June 26, 2008. On that date, a closely divided Supreme Court, in *District of Columbia v. Heller*, effectively revived the amendment, announcing for the first time that it protects an individual right to bear arms, and struck down a DC law banning possession of handguns. Two years later, in *McDonald v. City of Chicago*, the Court also invalidated Chicago's handgun ban and ruled that the Second Amendment applies to state and local as well as federal laws, overturning past precedent to the contrary. Before 2008, the Supreme Court had never invalidated any legislation under the Second Amendment. The Court's 1939 decision in *United States v. Miller*, upholding a prohibition on sawed-off shotguns, had been widely understood to mean that the amendment protected only the states' prerogative to maintain a militia, and not an individual right to bear arms unassociated with that purpose. As late as 1990, retired Chief Justice Warren Burger had dismissed as fraudulent the notion that the Second Amendment

97

protected an individual right to bear arms. Less than twenty years later, Burger's fraud had become an established constitutional right.[1]

In terms of practical effect, *Heller* was less momentous than *Obergefell*. By 2008, nearly all states recognized a right to bear arms under their own constitutions, and as most gun regulation is a matter of state law, most Americans enjoyed the right to have and use a gun long before *Heller* declared it a federal constitutional right. By contrast, no gay couples had a right to marry before Massachusetts recognized one in 2004, and gay couples in most states still lacked the right before the lower federal courts began ruling in their favor. As a matter of constitutional law, however, the *Heller* decision was in many ways just as remarkable as *Obergefell*. It turned constitutional doctrine on its head, and substituted a new view of the Second Amendment for one that had governed for most of the previous century. How did this come about?

The Second Amendment itself is ambiguous, even awkward, in its phrasing: "A well regulated Militia, being necessary to the security of a free State, the right of the people to keep and bear Arms, shall not be infringed." Both the majority and the dissenting justices in *Heller* took an "originalist" approach to the question of the amendment's meaning. On that view, the justices should interpret the Constitution by ascertaining what its words meant at the time they were adopted. The majority opinion, written by Justice Antonin Scalia, the high priest of originalism, relied entirely on such historical evidence to conclude that the amendment protects an individual right to bear arms. The principal dissent, written by Justice John Paul Stevens and joined by Justices Souter, Ginsburg, and Breyer, looked to the same historical record, but found support there for the opposite conclusion, namely, that the amendment guarantees only the rights of states to field militias, and not the rights of individuals to possess or use arms for non-militia purposes. Though the Court split 5–4, all nine justices spoke in originalist terms.[2]

The historical evidence relied on by the justices included the English Bill of Rights, a forerunner of our own; state constitutional provisions of the period; the drafting history of the Second Amendment; contemporaneous descriptions of the right in legal treatises; and the early interpretations of the provision by courts and other commentators. On the face of it, this was entirely a debate about whose version of history was more accurate.

Notably absent from all of the opinions is any reference to the longstanding campaign of the National Rifle Association to establish and defend an individual right to bear arms. There is no mention of the gun rights laws and precedents the NRA pioneered in the states, Congress, or the executive branch. And despite its dominance in the gun rights field, the NRA did not represent Dick Heller. In fact, much like the reaction of gay rights groups when Ted Olson and David Boies filed *Perry v. Schwarzenegger*, the constitutional challenge to Proposition 8, the NRA tried desperately to stop the *Heller* case.

Yet the NRA almost certainly had more responsibility for the result in *Heller* than did "originalist" theory. The historical record, after all, is, like the amendment itself, ambiguous, as the competing opinions demonstrate. "Originalism" cannot explain how a view dismissed as fraudulent by a conservative retired chief justice in 1990 became the law of the land less than two decades later. To understand this transformation, we must look, as with marriage equality, to civil society—and in particular to the NRA. The organization left no immediately visible marks on the decision, but we see its fingerprints everywhere once we begin to explore how this constitutional change came about. And as with same-sex marriage, the overwhelming majority of the work the NRA did to establish the right took place outside the federal courts. Here, too, constitutionalism was a multidimensional enterprise, taking place in a variety of forums and involving many tactics that have little directly to do with doctrinal analysis—originalist or otherwise.

By the time the Supreme Court ruled in 2008, the NRA had succeeded in transforming the gun rights landscape in a number of ways. It had encouraged legal scholarship advancing the view that the Second Amendment was intended to protect an individual right to bear arms. It had supported politicians who worked to change state laws and constitutions to respect an individual right to bear arms. It had secured influential endorsements of its view of the Second Amendment from Congress and the executive branch. It had helped ensure that the

Supreme Court's newest justices were selected in part on the basis of their sympathy to gun rights. Without all of these efforts, it is unlikely that the Court would have reached the decision it did in *Heller*. Perhaps even more significantly, as a result of this long-term campaign, the NRA remains today a more potent protector of gun rights than the Supreme Court itself.

The ascent and recent successes of the NRA would likely come as a shock to its founders. Established in New York in 1871, shortly after the Civil War, the NRA's initial focus was marksmanship, not gun rights. It was created by Union generals concerned that too many of their soldiers had been unable to shoot straight. As one founder, General Ambrose Burnside, said of his troops, "out of ten soldiers who are perfect in drill and the manual of arms, only one knows the purpose of the sights on his gun or can hit the broad side of a barn."[3]

The first evidence of the NRA advocating for the rights of law-abiding gun owners dates to the early twentieth century, when New York was considering requiring licenses to possess and carry guns small enough to be concealed. Commenting on what ultimately became the Sullivan Act, an NRA publication stated: "A warning should be sounded to legislators against passing laws which . . . seem to make it impossible for a criminal to get a pistol, if the same laws would make it very difficult for an honest man and a good citizen to obtain them. Such laws have the effect of arming the bad man and disarming the good one." Such arguments have become a consistant theme of NRA advocacy in the modern era. But this response was exceptional in the early history of the NRA, which for the most part steered clear of political advocacy.[4]

In its early days, the NRA also did not systematically oppose gun regulation. In the 1930s, for example, it endorsed the Uniform Firearms Act as model state legislation. The act included a waiting period for handgun sales; licensing requirements for gun dealers and for those seeking to carry concealed weapons; bans on the sale of machine guns, silencers, and sawed-off shotguns; and prohibitions on handgun sales to minors, drug addicts, or those "not of sound mind."[5]

When the NRA did begin to devote increased resources to defending gun rights in the late 1970s and early 1980s, the state of federal constitutional law was clear: the Second Amendment protected only the states' rights to maintain militias as a check on federal tyranny, and not an individual right to bear arms unconnected to that end. A federal court of appeals' discussion of the issue from 1942 is typical:

> It is abundantly clear both from the discussion of this amendment contemporaneous with its proposal and adoption and those of learned writers since that this amendment, unlike those providing for protection of free speech and freedom of religion, was not adopted with individual rights in mind, but as a protection for the States in the maintenance of their militia organizations against possible encroachments by the federal power.[6]

As another appellate court put it in 1971, "there can be no serious claim to any express constitutional right of an individual to possess a firearm." Still another, in 1988, stated that "for at least 100 years [courts] have analyzed the second amendment purely in terms of protecting state militias, rather than individual rights."[7]

Changing this status quo would be no easy task. The challenge the NRA faced was in many respects every bit as difficult as that faced by Lambda Legal Defense Fund and GLAD when they first began to campaign for marriage equality. Federal constitutional law was dead set against them. If the NRA was to achieve a constitutional right to bear arms, it would have to pursue other avenues than federal court litigation. As we will see, much like the gay rights groups, the NRA began with a state-by-state strategy.

7

One State at a Time

THE ADVENT OF THE MODERN-DAY NRA, NOW WIDELY REGARDED AS ONE OF THE MOST powerful lobbying organizations in the nation, can be traced to 1968. That year, in response to the assassinations of John F. Kennedy, Robert Kennedy, Malcolm X, and Dr. Martin Luther King Jr., Congress passed the Gun Control Act, the first major federal gun law since 1934. The act required anyone selling or buying a gun in interstate commerce to do so through a federally licensed dealer, prohibited mail order sales, and barred the sale of guns to convicted felons and the mentally ill. The NRA opposed certain aspects of the bill, but its executive vice president, Franklin Orth, wrote in the NRA's flagship publication, *The American Rifleman*, that "the measure as a whole appears to be one that the sportsmen of America can live with."[1]

Orth was wrong, at least from the standpoint of many NRA members. The passage of the Gun Control Act, together with the creation in 1974 of two national gun control organizations—the National Coalition to Ban Handguns and the National Council to Control Handguns—led many members to condemn Orth's willingness to compromise. In 1975, the NRA created a distinct lobbying arm for the first time, the Institute for Legislative Action, or NRA-ILA. When, the very next year, the NRA's old-guard leadership attempted to return the organization to a focus on hunting and conservation, and to move its headquarters from Washington, DC, to Colorado Springs, a revolt ensued. At the NRA's 1977 annual meeting in Cincinnati, Ohio, the membership voted to replace the more conciliatory leadership with hard-liners and overturned the decision to move.

The "Cincinnati revolt" focused the NRA on defending its vision of the Second Amendment as a protection of individual rights. As one insider, Joseph Tartaro, recounted, "To many who were paramountly interested in the NRA as a leader of the pro-gun political movement, much of what occurred [leading up to the 1977 meeting] smelled of retreat." The reformers had a "sense that the NRA was not only moving out of Washington, DC, where an eminent presence was considered politically necessary, but was also moving away from a strong defense of the Second Amendment."[2] The hard-line reformers made their intent clear from the very first resolution they successfully championed, which added to the organization's bylaws "a clear statement that one of the Association's purposes was 'to protect and defend the US Constitution, especially the political, civil and inalienable rights of the American people to keep and bear arms as a common law and Constitutional right both of the individual citizen and of the collective militia.'"[3]

The NRA continues to offer a wide range of services and activities that have nothing to do with advocacy—sponsoring shooting competitions and ranges, and providing firearms safety training and educational materials to millions. In fact, it devotes the lion's share of its budget to such endeavors. Only about 10 percent of the budget goes to its lobbying arm. But this faction has had enormous impact. Since 1977, the NRA has dominated the nation's debates about gun rights.[4]

How did the NRA make its vision of the Second Amendment the new constitutional normal? Like marriage equality advocates, it could not change Second Amendment doctrine simply by filing a lawsuit in federal court. The NRA did briefly try that route in the 1980s, but with as little success as the early marriage suits filed by gay couples. When Morton Grove, a Chicago suburb, banned handguns in 1981, gun rights advocates filed three lawsuits—two in federal court and one in state court—arguing that the ban violated both the Second Amendment and the Illinois state constitutional right to bear arms. The suits failed at every level. The US Court of Appeals for the Seventh Circuit ruled, relying on Supreme Court precedents, that the Second Amendment had no applicability to state or local governments, and that in any event it "extends only to those arms which are necessary to maintain a well-regulated militia."[5] The Supreme Court declined to review the decision.

Facing inhospitable federal courts, the NRA adopted a "federalist" strategy, amending state gun laws one state at a time. As leading gun rights advocate Dave Kopel argues on the NRA's website, "the preservation of Second Amendment rights nationally depends upon a national organization that has resources to fight locally." Guns, like marriage, are primarily regulated by states. According to former NRA President David Keene, "90 percent of the laws that the NRA has contended with over the course of the last few decades have not been the federal laws, but have been state and local restrictions." If the NRA could get the states to recognize an individual right to bear arms under their own constitutions, gun owners would, for all practical purposes, be protected against their principal regulators.[6]

In addition, a state-focused strategy allowed the NRA to pick its battles. Like marriage proponents, the NRA started in those states most likely to be sympathetic, and then used precedents won there to extend their gains to other states. Gun rights advocates had a head start as compared to gay marriage proponents, as plenty of states protected gun rights from the nation's beginning. While federal constitutional law did not recognize an individual right to bear arms when the NRA began its Second Amendment campaign in earnest in the late 1970s, many states already had gun rights provisions in their constitutions, and if those provisions could be interpreted to protect an individual right to bear arms, they would not only protect gun owners in that particular state, but might also lend credibility to an argument that the federal Constitution should be similarly construed.

Florida has generally been the NRA's starting line for legislative gun rights campaigns, in part because of Marion Hammer, the organization's first female president and long one of Florida's most influential lobbyists. A seventy-six-year-old grandmother who to this day carries a Smith & Wesson .38 Special in her purse, Hammer is the leading edge of the NRA's state strategy. She and her local NRA affiliate, the Unified Sportsmen of Florida, have been so successful in pressing for gun rights laws and defeating gun control legislation that Florida is sometimes referred to as "The Gunshine State." Florida is often the first place the NRA pursues specific gun rights protections, relying on Hammer and her supporters to set a precedent that can then be exported to other states. According to Richard Feldman, a former political organizer for the NRA, "There is no single individual responsible for enacting more pro-gun legislation in the states than Marion Hammer."[7]

Hammer's personal story mirrors the NRA's. She was a champion shooter in her youth, but had no particular interest in politics. For Hammer, just as for the NRA, that changed with the 1968 Gun Control Act. As Hammer explained to me, "When Congress decided to take away the rights of free men and women as a means of putting salve on their conscience or the nation's conscience, they stepped over the line. That disturbed me, and I became very committed to stopping that from happening in the future." She volunteered with the Unified Sportsmen of Florida (USF) and the NRA, but in her view, neither organization was equipped to challenge the Gun Control Act. Her description of the USF as of 1968 could just as accurately have described the NRA: "At that time, it was an organization primarily of shooters and instructors and hunters—people actively engaged in exercise of constitutional rights—but we didn't have a complement of legislative and political activists engaged in protecting those rights. That's what had to change. You can't just use rights and let somebody take them away from you. You need to work to protect those rights."[8]

Hammer has fought for gun rights ever since, even as she raised first her own children, and then, after her daughter died of a brain tumor, her grandchildren as well. USF was an all-volunteer organization when she first got involved. Today she is its only paid staff member. Yet USF is one of the most potent political forces in the state. Governors have credited Hammer with helping them get elected, and have eagerly signed into law gun rights measures that Hammer and USF endorse.

One of Hammer's and the NRA's important early successes at the state level involved the seemingly technical but politically critical issue of "preemption." After the NRA's unsuccessful challenge to Morton Grove's handgun ban, it devised a strategy of "preempting" such local gun ordinances by convincing state legislatures to pass laws requiring that any regulation of firearms be passed at the state level. As a policy matter, the NRA argued, it makes sense to have uniform gun laws throughout a state, so that individuals are not put in jeopardy of violating varying local ordinances simply by traveling from one town to another. But probably more important, as longtime NRA lobbyist Jim Baker explained to me, the NRA would rather fight the gun regulation issue at the state level. People in cities tend to favor more restrictive gun regulations, while people in rural areas tend to favor gun rights. Gun violence is often a more pressing problem in cities and police protection is more immediately available there, while in the country, the problems of gun violence are often less prevalent and there are fewer police. Because police response times are considerably longer, rural residents often feel the need to be prepared to defend themselves. As state legislation requires the support of representatives from rural as well as urban regions, state legislatures are less likely than cities to pass restrictive gun laws. The preemption laws deny gun control advocates the urban jurisdictions that are their preferred forum, and force them to operate in the state legislature, the NRA's home turf.

In 1979, only two states had full preemption laws, and five had partial preemption, prohibiting some but not all local-level gun regulation. The NRA made the passage of state preemption laws its "top legislative priority" in the mid-1980s and 1990s. By early 2005, forty-five states had full or partial preemption laws. After securing a preemption law, the NRA would then invoke it in state court to trump local ordinances, invalidating their restrictions on the right to keep and bear arms. The NRA effort went virtually unopposed, as gun control advocates concentrated on national legislation, and in any event did not have the money or staff to fight the NRA state by state.[9]

A second piece of the "federalist" strategy focused on securing state constitutional protections for gun owners. Some constitutions, such as those of Pennsylvania, Vermont, Kentucky, Ohio, Indiana, and Missouri, have always unambiguously protected an individual's right to bear arms. Pennsylvania's Declaration of Rights, adopted in 1776, is typical: it provides that "the people have a right to bear arms for the defense of themselves and the state." The reference to "defense of themselves" plainly contemplates a personal right to use arms for self-defense. But other state constitutions were more ambiguous, drawing the NRA's attention. In the 1980s and 1990s, eleven states—New Hampshire, Nevada, North Dakota, Utah, New Mexico, Delaware, Maine, Nebraska, Alaska, and Wisconsin—took up the NRA's call and amended their constitutions to explicitly protect an individual right to bear arms. And no state went the other way to restrict its gun rights protections. By the time the Supreme Court took up the question of the meaning of the federal Constitution, all but six states guaranteed a right to bear arms as a matter of state constitutional law, and nearly all of those protected an individual right.[10]

A third NRA state initiative was aimed at liberalizing the rules gun owners must follow to carry guns in public. Before the NRA began this campaign, "concealed carry" laws, one of the nation's oldest forms of gun control, generally required that a person obtain a permit to carry a concealed weapon, and either sharply limited who could get such a permit, or left licensing to the discretion of local officials. In the NRA's view, people should have a right to carry weapons unless they are disqualified for specific, limited reasons. Hammer explained the difference between the old approach and the NRA's favored "shall-issue" regime:

> The old law made permitting wholly discretionary. There were different standards in every county. People's ability to exercise their constitutional rights hinged on where they lived within the state. The right-to-carry law established uniform criteria statewide and

made licenses valid anywhere in the state. The new law said that if you qualify to own and possess a firearm, by virtue of not being a convicted criminal, user of illegal drugs, an alcoholic, or mentally ill, they had to issue you a license.[11]

The NRA announced its campaign to promote "shall issue" concealed carry laws in the *American Rifleman* in 1985. Hammer delivered the campaign's first victory in 1987, when Florida adopted a "shall issue" law. Over the next eight years, the NRA persuaded nineteen other states to follow Florida's lead. In late 2012, the US Court of Appeals for the Seventh Circuit, in *Moore v. Madigan*, struck down the last remaining state law prohibiting individuals from carrying concealed firearms, and in 2013, the Illinois legislature passed concealed-carry protections, making it the last state in the nation to do so. The NRA is still not satisfied; in its view, some state permit standards remain too restrictive. But it has made remarkable progress in shifting the understanding of concealed carry from a privilege subject to the discretion of local officials to a presumptive right.[12]

Still another NRA state-law initiative sought to ensure that individuals defending themselves with guns are not subject to what the organization deems overly restrictive legal definitions of self-defense. Again, Marion Hammer and Florida led the way. In 2005, at Hammer's urging, Florida adopted the first "stand your ground" law. The legislation is based on the "castle doctrine," a quaintly named rule dating to English common law that allows the use of lethal force in self-defense against an intruder in one's home, or "castle," without first requiring the homeowner to attempt a retreat. Stand-your-ground laws extend the "no-duty-to-retreat" principle beyond the home, to any place the individual has a legal right to be. (Contrary to widespread misperceptions, however, these laws still require proof of all the elements of self-defense before lethal force is excused; namely, that the individual faced an imminent threat of death or serious bodily injury, and honestly and reasonably believed that deadly force was necessary to avert the harm.) Since the Florida law passed, twenty-five other states have adopted similar legislation. Seven more states recognize the stand-your-ground principle by judicial decision. The killing of Trayvon Martin by George Zimmerman in Florida in 2012 prompted an outcry and condemnations of stand-your-ground laws, slowing the NRA's momentum. But the campaign continues.[13]

The NRA has also played effective defense at the state level, defeating gun control initiatives. As Chuck Cunningham, head of the NRA-ILA's State and Local Affairs Division, told me, "I got much of my information from the Brady Campaign [to Prevent Gun Violence] website—what they cite as victories, I put on my to-do list to repeal." In 1976, for example, gun control proponents put a handgun ban on the Massachusetts ballot. The NRA, declaring that Massachusetts was a "pilot battleground in the national effort to halt the increasing threat of firearms control laws," actively opposed the proposal. Almost 70 percent of Massachusetts voters rejected it. In 1982, the NRA defeated a similar gun control referendum in California, with another lopsided vote of 63–37 percent. In both instances, the NRA overcame what appeared to be long odds in relatively liberal states. These resounding defeats for gun control effectively put an end to statewide gun control referenda. The NRA was just too difficult to beat.[14]

A second successful defensive campaign arose in reaction to gun control advocates' attempts, beginning in the 1980s, to use personal injury lawsuits to hold gun manufacturers liable for injuries and deaths caused by their guns. The NRA responded by successfully lobbying state legislatures, and ultimately Congress, to pass laws making clear that manufacturers could not be held liable when the injuries were caused by the actions of criminals or others who misused their guns, rather than by a defective product. Here, again, the organization used state law to protect the right to keep and bear arms. Although the personal injury suits targeted manufacturers, not gun users, they could affect individuals' ready access to inexpensive firearms. If personal injury lawsuits against the gun industry were successful, manufacturers would be forced to spread the costs of potentially large jury awards by charging more for their products, or go out of business. At present, thirty-four states provide immunity to the gun industry for such injuries, or prohibit cities or other local government entities from bringing lawsuits against certain gun industry defendants. And in 2005, building on the state victories, the NRA persuaded Congress to provide immunity through national legislation.[15]

WHY HAS THE NRA been so successful at the state level? First, in every state, the NRA has a sizable advantage over gun control advocates. The NRA has active affiliate organizations in all fifty states. And it has always had a large membership—today, about five million people, or an average of one hundred thousand members per state. According to David Lehman, the NRA-ILA's deputy executive director and general counsel, beyond its membership, another "27 million Americans think they're members (membership expired and they don't know it, parent was a member and they thought it included them, thought they were automatically a member if they bought a gun, etc.); and 39 million Americans support the goals/objectives of the NRA." A July 2015 nationwide survey done for the NRA of people likely to vote in a presidential election found that 52 percent of likely voters favor the NRA's goals, and 76 percent agree that "every American has a fundamental right to self-defense and a right to choose the home defense firearm that is best for them."[16]

As we'll explore later in more detail, NRA members and supporters are especially responsive to the NRA's recommendations. Their willingness to take action—whether to vote, call a legislator, make a political donation, or participate in a town meeting—greatly amplifies the organization's political power. And with each incremental victory, the NRA shows its members and supporters that their personal involvement pays off, thereby encouraging them to take part in the next fight. The leading gun control organizations, by contrast, do not have substantial membership, let alone comparably responsive members, and lack a sufficient state presence to counter the NRA's voice.[17]

Much of the NRA's political influence derives from its single-mindedness and tenacity. As Chris Cox, the NRA-ILA's executive director, put it to me, "we have a track record of being focused, whether you call it myopic or laser-like. We've been called hard-headed. I'll accept that. We've been called dogged. I'll accept that. We've been called unforgiving at times. I'll accept that. We are going to do everything in our power to protect this right for our members."[18]

The organization's role in electoral politics reflects its tight focus, and undergirds its influence in state legislatures. The NRA assigns a letter grade from A through F to every major party candidate for every elected state and federal legislative or executive office throughout the nation. For a politician who has already served in office and addressed gun issues, the grade is based on his or her voting record. Others are assessed on the basis of their responses to an NRA questionnaire. If a candidate does not respond, he or she receives only a question mark. If the NRA learns that the Brady Campaign favors a candidate, that candidate immediately earns an F. The grades are sent out to members in election season, and posted on the organization's website. As a result, every candidate for state or federal office has to confront the issue of gun rights, and knows that if she is not supportive, she will have to fight the NRA. At the same time, every NRA member or supporter can find out very easily where his or her representative stands. And while other interest groups also grade elected officials, the NRA's supporters are more likely than most to act on such grades.[19]

The grades also inform the NRA's internal deliberations about which candidates to support or oppose, and about where the NRA's political action committee, the NRA Political Victory Fund (NRA-PVF), should spend its money. According to its lead state lobbyist, Chuck Cunningham, the NRA automatically endorses any incumbent with an A rating, no matter who the challenger is (and regardless of party). Thus, in Wisconsin in 2010, it endorsed a Democratic state legislator over a Republican challenger, even though both had A ratings, because the Democrat was the incumbent. As David Keene put it, "Our position is that if you support the Second Amendment, Republican, Democrat, whatever, if you support the Second Amendment, we don't desert you." Where candidates have different grades, the NRA endorses the one with the higher grade, again irrespective of party affiliation. In the 2010 Congressional elections, the NRA endorsed sixty-three

Democrats, sixty-one of them incumbents. In 1990, the NRA supported Bernie Sanders, a socialist, for Vermont's lone seat in the House of Representatives, because his opponent, Peter Smith, had supported an assault weapon bill. Although in today's polarized climate, there are fewer and fewer pro-gun Democrats or pro-gun-control Republicans, for the NRA, devotion to gun rights supersedes party loyalty.[20]

According to Cunningham, the NRA considers several factors in selecting the campaigns to which it devotes attention and resources: the degree of contrast between the candidates on gun issues; the competitiveness of the race; whether there are specific gun rights issues on the agenda; and whether party control of a legislature is at stake. The first factor is the most important. All other things being equal, the greater the contrast between two candidates' positions on gun rights, the more the NRA will spend to support its choice: it devotes about 80 percent of its funds to races between an A candidate and a D or F candidate.

The NRA adjusts elected politicians' grades as necessary, to make sure candidates it has graded or supported as pro-gun-rights remain true to their commitments. Where a candidate turns in a pro-gun questionnaire, but then votes differently in office, the NRA will try to make the candidate pay. Retribution is especially sure for candidates who soften after benefitting from NRA financial support or particular endorsement. Again, as Cunningham put it, "we'll spend the kitchen sink against those that turn on us to defeat them."

Debra Maggart is just one of many politicians who has learned that lesson. A strongly conservative Republican member of the Tennessee legislature, Maggart comes from a family that sells guns, and is a longtime hunter and member of her local gun club. For years, she had an A+ rating from the NRA. "You can't get more pro–Second Amendment than me," she told the *Washington Post*. But in April 2012, as chair of the Republican caucus in the Tennessee legislature, she tabled an NRA-backed bill that would have permitted gun owners to keep their guns in their locked cars. Three months later, billboards began appearing in her district picturing Maggart and President Obama. It read: "Rep. Debra Maggart says she supports your gun rights. Of course, he says the same thing. Defend Freedom. Defeat Maggart." The NRA paid for the ad, and campaigned heavily to unseat Maggart. She lost the Republican primary to the NRA-backed challenger by 16 percentage points.[21]

Chuck Cunningham has a framed political ad in his office at the NRA's national headquarters in Fairfax, Virginia, from a 1991 race for a seat in the Virginia Senate. Moody E. "Sonny" Stallings Jr. had won the prior election after sending the NRA a perfect questionnaire and seeking its endorsement. In office, however, he became a leading gun control advocate after defeating the NRA-endorsed incumbent. The ad asks, "Why Do Virginians Have a Tough Time Believing This Man? Because Sonny Stallings Has a Tough Time Telling the Truth." Stallings "was a one-term state senator," Cunningham notes with pride. "We spent a lot more on that election that we ordinarily would."[22]

WHEN I ASKED MARION Hammer what the NRA's state-level lobbying and electioneering had to do with the Second Amendment, she replied that the state laws she has pioneered are a way of implementing the constitutional right. As she put it, "sometimes to ensure the ultimate protection of the right, you have to treat it like a loaf of bread. You have to add slices so that it's understood even by those who don't believe in the Constitution. You can't infringe my right because it's enumerated in statutory law. The right to bear arms is guaranteed by the Second Amendment. The statutes further protect it." To the average gun owner, what matters is that he has the freedom to own and use his gun as he deems fit; he may not know or care whether the laws that protect that freedom are state or federal, statutory or constitutional. And because most gun regulation occurs at the state level, the NRA's state strategy is central to expanding gun owners' rights.

As with marriage equality, the NRA's state-level strategy also helped transform federal constitutional law. From an originalist view of constitutional interpretation, this should not be possible. The only state laws that ought to be relevant to an originalist, and the only state laws expressly relied on by the justices in *Heller*, were those dating from the time of the founding of our constitutional republic; such laws might shed light on what the Constitution's Framers understood the Second Amendment to protect. Thus, both Scalia for the majority and Stevens in dissent cited state constitutional provisions from the Framing period to support their competing conceptions of the federal right. But even an organization as powerful as the NRA could not go back in time and improve state law at the time of the Framing.[23]

Contemporary state law, however, can be revised, and it can and often does affect the development of federal constitutional law even if not overtly. When many states have adopted a rule as a matter of state law, the Supreme Court will cause less disruption by embracing a similar rule as a matter of federal constitutional law. The fact that the NRA had already succeeded in prompting most states to protect gun rights made it easier for the Court to reach its decision in *Heller*, despite the formally originalist approach Scalia took in writing the majority opinion. Striking down the District of Columbia's near-absolute ban on handguns did not threaten a major nationwide upheaval, because the NRA had already made sure that few such bans existed anywhere else.

Relatedly, the NRA's state-law efforts since its transformation in 1977 made the idea of an individual right to bear arms more credible and legitimate by the time *Heller* reached the Court three decades later. By forging an intricate and expanding web of state laws that safeguarded the freedom of gun owners to keep and bear arms, the NRA's day-to-day state-level advocacy fostered a legal culture in which the right to bear arms enjoyed a privileged place.[24]

And there is still another way—perhaps the most important of all—in which the NRA's advocacy at the local level protects the constitutional right to bear arms. By giving its members and supporters multiple opportunities to lobby for their rights at the state level, and by delivering regular victories, the NRA reinforces in them a sense of the right as a living, concrete, and vital aspect of their own identities as Americans. Each battle teaches the lesson Judge Learned Hand offered in his 1944 speech on "The Spirit of Liberty," namely that "liberty lies in the hearts of men and women."

Near the end of my conversation with her, Marion Hammer captured this notion nicely:

HAMMER: The overriding issue is freedom. That's what the Constitution is about. That's what every amendment is about. And freedom is the most important thing that we possess and it is that for which we must fight. My father was killed at Okinawa fighting for freedom in World War II. Today, we're at war fighting for freedom against those who would deprive us of freedom for their convenience or political aspirations. And the Second Amendment protects freedom.

ME: So you're following in your father's footsteps?

HAMMER: I would see it that way.

8

Revisionist History

WHEN I ASKED NRA OFFICIALS HOW THEY HAD SUCCEEDED IN CHANGING CONSTITU-
tional law, they tended to give me funny looks. In their view,
they did not attempt to change the Constitution at all, but
merely to enforce it—or at most, to recover its lost meaning. Marion
Hammer's expression of that view is typical:

> Something in the beginning of our conversation that you said in-
> trigued me. You talked about what the Constitution means or should
> mean. Well, it means what the Founding Fathers intended for it to
> mean. Nothing more and nothing less. Whether people like it or not,
> it is what it is. And trying to change it to fit the political beliefs of
> people today is not what the Founders intended. They intended to
> protect basic rights, and those rights should not change.

Unlike marriage equality advocates, who necessarily promoted an
evolving understanding of constitutional rights, most gun rights advocates object altogether to such a conception. They tend to favor the
originalist understanding that the Constitution protects what it was
designed to protect when it was adopted—as Hammer said, "nothing

more and nothing less." And they argue that the language of the Second Amendment, properly understood, was always meant to protect an individual right. In their view, the many judges who had, before *Heller*, rejected an individual right to bear arms were simply mistaken. Like marriage equality advocates, the NRA was committed to changing an existing conception of constitutional law. But in their eyes, the claim rested not on recognition of new rights under a "living Constitution" but on restoring the Constitution's properly understood original meaning.

GIVEN THIS VIEW, ONE way for the NRA to pursue its mission was to examine contemporaneous understandings of the Second Amendment when it was adopted in 1791. Before the NRA got involved, the ground was fallow. As Stephen Halbrook, the nation's leading gun rights scholar, told me, when he was an undergraduate with a passion for history at Florida State University in the 1960s, Second Amendment scholarship was virtually nonexistent: "I went to the Florida Supreme Court library and looked up law review articles on the Second Amendment. There were about three, and they weren't any good."[1]

Halbrook defies all stereotypes about gun rights advocates. He did not come to the issue with a particularly abiding interest in guns, or even as a conservative. The son of hardware store merchants in Florida, Halbrook was initially a pre-law major at FSU, but his opposition to the Vietnam War—he recalls protesting in front of the FSU ROTC headquarters the night that four anti-war protesters were shot and killed by the National Guard at Kent State University in Ohio—turned him toward radical political philosophy. Halbrook graduated in 1972 with a PhD in philosophy, having read all of Karl Marx's multivolume *Das Kapital*. He then taught political philosophy for nearly a decade at two historically black colleges: Tuskegee and Howard. He researched Latin American revolutionary movements, and coedited a book called *Social Philosophy from Plato to Che*. While teaching at Howard, Halbrook also attended Georgetown Law at night, where he rekindled his interest in Second Amendment history.[2]

In 1977, Halbrook met Don Kates at a Second Amendment symposium in Colorado. Kates also has an unlikely background for a gun rights scholar, having worked with the renowned civil rights lawyers William Kunstler and Arthur Kinoy, cofounders of the Center for Constitutional Rights. Kates and Halbrook hit it off, sharing an interest in the historical origins of the Second Amendment. Halbrook published his first law review article on the subject in 1981, just a few years after graduating from law school. By 1989, he had written six law review articles and a book on Second Amendment history—while simultaneously teaching political philosophy and opening his own law practice.[3]

Kates was slightly less prolific, but by Halbrook's account, he was responsible for an important breakthrough in Second Amendment scholarship when, in 1983, he had an article on the original meaning of the Second Amendment accepted for publication by the prestigious *Michigan Law Review*. Until then, revisionist Second Amendment scholarship had appeared only in far less prominent journals.[4]

With a handful of other scholars, Halbrook and Kates transformed the field of Second Amendment scholarship. Before 1969, there were only twenty-five law review articles on the Second Amendment, and all but three argued that the Second Amendment protected only a right of the states to maintain a militia. Between 1970 and 1989, however, fifty-two articles were published on the subject, with twenty-seven adopting the view that the amendment protected an individual right to bear arms. By 2000, Halbrook and Kates by themselves had "written or edited eight books, twenty-three law review articles, and countless op-ed pieces and other writings about the right to bear arms."[5]

Halbrook and Kates argued that the Second Amendment, properly understood, protected both the states' right to maintain a militia and an individual right to bear arms for self-defense. They pointed to the text of the amendment itself, which conferred the right to keep and bear arms on "the people," just as the First and Fourth Amendments conferred speech and privacy rights, indisputably individual rights, on "the people." They argued that the "militia," as it was understood at the time of the Constitution's adoption, consisted of all able-bodied white men, not a select group of military inductees, further supporting the notion that the Framers of the Second Amendment intended to confer the right on individuals. They cited the antecedent right to bear arms in the English Bill of Rights, which was indisputably an individual right. They quoted contemporaneous constitutional scholars, who had discussed the Second Amendment in terms that supported an individual-rights view. And they maintained that the right to use arms in self-defense was considered a natural right—one that precedes any written legal affirmation—at the time the Constitution was drafted. They thus suggested that the Second Amendment did not so much create the right as limit the power of government to infringe on a pre-existing natural right. Judicial decisions seen as rejecting the individual-rights view, they argued, were either misunderstood or conclusory, and should not settle the issue.[6]

There are counters to their arguments, to be sure. Other scholars and jurists, including Northwestern history professor Garry Wills and Supreme Court Justice John Paul Stevens, have argued that the first clause of the Second Amendment, referring to militias, qualifies the right identified in the amendment's second clause. They note that some state gun rights provisions in existence at the time of the Framing guaranteed an individual right to bear arms to defend oneself, but that the Second Amendment, by contrast, is silent on self-defense and invokes only defense of the state through organized militias. And they point to a long line of jurists and scholars who, until the scholarship of the 1980s, almost universally took the view that the amendment was limited to the collective rights of the states.[7]

The critical point here is not who has the better argument, but rather that a handful of scholars succeeded in changing the academic landscape on this question by the time it reached the Supreme Court. When Halbrook and Kates began their research in the 1970s, there was one widely shared view of the Second Amendment. Twenty years later, the situation had changed so markedly that one law professor labeled the individual-rights view the "standard model" of the Second Amendment. And in *Heller*, that shift became formal constitutional law.[8]

Halbrook and Kates both became closely associated with gun rights organizations. As a solo practitioner, Halbrook has often represented the NRA in gun rights litigation; today, his practice is exclusively gun-related, and he consults regularly with the NRA. His office in a Virginia suburb sports the usual decorations—his law diploma and drawings of Halbrook in court—but also Swiss shooting medals, duck decoys, and two nineteenth-century percussion shotguns. If the NRA had its way, Halbrook would have argued *Heller*. With the NRA's assistance, Halbrook filed probably the most influential friend-of-the-court brief in that case—on behalf of a majority of the US senators and representatives, as well as Vice President Dick Cheney. And he was the NRA's lawyer in *McDonald v. City of Chicago*, which applied the Second Amendment to the states.[9]

The NRA also long supported Halbrook's scholarship. He received his first grant from the organization in the early 1980s to do research at the Library of Congress and the University of Wisconsin's Documentation Center on the Constitution, just as he was beginning his study of the Second Amendment in earnest. He notes that the group imposed no demands on his findings or results, and that the grant made it possible for him to contribute to amicus briefs as well as to write several law review articles. For his part, Kates has also been retained by the NRA to represent gun owners; represented the Second Amendment Foundation, another gun rights group, in the Morton Grove case; and wrote a regular column for *Handguns* magazine. Nor were these ties aberrational; most of the scholars who first advanced an individual-rights understanding were associated with the NRA or other gun rights groups.[10]

In time, however, more independent scholars began to adopt the individual-rights view. Joyce Malcolm, for example, came to the issue of the Second Amendment as a young historian studying the English Civil War. Her doctoral work examined how the concept of individual rights emerged in seventeenth-century England. The English "right to bear arms," she argued, began not as a right but as an obligation to be armed, so that one could help defend one's country when called upon by the King. But after the "Glorious Revolution" of the late seventeenth century, King William and Queen Mary agreed to an English Bill of Rights that, among other things, reformulated the duty to possess and bear arms as a right that could not be denied (at least to Protestants) by the Crown. While Malcolm was researching this subject, an eminent scholar of English history suggested that she might also examine whether the English right had crossed the Atlantic, and whether it might inform our understanding of the Second Amendment. She took up the subject "with some trepidation," she told me later, as it was outside of her field. The project was promising enough, however, to attract support from the National Endowment for the Humanities and a fellowship from Radcliffe College. In 1983, she wrote a law review article setting forth her initial findings, and in 1996, Harvard University Press published her book, *To Keep and Bear Arms: The Origins of an Anglo-American Right.*[11]

While Malcolm was neither a gun enthusiast nor a member of the NRA, her message was welcomed by the organization. If the English Bill of Rights was a model for the Second Amendment, that would support the individual-rights view. The English, after all, did not have states or state militias, and Malcolm recounted that leading legal scholars of the founders' generation, including William Blackstone, understood the English right to bear arms as an individual right.Gun rights advocates began to invite Malcolm to participate in symposia, panels, and conferences on the subject. That she had come to her conclusions so independently only added to her credibility.[12]

Perhaps the most valuable independent support, however, came in 1989, when Sanford Levinson, a well-respected liberal law professor at University of Texas, published "The Embarrassing Second Amendment" in the *Yale Law Journal.* What was embarrassing, according to Levinson, was the fact that the historical evidence for an individual right to bear arms was much stronger than most legal scholars had thought, and contradicted liberal dogma. Levinson's article, which relied largely on the sources that Halbrook, Kates, and others had unearthed, was significant not so much for what it said as for who said it and where he said it. The *Yale Law Journal* is one of the nation's top law journals, published by one of the nation's leading law schools, where faculty and scholarship typically have a liberal bent. The fact that the *Journal* had published such an article gave the individual-rights view further legitimacy. To this day, Levinson's twenty-three-page essay may well be the most influential Second Amendment article in the literature.[13]

The NRA increased its support of Second Amendment scholarship in the 1990s. Halbrook continued to receive grants; in 1991 and 1992 alone, the NRA gave him more than $38,000. The NRA also funded a new organization, Academics for the Second Amendment, or A2A, headed by Joseph Olson, a law professor and NRA board member. In 1994, the NRA launched an annual Second Amendment essay competition, with a generous first prize of $25,000. During the 1990s, Second Amendment scholarship flourished and the balance tipped decidedly in favor of the individual-rights view. Of the eighty-seven gun-rights-related law review articles published during the decade fifty-eight adopted an individual-rights position, while only twenty-nine took a state-militia view.[14]

Soon, the NRA found its cause joined by still more unlikely allies. In the 1990s, Yale Law Professor Akhil Amar, Harvard Law Professor Laurence Tribe, Duke Law Professor William Van Alstyne, and Pulitzer Prize–winning historian Leonard Levy, all eminent scholars, none associated with conservative or gun rights causes, each expressed some support for the individual-rights view. Amitai Etzioni, a professor at George Washington University who favored gun control, was so disturbed by this turn of events that he published an essay in the *Chronicle of Higher Education* questioning the ethics of the research: "although no one would contest the revisionist scholars' right to engage in such research, I can't help but wonder if they are *right* to engage in such research. . . . With so much at stake, should scholars refrain from conducting studies that might have grave unsettling social consequences?" Etzioni's concern was not that the scholarship was tainted or deficient, but that it might be too effective. The position that Warren Burger had dismissed as a fraud, and that the federal courts had consistently rejected, now had considerable scholarly backing from across the ideological spectrum. It had to be taken seriously.[15]

Critics have implied that there was something nefarious about the NRA's funding of pro-gun-rights scholarship that supported its view of the Second Amendment. But the NRA's actions are not unusual; non-profit organizations, foundations, and advocacy groups regularly award grants for research and scholarship that they hope will advance their agendas. Liberal foundations like the Ford Foundation and the Open Society Foundations have long done just that, as have conservative foundations and think tanks like the Olin Foundation and the Cato Institute. And it's common for legal scholars to accept fellowships or grants from such foundations to support their scholarship, as well as to write amicus briefs, present congressional testimony, or assist with litigation supporting legal positions of organizations with which they agree. In any event, the NRA's grants were unlikely to tempt scholars to compromise their principles. As Halbrook told me, the bulk of his scholarship was done without any compensation. No one has ever gotten rich writing law review articles. One does it for the intrinsic value of the search for truth, and with the hope that one's articles might actually help change our understanding of some aspect of law. By that standard, Halbrook, Kates, Malcolm, and other scholars advancing an individual-rights view were wildly successful. They challenged received wisdom and, by 2008, their view had become not only the reigning academic understanding of the Second Amendment but the law of the land.

Joyce Malcolm signed an amicus brief on the English foundations of the Second Amendment in the *Heller* case, and Justice Scalia cited her book in his opinion (as had the Justice Department's Office of Legal Counsel in a 2004 opinion supporting the individual-rights view). The day the Supreme Court decision came down, Malcolm appeared on a BBC news program with Walter Dellinger, the former acting solicitor general under President Bill Clinton. Dellinger had represented the District of Columbia in the *Heller* case in the Supreme Court. As they left the studio together after the segment, Dellinger turned to Malcolm and said, "you know, it was the scholarship that won the case."[16]

As the range of scholars who eventually supported an individual-rights view attests, this was not a public relations ploy dressed up as scholarship. Malcolm, Halbrook, Kates, and others found significant evidence to support a revisionist view of the Second Amendment. The historical research they pioneered, and that, once it learned of it, the NRA supported at every turn, transformed an issue long deemed resolved into an open question. Their research did not guarantee a victory in the Supreme Court, much less in the court of public opinion. After all, the vote in *Heller* was 5–4; reasonable people could and did disagree, and many other factors contributed to the victory. But as Dellinger conceded to Malcolm, the Second Amendment scholarship plowed critical ground for the change.[17]

ALTHOUGH PROFESSORS MIGHT WISH it so, legal scholarship rarely plays as central a part in constitutional change as it did in the Second Amendment saga. But this account illustrates that legal scholars can sometimes be an important part of a campaign to reform constitutional law. They have no formal authority, of course; they exercise only the power to persuade. But they have the expertise and training to engage with constitutional doctrine in a meaningful way. In this setting, the Second Amendment scholars' work was an essential part of the picture. With substantial state-level reforms supportive of an individual right to bear arms, and a significant body of scholarship, the NRA had two pieces in place for its effort to secure recognition of a constitutional right to bear arms. But the issue was ultimately one of federal law. In that arena, too, the NRA was no less committed, and no less effective, in furthering its cause.

9

Federal Forums

ON A CLEAR DAY IN MID-DECEMBER 2012, TWENTY-YEAR-OLD ADAM LANZA SHOT HIS way through the front door of the Sandy Hook Elementary School in Newtown, Connecticut, and then headed for class-rooms, evidently with the intent to kill as many people as he could. Before he killed himself, Lanza murdered twenty children, mostly first-graders, and six teachers or administrators. There had been many mass shootings before Sandy Hook. Earlier that year, James Holmes killed twelve and injured seventy during a midnight showing of *The Dark Knight Rises* in Aurora, Colorado, and a white supremacist opened fire at a Sikh mosque in Wisconsin, killing six and injuring four. But the youth of the Newtown victims made this tragedy especially horrific. The nation was shocked, saddened, and angry. Politicians vowed to respond with gun control legislation. The impetus for reform seemed unstoppable.

President Obama assigned Vice President Joe Biden to craft a re-sponse, and within months politicians from both sides of the aisle came together to support a bill that would extend the requirement of back-ground checks of prospective gun buyers to "private sales" at gun shows and on the Internet. Federal law already demanded background checks for purchases at licensed gun dealers, but gun shows feature sales by non-licensed private dealers and may account for approximately 20 percent of gun sales. Gun shows—typically held at expo centers, fairgrounds, or community halls—provide an easy way for ineligible buyers to elude checks. In light of the horror at what happened at Sandy Hook, the bill seemed a modest reform, one that would only close a loophole in a pre-existing regulatory scheme. An April 2013 *Washington Post* poll reported that 86 percent of Americans supported the measure. Robert Levy, the libertarian lawyer who financed *Heller*, wrote an op-ed in the *Washington Post* urging the bill's passage. Yet that same month, the bill died when it failed to attract the sixty votes in the Senate necessary to overcome a filibuster. The NRA had convinced four Democrats and all but four Republican senators to vote against the bill—despite polls showing that even a majority of NRA members backed it. The result was a stark reminder of the NRA's influence in Washington.[1]

The NRA vigorously opposed the background check bill, even though the bill's sponsors—Senators Joe Manchin III, Democrat of West Virginia, and Patrick J. Toomey, Republican of Pennsylvania—were gun rights supporters with A ratings from the group. The NRA criticized the existing background check system as broken; in its view, the scheme didn't actually block sales to felons, the mentally ill, and others legally ineligible to buy guns, because states were so delinquent about keeping track of who was ineligible. The NRA also charged that the bill was a first step on a slippery slope toward a gun registry, which in turn it saw as a step along the road toward confiscation. Congress has not seriously considered any gun control legislation since the NRA's post–Sandy Hook victory. When a young white supremacist shot and killed nine people at the Emanuel A.M.E. Church in Charleston, South Carolina, in June 2015, the political response was to take down the Confederate flag from South Carolina's State House, not to regulate guns.[2]

THE NRA HAS LONG been as powerful in the national legislative and executive branches as it has been in the states. Since the organization committed itself to a vigorous defense of the Second Amendment in 1977, it has won numerous federal victories. Each one made it that much easier for the Supreme Court to recognize an individual right to bear arms when it took up the question in 2008. In 1980, Ronald Reagan, a member of the NRA, and the first presidential candidate to receive the organization's endorsement, handily won the presidency. On his coattails, Republicans took control of the Senate for the first time since 1954. Senator Orrin Hatch of Utah, a long-time NRA member, assumed leadership of the Subcommittee on the Constitution of the Senate Judiciary Committee, and one of his first acts was to conduct a study of the Second Amendment. The resulting report was the first such congressional report to support the NRA's individual-rights view.[3]

Citing evidence dating to AD 872, but concentrating on the Framers' generation, the committee report found it "inescapable that the history, concept, and wording of the second amendment . . . as well as its interpretation by every major commentator and court in the first half-century after its ratification, indicates that what is protected is an individual right of a private citizen to own and carry firearms in a peaceful manner." The report itself is only twelve pages. The bulk of the evidence for its conclusion appears in several lengthy essays included in an appendix. All three of the submissions supporting an individual-rights view are by lawyers affiliated with the NRA. According to the NRA's director of federal lobbying, Jim Baker, the organization did all it could to support Senator Hatch's undertaking—and it shows. Virtually every sentence in the report supporting the committee's conclusion can be traced to the NRA.[4]

The NRA showed its appreciation in Senator Hatch's next election, spending $22,081 in aid of his 1982 Senate campaign. That may not sound like much in today's terms, but the NRA was the only nonprofit listed as a large campaign donor to Hatch in that election by *The Almanac of American Politics*. Its outlay was fully one-third of the amount the Republican Party itself spent on Hatch's behalf.[5]

In 1986, the NRA achieved its first major federal legislative victory when it persuaded Congress to pass the Firearms Owners' Protection Act, which eased several restrictions imposed by the 1968 Gun Control

Act. The new law relaxed limits on transportation of long rifles across state lines, eliminated federal recordkeeping requirements for ammunition sales, and provided a safe harbor for people traveling by car with guns by barring their prosecution for infringing strict local gun laws so long as they kept their guns properly stored in their vehicles. And importantly, the act did so in the name of protecting the people's right to bear arms, by including a "finding" that US citizens' rights "to keep and bear arms under the second amendment to the United States Constitution . . . require additional legislation to correct existing firearms statutes and enforcement policies."[6]

During President Bill Clinton's first term, the NRA suffered two of its relatively rare losses at the federal level—but even these it arguably turned into qualified victories. In 1993, Congress passed the "Brady Bill," named for James Brady, Reagan's former press secretary, who was paralyzed in 1981 when one of John Hinckley's bullets, intended for President Reagan, hit Brady in the head. Brady and his wife, Sarah, became the nation's leading gun control proponents, and in 1993, Congress passed the Brady Bill, mandating waiting periods for gun purchases and requiring state and local police to conduct the requisite background checks until a federal computer program could be developed to handle the task. The NRA could not defeat the bill, but its lawyer—Steve Halbrook—challenged the constitutionality of the law. In *Printz v. United States*, the Supreme Court agreed with Halbrook, and ruled that Congress had violated states' rights by compelling state officials to carry out the background checks. The suit did not invalidate the background check requirement altogether, but only the temporary requirement that state officials do the checking until a national computerized system was up and running. Yet it was a victory nonetheless. And even though the NRA and Halbrook did not raise a Second Amendment challenge to the law—they didn't feel the time was right—Justice Clarence Thomas wrote a separate concurrence stating his view that the Second Amendment protects a "personal right" to bear arms.[7]

In 1994, the NRA lost again, when it was unable to block a federal law prohibiting the manufacture of semi-automatic "assault weapons" for civilian use. But again, the group transformed its loss into a victory. The assault weapons law was flawed to begin with, a largely symbolic measure with little practical impact. Functionally, an "assault weapon" loads a fresh bullet into the firing chamber with each trigger pull, and is therefore considered "semi-automatic." Most modern-day guns in America operate in this manner, and Congress could not realistically prohibit all such weapons. Instead, it chose to ban only those with military-style designs. In the end, the law banned nineteen guns by name, and exempted 661 other models. And because the law's general prohibition turned on a gun's appearance, it was easily evaded by gun manufacturers making slight design modifications. As one commentator put it, "the assault weapon ban was a little bit like a law designed to reduce dog bites that only outlawed the sale of Doberman pinschers with clipped ears."[8]

Even though the law was largely toothless, its passage sparked a costly backlash against those who had supported it. The midterm elections followed shortly thereafter, and the NRA called on its followers to show their disapproval. The NRA particularly targeted twenty-four members of Congress who voted for the assault weapons ban, and nineteen of them lost. Republicans took control of the House of Representatives for the first time since 1954. In his memoir, Clinton credited the NRA, writing: "On November 8, we got the living daylights beat out of us, losing eight Senate races and fifty-four House seats, the largest defeat for our party since 1946. . . . The NRA had a great night." Many factors surely contributed to the 1994 returns. Whether Clinton's diagnosis was accurate or not, the experience dampened Congress's enthusiasm for gun control legislation for years. In 2004, when the assault weapons ban came up for renewal, it died; the Democrats had learned their lesson.[9]

It took another Republican presidential victory to get the executive branch formally behind the NRA's view of the Second Amendment. As an enforcer of gun laws, the Justice Department had long opposed the NRA's view. Shortly before the 2000 election, the Justice Department reasserted its position in a closely watched case in the US Court of Appeals for the Fifth Circuit, *United States v. Emerson*. As Chris Cox told me in an interview in the NRA-ILA office he heads, the brief was a political gift. The NRA used it in the 2000 campaign to show its members and supporters that they could not trust Al Gore on gun rights. The NRA also spent over $2 million in support of Bush's election, and over $200,000 attacking Gore—in total, about 16 percent of what the Republican National Committee spent, and about one-third of all outside group spending in support of Bush. Given how close the election was, the NRA's money and advocacy was crucial. Once again, in Clinton's view, it made the difference. In an interview a few years later, he said: "I believe Al lost Arkansas because of the National Rifle Association . . . and maybe Missouri, and maybe Tennessee, and maybe New Hampshire (in addition to the Nader vote). . . . I don't think the NRA got near as much credit as they deserve for Bush's election. They hurt us bad."[10]

On taking office, President Bush, like Reagan an NRA member, named the former Missouri senator and fellow NRA member John Ashcroft as his attorney general. In the Senate, Ashcroft had been a reliable voice for gun rights. With Bush and Cheney in the White House, and Ashcroft the attorney general, would the administration continue to back its predecessor's view that the Second Amendment did not protect an individual right? Jim Baker, then executive director of the NRA's advocacy office, wrote Ashcroft a letter in April 2001 requesting his views on the Second Amendment. In a letter dated May 17, 2001, shortly before the NRA's annual convention, Ashcroft replied that it was "unequivocally my view that the text and the original intent of the Second Amendment clearly protect the right of individuals to keep and bear firearms." Echoing the reasoning and findings of Hatch's committee, Ashcroft's 2001 letter cited the amendment's protection of the rights of "the people," the views of the Framers and early courts, and the views of scholars, including Don Kates, Sanford Levinson, and Akhil Amar. When the Violence Policy Center, a gun control group, issued a critique of Ashcroft's letter, Steve Halbrook in turn published a point-by-point defense, offering detailed evidence for each of Ashcroft's points—in effect reprising the work he and other NRA lawyers had done to buttress the Hatch committee report on the Second Amendment twenty years earlier.[11]

In October 2001, the US Court of Appeals for the Fifth Circuit issued its decision in *Emerson*, becoming the first federal appeals court to adopt the individual-rights view of the Second Amendment. Ashcroft promptly sent a memo to all US prosecutors saying that it reflected his view of the Second Amendment and urging them to coordinate all briefing in Second Amendment cases. In May 2002, the solicitor general filed two briefs with the US Supreme Court explaining that, contrary to earlier filings, the Justice Department now took the position that the Second Amendment protected an individual right to bear arms.[12]

In 2004, the Justice Department's Office of Legal Counsel (OLC), which advises the executive branch on constitutional law, issued a formal opinion reaffirming Ashcroft's individual-rights view. Instead of a two-page letter, the OLC memorandum spanned 105 pages and boasted 437 footnotes. It analyzed the text and structure of the Second Amendment, the historical origins of the right in England, the history of the Second Amendment's drafting, and early interpretations of the right by commentators and courts. Its carefully crafted and exhaustively researched arguments, which rested on the analysis and evidence developed by the Second Amendment scholars, reaffirmed the decision in *Emerson* and prefigured the reasoning Justice Scalia would use in his opinion for the Court in *Heller*.[13]

In 2005, the NRA got Congress as a whole on board. After extensive lobbying by the NRA, Congress passed federal legislation barring suits against gun manufacturers for injuries resulting from the unlawful use of guns. The Protection of Lawful Commerce in Arms Act's preamble expressly endorses the view that the Second Amendment protects an individual right to bear arms—the very issue the Supreme Court would take up only three years later in *Heller*.[14]

As a result of the NRA's efforts at the national level, both the executive branch and Congress had endorsed an individual-rights view of the Second Amendment by the time the Supreme Court addressed the issue. Those successes, along with the widespread protection of gun rights the NRA had achieved in the states and the new gun-rights scholarship it had supported, set the stage for a Supreme Court victory. So it was a surprise to many that when the opportunity came, the NRA balked.

10

Supreme Recognition

THE NRA WORKED TIRELESSLY FOR DECADES, IN EVERY STATE IN THE UNION AND INSIDE the Beltway, to advance recognition of an individual right to bear arms. Yet when a team of conservative lawyers in 2002 proposed bringing the issue to the Supreme Court by challenging the District of Columbia's ban on handguns, the NRA adamantly resisted. Like the gay rights groups who opposed Boies and Olson's filing of the challenge to California's Proposition 8, the NRA worried that the time was not yet right. The leadership felt that they had still more work to do before they could be confident of victory, and they did not want to risk defeat. *Heller* was filed over NRA objections. But even so, *Heller*'s success owes more to the NRA than to the able lawyers who filed and litigated the case.

HELLER WAS THE BRAINCHILD of Clark Neily and Steve Simpson, two lawyers with the Institute for Justice, a conservative public interest law firm in Washington, DC. In 2002, they approached Robert Levy, then a senior fellow at the libertarian Cato Institute, with the idea of challenging the District's ban on handguns. In their view, all the conditions for a successful constitutional challenge were present. Attorney General Ashcroft had placed the Justice Department squarely behind the individual-rights view. The Fifth Circuit in the *Emerson* case had become the first court of appeals to adopt that view in October 2001, and its opinion had laid out a detailed historical case. Legal scholarship increasingly supported the individual-rights view; as we have seen, by 2002, several law professors, including prominent liberals, had endorsed the view. The DC ban was the most restrictive in the nation, making it especially vulnerable to challenge. The majority of the judges on the DC Circuit, which would hear any appeal in the case, were conservatives appointed by Presidents Reagan and George H. W. Bush. And a majority of the justices on the Supreme Court were similarly appointed by Republican presidents.[1]

Levy was intrigued. As he told me years later, he had not previously had much interest in gun rights. But he was a libertarian, generally skeptical of government regulation of private affairs, and Neily and Simpson convinced him that this was a propitious opportunity. Levy was well into his second career as a lawyer, but Neily and Simpson approached him primarily to see if he'd be willing to finance the challenge. Born to working class parents in DC, Levy had initially earned a graduate degree in business at American University and started an investment advising firm. The firm, CDA Investment Technologies, was a huge success. Thomson Corporation bought the business for a handsome amount, and in 1991, Levy retired and enrolled at George Mason University's law school. He graduated at the top of his class, clerked for two eminent judges in the District of Columbia, and was, in 2001, a senior fellow at the Cato Institute.

A Second Amendment challenge was not something the Institute for Justice would take on, as it fell outside the group's focus on economic liberty and property rights. So Neily and Simpson could not do it themselves. Levy agreed to fund the litigation, and together they set about looking for a lawyer to handle the case. When the NRA learned what they were up to, it strongly urged the trio to desist. The NRA was of course no fan of the District's handgun ban, which had been around since 1976, but it believed more groundwork needed to be done before presenting the issue to the Supreme Court. As Levy explained, the NRA was "not confident about the five votes. They felt that we could end up winning in the appellate court and they feared that you'd win the battle and lose the war. In retrospect, they were pretty damn close to right. It was 5–4." Former NRA president David Keene agreed: "We didn't want to go to the Supreme Court until we were ready, until the public was ready. . . . The Supreme Court may not always follow the election returns, but public sentiment has a great deal to do with where the Court is ultimately gonna come down, if it's a close question." Most troublingly to the NRA, when the *Heller* case was being planned in 2002, the likely fifth vote on the Supreme Court was Justice Sandra Day O'Connor, a somewhat unpredictable moderate, and there was no certainty that she would vote in favor of an individual-rights view. On the contrary, Chris Cox, the NRA-ILA's executive director, told me, "our indications were that O'Connor would not be with us."[2]

Levy, Neily, and Simpson were not deterred. They recruited Alan Gura, a young graduate of Georgetown Law who had impressed them when he interned at the Institute for Justice. Gura, like Levy an ardent libertarian, had a small private law practice. Levy hired him "at more or less subsistence wages," but promised that if the case made it to the Supreme Court, it would be Gura's to argue. They identified a handful of exemplary plaintiffs, including Dick Heller, a security guard at a federal building who lived across the street from an abandoned housing project and wanted a gun to protect himself from drug dealers; Shelly Parker, an African American who lived in a poor neighborhood beset by rampant drug dealing and had been personally threatened by the dealers; and Tom Palmer, a gay man who wanted to arm himself against anti-gay violence.[3]

When the NRA was unable to dissuade Levy and Gura from filing, it retained Steve Halbrook to file a parallel lawsuit, and tried to have the cases consolidated in an attempt to wrest control. The courts declined and ultimately dismissed the NRA suit on procedural grounds. The NRA was not done yet, however. It lobbied Congress to use its oversight authority in the District to repeal the handgun ban, in order to render the lawsuit moot before it could reach the Supreme Court. The NRA redoubled these efforts when the Court of Appeals for the DC Circuit struck down the DC ban in March 2007, becoming only the second court of appeals in modern times to recognize an individual right to bear arms under the Second Amendment. Gun control advocates, also fearing an adverse decision from the highest court, urged DC Mayor Adrian Fenty not to seek Supreme Court review, but he pressed ahead. Meanwhile the NRA's lobbying effort in Congress ended in April 2007, when a student at Virginia Tech killed thirty-two students and teachers and injured seventeen others in the deadliest mass shooting by a single assailant in US history. In November 2007, the Supreme Court granted review in *Heller*.[4]

Having failed to stop the case from making it to the Supreme Court, the NRA now directed its energies toward winning it. It filed an amicus brief on its own behalf, arguing that the Second Amendment guaranteed an individual right to keep and bear arms for self-defense, and maintaining that "strict scrutiny," the most skeptical form of review that exists in constitutional law, should apply to any infringements on that right. David Hardy, who had contributed to Orrin Hatch's 1982 study of the Second Amendment, filed an amicus brief on behalf of Academics for the Second Amendment, the organization supported by the NRA. And most impressively, Steve Halbrook filed an amicus brief, organized by the NRA, on behalf of 55 senators, 250 members of the House of Representatives, and Vice President Dick Cheney, in his capacity as president of the Senate. The Bush administration, through the solicitor general, was defending the District's law, so the vice president and the president were on opposite sides of the case—the only time that has ever happened. Halbrook's brief stressed Congress's own formal recognition of the rights of individual citizens to keep and bear arms, including in the preamble to the 2005 Protection of Lawful Commerce in Arms Act.[5]

The NRA's many accomplishments in the states, the academy, Congress, the executive branch, and electoral politics all made a positive decision in *Heller* more likely. But the NRA played still another crucial part in the victory—namely, by helping determine who would decide the case. By the time *Heller* reached the Supreme Court in 2007, O'Connor had retired and Chief Justice William Rehnquist had died. That gave Bush the chance to nominate two new justices. And he owed both his 2000 election and 2004 reelection in no small measure to the NRA, which was one of his largest supporters in each election.[6]

As a result, Bush was unlikely to nominate a justice who might be unreliable on Second Amendment issues. Yet in the NRA's view, he initially did just that, when he named Harriet Miers, his White House counsel, to replace the retiring Justice Sandra Day O'Connor. The NRA was joined by many conservatives in considering Miers insufficiently reliable. Questions also arose about whether her thin written record showed sufficient qualification for the position, and Miers soon withdrew from the process. Bush tried again, this time nominating DC circuit judge John Roberts and, when Chief Justice Rehnquist died, Third Circuit judge Samuel Alito. According to Chris Cox, the NRA investigated both nominees and concluded that it was comfortable with their appointments. Had it felt otherwise, Cox explained, the NRA would have objected, as it had with Miers. In 2008, both Roberts and Alito voted with the five-member majority in *Heller*. In retrospect, had Bush not received the NRA's support in 2000 and 2004, he might have lost either election, a Democratic president would have selected the Court's two replacements, and the Court's decision in *Heller* might well have turned out differently.[7]

The day of the *Heller* victory, Alan Gura filed a new lawsuit, this time against the City of Chicago, challenging the constitutionality of its handgun ban, noting that it was nearly identical to the one the Court had struck down in *Heller*. The next day, the NRA filed two similar lawsuits, one also challenging Chicago's handgun ban, the other challenging a similar ban in Oak Park, a suburb of Chicago. The issue in all three cases was whether the right to bear arms recognized in *Heller* applied to the states.[8]

Early Supreme Court decisions had interpreted the Second Amendment, along with the rest of the Bill of Rights, as applying only against the federal government and not the states. The idea was that the Constitution created new federal power, and its amendments limited only that power. By 2000, however, that view had long passed into history with respect to nearly the entire Bill of Rights other than the Second Amendment. Over the course of the twentieth century, and especially in the 1960s and 1970s, the Court had ruled that most of the rights in the Bill of Rights also constrained state governments. The Court had interpreted the Fourteenth Amendment's guarantee of due process, adopted in 1868, to "incorporate" the "fundamental" rights in the Bill of Rights, thereby making them binding on the states. But because the Court had not recognized an individual right to bear arms until 2008, it had not confronted, in the modern era, whether the Second Amendment limited state regulations of firearms.

Alan Gura's and the NRA's cases were consolidated before the US Court of Appeals for the Seventh Circuit as *McDonald v. City of Chicago*. When that court ruled that the right to bear arms did not apply to state regulations, the Supreme Court granted review. Once again, the NRA was able to convince sizeable majorities of both houses of Congress to file a joint amicus brief supporting its cause. This time, the congressional amicus brief was filed on behalf of 58 Senators and 251 members of the House of Representatives—the most members of Congress to sign an amicus brief to that point in time. The amicus brief was written by Paul Clement, who had defended the DC handgun ban when he was Bush's solicitor general, but was now in private practice and on the NRA's side. Gura again argued the case in the Supreme Court, but the NRA was also a party to the appeal, represented by Steve Halbrook. The Court sided with gun rights advocates, by the same 5–4 margin. And again, the Court relied heavily on the Second Amendment scholars' historical research—especially Halbrook's, which the majority opinion cited six times. With the victory in *McDonald*, the Second Amendment—and the individual-rights interpretation the NRA championed—applied throughout the United States, to all official actions, local, state, or federal.[9]

BOTH *HELLER* AND *MCDONALD* were major victories. For the NRA, however, just as for Evan Wolfson and the gay rights groups after

Obergefell, there was still plenty to do. For one thing, while the Court had now recognized an individual right to bear arms, its decisions did not specify how courts should review laws implicating Second Amendment rights. Because the DC and Chicago laws were so extreme, the Court did not have to address gun regulations that fell short of complete bans. Justice Scalia's opinion in *Heller* nonetheless acknowledged that the right to bear arms was not absolute, and that a host of gun regulations were presumptively reasonable, including bans on possession by convicted felons and the mentally ill; prohibitions on carrying guns in sensitive areas such as airports and government buildings; bans on particularly dangerous and unusual weapons; and licensing requirements for commercial sales. The Court's approval of such a wide range of gun regulations led Dennis Henigan, head of the Brady Campaign to Prevent Gun Violence, to declare the decision something of a victory for gun control after all. As he noted, Scalia's list "encompassed our entire agenda. It basically made it very easy for lower courts without a whole lot of difficulty to find that whatever gun law is at issue in the particular case in front of them . . . had been blessed."[10]

Second Amendment law is still in its infancy—akin to where First Amendment law was in the early twentieth century, when the Court had first recognized the right but had not yet elaborated what standard of review applied, or what sorts of regulations of speech were permissible. The contours of the right to bear arms remain largely undeveloped. In the NRA's view, a restriction on guns should be treated like most restrictions on speech: it should be presumptively invalid, and justifiable only if the government can show the regulation is necessary to further a compelling interest. But in the wake of *Heller* the lower courts have on the whole been much more deferential. They have upheld restrictions on sales of guns to felons, minors, and the mentally ill; requirements that individuals demonstrate a "justifiable need" for a license to carry a concealed weapon; bans on possession of machine guns; and prohibitions on carrying weapons on university campuses and in national parks.[11]

None of this is entirely surprising. As Chris Cox put it, most of the judges on today's federal courts learned and practiced law in a world that dismissed the Second Amendment as irrelevant; changing these judges' attitudes will take time. It also seems likely that judges will continue to be sensitive to the states' interests in placing reasonable restrictions on inherently dangerous products—especially as guns become ever more lethal and the incidence of mass shootings seems to rise.

In any event, given the federal courts' deferential attitude post-*Heller*, the NRA's most important work in protecting the right to bear arms continues to take place, as it always has, primarily outside the courts. The NRA continues to be a more important safeguard of the right than the judiciary, even after the Supreme Court victories. It has successfully blocked legislation—such as the universal background check law proposed after the Sandy Hook shootings—that the courts would plainly deem constitutional. It has successfully persuaded legislatures to enact many gun protections—including laws on concealed carry permits, self-defense, firearms preemption, and immunity for gun manufacturers—that are not required by the Second Amendment as the courts understand it, even under *Heller* and *McDonald*. And its political influence is such that it deters many politicians from even considering gun regulations, no matter how constitutionally valid, for fear that they might be targeted by the NRA in their reelection campaigns. The significance of the victories in *Heller* and *McDonald* should not be underestimated. But it remains the case that the most effective guardian of Second Amendment rights is not the courts, but the NRA.

11

People Power

WHAT IS THE SOURCE OF THE NRA'S REMARKABLE ABILITY TO SHAPE GUN RIGHTS? Pointing to the NRA's massive annual budget, critics often argue that its influence is a reflection not of the power of its ideas but the size of its purse. In 2013, the NRA reported revenue of just under $350 million and expenditures of $290 million. The leading gun control organization, the Brady Campaign to Prevent Gun Violence, by contrast, reported revenue and expenditures for the same year of about $3 million. If the NRA spends one hundred dollars for every one that its principal opponent spends, is it any wonder that it usually wins? Is its success, then, simply a function of its vast resources? If so, then the NRA's story is less a reflection of the power of citizens banded together to advance constitutional law than it is a reminder of the all-too-common story that money drives our politics.[1]

It is, of course, difficult to disentangle the influence of popular support from the influence of money. This is particularly true in the case of the NRA, because about half of its annual revenue comes from its five million dues-paying members and fee-generating services (in 2013, more than $180 million). And according to NRA Deputy Executive Director and General Counsel David Lehman, 80 percent of the NRA's

140

contributions come from members. So in a sense, for the NRA popular support and money are inextricably interrelated: the NRA has more money because it has more popular support. These figures make clear that the NRA is not merely the mouthpiece of a few wealthy individuals or corporations.[2]

In addition, a relatively small portion of the money raised each year actually goes to lobbying for Second Amendment rights. The NRA-ILA—the Institute for Legislative Action, the heart of the NRA's constitutional defense of the right to bear arms—makes up only about 10 percent of the NRA's overall budget, or about $30 million. That's still ten times that of the Brady Center, but not one hundred times. For four decades the NRA-ILA has helped to shape federal and state constitutional and statutory law on the right to bear arms and has played a decisive role in major elections. But it is not a large office, at least relative to the rest of the NRA. In 2015, the NRA-ILA had seventy-eight staff members, which amounts to about 10 percent of the organization's employees, not counting the organization's approximately 150,000 volunteers. The NRA's Second Amendment lobbying arm doesn't have nearly the money or the staff many of its critics assume it has.[3]

Critics also charge that the NRA's influence stems from gun industry largesse. Gun manufacturers and dealers do support the NRA in a number of ways, including with direct contributions. But the gun industry's donations constitute only a small fraction of the NRA's overall resources. According to a 2011 report by the Violence Policy Center entitled "Blood Money: How the Gun Industry Bankrolls the NRA," the firearms industry contributed "between $14.7 million and $38.9 million" to the NRA from 2005 to 2011. That averages $2.5 million to $6 million a year, or between 1 and 5 percent of the NRA's annual revenues—not small change, to be sure, but hardly a case of "bankrolling."[4]

The NRA receives additional corporate support from the gun industry by selling ads in its magazines. Gun industry ads brought in $20.9 million in 2010. But that is only another 7 percent of the NRA's annual budget. Some gun manufacturers and dealers offer gun purchasers the opportunity to round up their bills as a way of donating to the NRA, just as grocery store chains ask customers at the cash register if they want to add a small additional donation to various nonprofits. These "round-up" donations, however, come from citizens, not the gun manufacturers or dealers themselves. Most of the organization's resources come not from the gun industry, but from the millions of ordinary citizens who are its members and supporters.

THE REAL SOURCE OF the NRA's influence is its remarkable ability to mobilize its members and supporters at the ballot box. Former NRA president David Keene put it this way:

> The power of the National Rifle Association doesn't come from money, which doesn't mean we don't have to spend money, because we do. But it comes from votes. It comes from people. It comes from the . . . narrative that we have. In the recent Colorado recalls [elections to remove from office legislators who had supported new gun laws following the Aurora shootings], the anti-gun people outspent the pro-gun people by better than six to eight to one and didn't make any difference, because we had the votes. We had the people. . . . Politicians . . . can raise money in a lot of different ways from a lot of different places. But if you tell a politician you've got eight thousand members in his district, he's willing to think about things other than money, because . . . his job depends on whether those people are gonna vote for or against. That's where the real power of an advocacy group in a free society comes from.[5]

Or as Chris Cox put it, "If you want to speak with a louder voice, get together. It's Democracy 101."

Dennis Burke, an aide to former senator Dennis DeConcini, agreed, saying, "I don't think [politicians] care about the contributions they get from the NRA. They care about the piles of mail, these nasty calls, and people picketing their state offices. Politicians are risk averse." After the NRA succeeded in persuading Congress to pass the Firearms Owners Protection Act in 1986, one congressman told the *Washington Post*: "We made the hard political calculus, 'Do I want to spend the next five months debating one crummy vote on gun control? The NRA's got the network, the head counts, they know who's wavering. . . . It's the kind of an issue that could defeat me when nothing else could." [6]

For many NRA members and supporters, the right to bear arms is a make-or-break issue. They will vote for candidates who support gun rights, and vote against those who do not. They will be guided by the NRA's candidate grades, which are determined exclusively by the candidates' views on guns. By contrast, most gun control supporters do not see gun control as their most important concern; gun control is more likely to be one of many policy preferences, and is therefore less likely to drive their political behavior. The Pew Research Center found in a 2013 survey, for example, that "a quarter of those who prioritized gun rights said they had, at some point, contributed money to an organization that took a position on the issue, compared with 6% of gun control supporters," and that "gun rights proponents outnumbered gun control supporters by 45% to 26% when it came to those who said they were involved in one or more instances of activism." [7]

As David Keene said in a conversation at the Open Society Foundations in 2013, "The difference between the NRA and other groups is that we've developed a community [and] when they see Second Amendment rights threatened they vote. They cross party lines. They do whatever they need to do. They get out. They give money. They're active at the state level. They're active at the national level." [8]

Gun rights proponents may feel more strongly because they have something tangible they are afraid they'll lose: their guns. As Chris Cox put it, "from a philosophical standpoint, are you willing to fight more for something you have or to take something away from someone else? That's why we not only have more people who support us, but we have the passion, because you're fighting to keep something you're going to lose rather than for something you don't have to begin with." Over a third of all Americans report having a gun in their household. That's a lot of people with something tangible to lose.[9]

Gun regulation does not mean gun confiscation. But the NRA and many gun rights advocates are quick to claim that there is a natural progression from regulation to confiscation. When Congress was considering the Brady Bill, for example, which imposed waiting periods on gun purchases, Wayne LaPierre, the NRA's chief executive officer, warned that it was "nothing more than the first step toward more stringent 'gun control' measures. Some people call it 'the camel's nose under the tent,' some call it 'the slippery slope,' some call it a 'foot in the door,' but regardless of what you call it, it's still the same—the first step." When Barack Obama proposed closing the loopholes on background checks after the Sandy Hook shooting, LaPierre argued that the only purpose of the background check was to create a gun registry, and "in the end, there are only two reasons for government to create that federal registry of gun owners—to tax them and to take them."[10]

Liberals may unintentionally contribute to the NRA's strength. Dan Baum, author of *Gun Guys*, a portrait of gun enthusiasts, argues that liberals' often dismissive attitudes toward gun owners have led the latter to band together. Baum offers some examples:

> Newspaper editorialists called gun owners "a ridiculous minority of airheads," "a handful of middle-age fat guys with popguns," and "hicksville cowboys" with "macho" hang-ups. For Gene Weingarten of *The Washington Post*, gun guys were "bumpkins and yeehaws who like to think they are protecting their homes against imagined swarthy marauders desperate to steal their flea-bitten sofas from their rotting front porches." Mark Morford of *SF Gate* called female shooters "bored, under-educated, bitter, terrified, badly dressed, pasty, hate-spewin' suburban white women from lost Midwestern towns with names like Frankenmuth."

As Baum notes, it is "impossible to imagine getting away with such cruel dismissals of, say, blacks or gays, yet among a certain set, backhanding gun owners was good sport, even righteous." If liberals dismiss gun owners' interests, and stereotype them in patently disrespectful ways that would be unacceptable for nearly any other group, those who care about gun rights are likely to be even more adamant about the need to defend their rights.[11]

Kayne Robinson, a former NRA president and executive director, confirmed this, telling me that "the threat is the thing. The most important thing in motivating the members is the threat. Understanding the gravity of the threat is what produces action." As an example, he pointed to the 1968 Gun Control Act as the principal motivating force in the NRA's transformation into a political advocacy organization in the 1970s. But the point is a more general one. According to several NRA officials with whom I spoke, new memberships spike whenever there is a mass shooting. Gun owners fear that the shootings will lead to efforts to limit their rights, so they turn to the NRA—just as those concerned about civil liberties join or increase their support to the ACLU in times of national security crises. In this way, the NRA performs a checking function; it is strongest when the people's perceived need for it is greatest. As a *Washington Post* account of the organization's successful advocacy put it, "the NRA learned that controversy isn't a problem but rather, in many cases, a solution, a motivator, a recruitment tool, an inspiration."[12]

The NRA's success also surely stems in part from its ability, as David Keene suggests, to build a sense of community and identity among its members and supporters. Just as gay and lesbian identity and community proved a powerful motivator in the fight for marriage equality, so, too, the sense of identity fostered by the NRA is an invaluable asset. As Keene says, the NRA is not just an organization, but "a family." In this regard, the NRA has several advantages over most other constitutional rights organizations. First, it has a long history of building a sense of identity around guns, dating back to the nineteenth century, long before it even had much of a political role. Families have passed down their loyalty to the NRA for generations. Second, the group's focus lends itself to a wide range of nonpolitical activities, including hunting, shooting competitions, training, collecting, and gun shows. Most constitutional rights groups hold an annual convention or dinner and sponsor an occasional panel, but that can hardly compete with the wide range of bonding activities that the NRA offers its millions of members every year.

The peculiarly American romance with guns, which the NRA invokes in its literature and messaging, also contributes to the organization's success. The image of the cowboy or the rifleman is iconic in American culture. We have long associated the gun with the pre-revolutionary citizen-soldier, the frontier, self-sufficiency, and individual freedom. It is a critical component of our libertarian heritage rooted in the American Revolution, and its appeal goes far beyond guns themselves.

THE FACT THAT THE NRA sees itself as protecting a constitutional right, as opposed to some lesser interest, also adds to its power and influence. The amendment, or at least the part of it the NRA prefers, is etched in stone above the entry to its national headquarters in Virginia. As Kayne Robinson observes: "We have the constitutional right. No one else has that. The difference it makes in terms of your credibility is immense." Chris Cox argues that members are motivated by "believing it's fundamental and uniquely American, and wanting to pass it down to the next generation intact." Chuck Cunningham agrees that the ability to point to the right's protection in the Constitution gives the NRA a legitimacy and power that it might not otherwise have. Of course, it was the NRA itself that transformed the modern understanding of the Second Amendment into an individual right. But as Cunningham points out, the organization and its members saw the right as constitutionally based long before 2008. For the NRA and its members and supporters, the right to bear arms has long been a central tenet of their constitutional faith.[13]

The NRA's conception of the Second Amendment involves not only the right to own guns, but the right to defend oneself, and this, too, is part of the idea's attraction. As Robinson told me, a "key aspect" of the NRA's appeal "is our concept of the right of self-defense. This is a very, very big deal." Keene agrees: "our narrative has been that firearms ownership is part of the American DNA, that is why this country is what . . . it's been, that families had been hunting and shooting together for hundreds of years. . . . The Second Amendment . . . is merely an incorporation of something that goes back far, far, into history before that Constitution was written, which is the right to defend yourself, your community and your family."[14]

Finally, and perhaps most important, in many NRA members' eyes, the Second Amendment is a cornerstone of freedom itself. NRA leader Wayne LaPierre's comments from a 2013 speech are typical: "Our Founding Fathers knew that without Second Amendment freedom, all of our freedoms could be in jeopardy. Our individual liberty is the very essence of America. It is what makes America unique. If you aren't free to protect yourself—when government puts its thumb on that freedom—then you aren't free at all." Richard Feldman, a former NRA lobbyist, explains the role this message plays in the NRA's appeal: "they have turned this into a symbolic issue. It's no longer about guns. It's about freedom and responsibility and liberty."[15]

ALL OF THESE FACTORS contribute to the NRA's decided advantage in the gun debate. But the NRA had to recognize and put them to use in the first place. Securing an individual right to bear arms has been not only a long-term goal but an organizing principle and source of legitimacy. By harnessing the committed support of its members—who express that support in many ways, including political action and donations—the NRA has met with success at every level of American government and law, from local municipalities to the Supreme Court.

The Constitution is, of course, supposed to place its guarantees above the ordinary political process. But as the NRA's story illustrates, the vitality of a constitutional right turns in significant part on the extent to which the people, or at least a significant portion of the people, view the right as fundamental and as warranting their attention, support, and political action. Ideally, the people will consider fealty to the right as a core part of their very identity. Through its membership services, its nourishing of a sense of identity and community, its active engagement in electoral politics, and its advocacy in a wide range of federal, state, and local arenas, the NRA has made the right to bear arms one of the most salient issues in the American political landscape. By directly involving its members and supporters in the defense of gun rights wherever such issues arise, and by tracking every state and federal politicians' fidelity to gun rights, the NRA has ensured that the constitutional right to bear arms is protected not just by the courts, but by the political process. The NRA, more so than any court, is the Second Amendment's best protector. It ensured gun rights long before the Supreme Court recognized the right in 2008, and it continues to be the amendment's first line of defense. As Chris Cox put it, NRA members "know that if it weren't for this organization, we would have lost this right a long time ago. And I don't think any of our opponents would deny that."

PART THREE

HUMAN RIGHTS IN
THE WAR ON TERROR

WHEN NINETEEN AL QAEDA OPERATIVES HIJACKED FOUR PASSENGER AIRPLANES AND turned them into weapons of terror on September 11, 2001, they changed the face of America. In short order, President George W. Bush declared a "war on terror," Congress authorized the use of military force against Al Qaeda and those who harbored it, and the United States invaded Afghanistan. Fourteen years later, the war drags on. And Al Qaeda's affiliates have spread, operating from the largely ungoverned areas of Pakistan's mountainous region bordering Afghanistan, as well as Yemen, Somalia, and other locations.

Civil liberties are often among the first casualties of war. In times of fear and crisis, citizens defer to authority, and are willing to sacrifice liberty for the promise of greater security—especially when the liberty they sacrifice is not their own. The phenomenon is hardly unique to the United States, and dates back at least to the Romans, who gave us the Latin phrase *inter arma enim silent leges*, or "in wartime, the law is silent."[1]

The American Civil Liberties Union (ACLU), the Center for Constitutional Rights (CCR), Human Rights Watch (HRW), and other organizations dedicated to civil liberties and human rights knew that the rights they were created to protect would be at risk after 9/11. The political branches have often overreacted in times of crisis, and courts have historically deferred, tolerating significant infringements on civil liberties. In the Civil War, President Abraham Lincoln suspended the writ of habeas corpus, an authority the Constitution gives only to Congress, and aggressively censored dissent. In World War I, the Supreme Court upheld legislation making it a crime to speak out against the war effort, and many Americans were jailed for their views. In World War II, the Court upheld the internment of more than 110,000 Japanese Americans and Japanese immigrants, based not on any individualized suspicion but solely on their Japanese ancestry. In the Cold War, when Congress made association with the Communist Party a crime, the Court initially declined to intervene. The historical record, in short, was consistent, and—from the point of view of organizations devoted to the protection of civil liberties—dismal. In wartime, civil liberties had been sacrificed, and the courts had largely played a rubber-stamp role.[2]

There are some exceptions. During what we now call the Korean War, the Supreme Court invalidated President Harry Truman's seizure of the nation's steel mills in the face of an impending strike. But the decision involved only a domestic labor initiative, and the Court stressed that our involvement in Korea was not a war, but, in Truman's own words, only "a police action." Courts have also played a somewhat more active role at the ends of wars. Near the end of the Civil War, the Supreme Court ruled in favor of Lambdin Milligan, who, the Court held, could not be tried in a military tribunal because he was a civilian. At the end of World War II, the Court ruled that the government could not continue to intern Japanese Americans who had been determined to pose no threat. The Court became more protective of speech and associational rights after the Senate censured the anti-Communist senator Joe McCarthy and McCarthyism was on the wane. And at the close of the Vietnam War, the Court allowed the *New York Times* and

Washington Post to publish a confidential Pentagon internal review of the war effort that had been leaked by whistleblower Daniel Ellsberg. But these are exceptions; during war, the courts—and Congress—had nearly always deferred to the executive.[3]

Those who wanted to protect civil liberties and human rights in the wake of 9/11 faced considerable headwinds: as with gay rights and gun rights advocates in the 1990s, neither history nor the law was on their side. The challenge they faced was in several respects even more daunting. The marriage equality and Second Amendment campaigns focused on one specific right. The threats to civil liberties and human rights in wartime, by contrast, were many; they included preventive detention, unfair trials, torture and other cruel interrogation techniques, illegal abductions or "renditions," excessive secrecy, dragnet surveillance, ethnic and religious profiling, and the punishment of speech and association. The government set the agenda through its security initiatives, and civil liberties organizations were usually on the defensive, responding to whatever new incursion the government introduced. Unlike the gay rights and gun rights groups, they did not have the opportunity to plan and carry out a long-term, incremental strategy of their own devising.

In addition, probably the most productive tactic these other groups used—working through the states—was largely unavailable to civil liberties lawyers and organizations. National security is principally a federal prerogative, and federal security programs cannot be challenged for transgressing state laws. A state-by-state strategy was not a realistic option. What's more, the victims of the government's actions were largely foreign nationals. Unlike the NRA and Freedom to Marry, civil liberties organizations did not have a natural constituency of self-interested citizens to mobilize.[4]

What civil liberties and human rights groups shared with gay rights and gun rights advocates was a need to find alternative forums to advance their claims. Where the latter groups turned to the states, civil liberties and human rights groups turned to foreign audiences and governments, exhorting them to bring pressure to bear on the United States to conform its actions to basic human rights. They successfully framed the debate as pitting the rule of law against "law-free zones," and recruited unlikely allies, especially from retired military leaders, to serve as credible messengers. They pursued transparency, obtaining documents under the Freedom of Information Act (FOIA), and disseminating them to bring attention to the administration's controversial initiatives. They relied on the public shaming tactics that human rights groups often use where more formal avenues of redress are unavailing. And when, under President Obama, the option was available, they played an "inside game," seeking reforms from within through the assistance of sympathetic officials, even as other activists continued the drumbeat of criticism without.

Like gay rights and gun rights groups, civil liberties and human rights groups also turned to the federal courts with constitutional claims. Here, too, such lawsuits were a relatively minor part of the overall effort. But unlike the other campaigns, civil liberties advocates did not have the luxury to delay filing federal lawsuits until they had made sufficient progress in alternative venues. When a client is in detention, his lawyer cannot tell him to wait three to five years to see what sort of momentum might develop. Accordingly, civil liberties groups filed federal lawsuits from the very outset of the war on terror. Indeed, our story begins with one such suit.

12

"Completely Hopeless"

PRESIDENT GEORGE W. BUSH WAS NOT THE FIRST PRESIDENT TO USE GUANTÁNAMO BAY Naval Base, on Cuban land indefinitely leased to the United States, as a "law-free zone." His father, President George H. W. Bush, had come up with the idea some ten years earlier. When a military coup in Haiti in 1991 prompted thousands of desperate Haitians to board overcrowded, often unseaworthy boats for America's shores, the first President Bush ordered the Coast Guard to interdict them at sea. The Coast Guard perfunctorily screened the refugees on board to see if any had a credible claim for asylum, and turned back those who did not. Those refugees deemed to have credible asylum claims were either brought to the United States or held at Guantánamo Bay while their claims were more fully assessed. Some tested positive for HIV; they were held at Guantánamo indefinitely, regardless of the outcome of the further assessments of their asylum claims.

When the first Haitian refugees arrived at Guantánamo, Michael Ratner was a lawyer in his fifties, working with the New York–based Center for Constitutional Rights (CCR), and co-teaching a human rights clinic at Yale Law School with Professor Harold Koh. Ratner, the son of a Cleveland real estate magnate, graduated at the top of his

Columbia Law School class in the 1960s. His brother Bruce followed in their father's footsteps, and became one of New York City's most powerful developers, building the Barclays Center in Brooklyn, and buying the then–New Jersey Nets and bringing them to Brooklyn. Michael chose a different course, becoming a public interest lawyer. At CCR, he represented progressive activists whom the government had targeted for their political activities, and regularly sued the federal government over its foreign policy. He filed suits to challenge Ronald Reagan's funding of the contras in Nicaragua, the elder Bush's first Gulf War in Iraq, and Bill Clinton's bombing of Kosovo. He was not afraid of bringing cases that had little chance of success, if he could devise a legal theory to support what seemed right as a matter of principle and effective as political advocacy.

It was with that view that Ratner took on the Haitian detentions at Guantánamo. A federal appeals court in Miami had already ruled that, as foreigners outside the United States, the Haitians had no enforceable rights. Despite that precedent, Ratner and Koh, with the law school clinic's students, filed suit in New York, hoping to win a more favorable ruling from a different court.

The Haitian suit prefigured the lawsuit Ratner would file a decade later against the younger Bush's detention of alleged enemy combatants in the war with Al Qaeda. In both cases, government lawyers argued that because the detainees were foreigners and were held on land that technically belonged to Cuba and was only leased to the United States, they had no legal rights enforceable by an American court. And in both instances, Ratner and his co-counsel initially made limited procedural claims—in the Haitian case, that the detainees had a right to a lawyer; in the later case, that the detainees in the war on terror had a right to judicial review of their detentions.

In the Haitian case, the court ordered the government to provide access to lawyers. Once lawyers made it to the island, they reported on the atrocious conditions there, and those reports ultimately led to the release of all the Haitians. Ratner's victory in the Haitian case, however, was of little legal help a decade later. The court had afforded the Haitians constitutional protections only because they had made an initial showing that they faced a credible threat of persecution if returned to Haiti, and therefore were entitled under law to a full review of their asylum claims. And the Haitian case did not involve war powers. The new Guantánamo detainees had made no showings that they were eligible for asylum, and were effectively prisoners of war.[1]

Ratner nonetheless felt compelled to act. The new detainees had been denied any rights whatsoever. They were given neither lawyers nor hearings. Their identities were secret. The administration allowed no one to talk to the men to learn who they were, how they were captured, what they were doing when taken into custody, and how they were treated. In February 2002, Bush declared that Al Qaeda detainees were not protected by the Geneva Conventions, which require humanitarian treatment of all wartime detainees. The detainees were entirely cut off from the world at large—held incommunicado on an isolated island base in the Caribbean. Like the Haitians brought to Guantánamo in the early 1990s, these new detainees were, to Ratner, evidence of the failure of the United States to live up to its values.

RATNER HAD BEEN CONTEMPLATING a lawsuit even before the military brought anyone to Guantánamo. In November 2001, President Bush issued "Presidential Order No. 1," an executive order establishing a military tribunal to try alleged war criminals, including for capital offenses. Under this scheme, the executive branch would be judge, jury, and executioner. It would authorize the prosecutions, pick and supervise the judges, review convictions on appeal, and carry out the executions. The order expressly prohibited judicial review. It was so extreme that even William Safire, the conservative columnist for the *New York Times*, editorialized against it. Within a week of the order's issuance, Ratner had begun discussing potential legal challenges with two experienced death penalty lawyers: Clive Stafford Smith, a British lawyer who was defending death row inmates in Louisiana, and Joseph Margulies, who had a civil rights and criminal defense practice in Minneapolis.[2]

Once detainees began arriving at Guantánamo in January 2002, Ratner and his colleagues began focusing on the issue of detention without trial. The Geneva Conventions, a series of treaties governing the treatment of prisoners in wartime, provide that where there is any doubt regarding a detainee's status in an armed conflict, he is entitled to a hearing to determine whether he is appropriately subject to detention as a prisoner of war. The principle that imprisoned individuals deserve an opportunity to challenge the legality of their detention is as old as the Magna Carta. Ratner and his team began looking into whether they could file petitions for habeas corpus on behalf of the detained. Habeas corpus, a right recognized by English common law, adopted by the colonies, and enshrined in the Constitution, permits any imprisoned person to go to a court to demand a justification for why he is being confined, and empowers courts to order the release of those unlawfully detained. The Constitution prohibits the suspension of habeas corpus, "unless when in Cases of Rebellion or Invasion the public Safety may require it." Congress had not suspended habeas corpus, and in any event, the terrorist attack on 9/11 was neither an invasion nor a rebellion.

The late New York senator Daniel Patrick Moynihan once said that if he had to choose between living in a country where he had the right to vote, but no habeas corpus, and one where he had a right of habeas corpus but no vote, he'd choose the latter. In Moynihan's view, habeas corpus was more important even than democracy itself. That's because the very notions of freedom, democracy, and limited government are incompatible with the power to detain without explaining why. To Ratner and his colleagues, these values are so fundamental that they are worth fighting for even when—and perhaps *especially* when—they are least likely to be respected.

Finding detainees to represent proved difficult, given the military's refusal to allow access to the base or to make public the names of those held there. How can you sue on behalf of a prisoner you cannot name? The breakthrough came from halfway around the world. The Bush administration notified the United Kingdom and Australia, two of its closest allies, that some of their citizens were among the detained.

When those countries in turn informed the detainees' relatives, the relatives reached out to lawyers, and the secret was out. Ratner saw a quote in a news article from an Australian lawyer representing the family of a detainee named David Hicks, and immediately called to offer his assistance. Shortly thereafter, Stephen Watt, another CCR lawyer, similarly identified and contacted the lawyer for Mamdouh Habib, another Australian detained at Guantánamo. The families of two British detainees, Shafiq Rasul and Asif Iqbal, contacted British lawyer Gareth Peirce, and she and Ratner were soon in touch as well.

Each of the men had been captured in Afghanistan or Pakistan. David Hicks, born in Adelaide, had converted to Islam in 1999 and traveled to Pakistan and Afghanistan, where he attended training camps run by the terrorist groups Lashkar-e-Taiba and Al Qaeda. He was arrested by the Northern Alliance and turned over to US forces in December 2001. Mamdouh Habib, a dual national of Egypt and Australia, was arrested while traveling in Pakistan, rendered to Egypt and Afghanistan, and eventually brought to Guantánamo. Shafiq Rasul and Asif Iqbal were young men from Tipton, England, who had traveled to Afghanistan in 2001. Within weeks of these men's arrival at Guantánamo, on February 19, 2002, Ratner, Margulies, and CCR filed suit in a federal court in Washington, DC, challenging the detentions on behalf of their family members. A few months later, in May 2002, Tom Wilner, a litigator with Shearman and Sterling, a prestigious American corporate law firm, filed a similar suit on behalf of the families of twelve Kuwaiti citizens held at Guantánamo. The cases were consolidated before US District Judge Colleen Kollar-Kotelly. Both lawsuits asserted that the detainees had a right to judicial review via the writ of habeas corpus.

In Ratner's view, the cases were "completely hopeless." The law was dead set against them. The Supreme Court had ruled after World War II that enemy prisoners of war could not seek habeas corpus review in US courts. Justice Robert Jackson, writing in 1950 for the Court in *Johnson v. Eisentrager*, stated in no uncertain terms: "Nothing in the text of the Constitution extends such a right, nor does anything in our statutes." Jackson explained that "it would be difficult to devise more effective fettering of a field commander than to allow the very enemies he is ordered to reduce to submission to call him to account in his own civil courts and divert his efforts and attention from the military offensive abroad to the legal defensive at home." Given that precedent, not to mention the long history of deference to the executive in times of crisis, the government could feel confident about how these new habeas petitions would fare. It promptly moved to dismiss.[3]

Politically, the detainees' case was no stronger. Memories of the collapsing World Trade Center towers and of the many people who had leapt to their deaths in desperation were still raw, and there was little sympathy for anyone said to be associated with the perpetrators of that heinous act. Moreover, the only people the government imprisoned at Guantánamo were foreign nationals, so the rights of US citizens were not implicated.

Ratner and Margulies contended that *Eisentrager*'s ruling denying habeas review should be limited to aliens from enemy nations in a formally declared war—"enemy aliens"—who had been tried and convicted of war crimes. Their own clients, they stressed, were citizens of friendly nations and had never even been charged with, much less convicted of, war crimes. Judge Kollar-Kotelly did not see a difference. In her view, *Eisentrager* established that foreigners detained outside the United States had no right to habeas corpus; she dismissed the case. The detainees appealed, but a three-judge panel of the US Court of Appeals for the DC Circuit unanimously affirmed, also relying heavily on *Eisentrager*. The detainees had not won a single judge's vote.[4]

The lawyers nonetheless pressed on, petitioning for review in the Supreme Court. There, they had even less chance than in the lower courts. The Supreme Court does not have to hear any appeal, and almost never accepts review where the federal government has prevailed and there is no disagreement among the lower courts on the law.

Yet on November 10, 2003, to everyone's surprise, the Court agreed to review the case. And on June 28, 2004, the Court issued its decision in *Rasul v. Bush*, ruling by a vote of 6–3 that the habeas corpus statute afforded the detainees a right to court review of their detentions.

Rasul was only the beginning. Over the next four years, the Court decided three more equally significant "enemy combatant" cases against the Bush administration, a wholly unprecedented run of losses for a president during wartime. The same day that it decided *Rasul*, the Court also rejected the Bush administration's assertion, in *Hamdi v. Rumsfeld*, that it could hold a US citizen in military detention as an "enemy combatant" without a hearing. Yaser Hamdi, born in Louisiana but raised in Saudi Arabia, was captured on a battlefield in Afghanistan, allegedly fighting for the Taliban, and held in military brigs in Virginia and South Carolina without a hearing or access to a lawyer for more than two years. The Supreme Court ruled that Hamdi was constitutionally entitled to a fair hearing, and in the face of that threat, the administration released him on a promise that he return to Saudi Arabia and remain there.[5]

Two years later, in 2006, in *Hamdan v. Rumsfeld*, the Court declared invalid President Bush's military commissions order, the one that had first drawn Ratner's attention. In reaching its decision, the Court ruled that the Geneva Conventions' protections for prisoners in wartime applied to Al Qaeda detainees, directly contradicting the president's determination. And then, in 2008, in a pair of consolidated cases handled for the detainees by former solicitor general Seth Waxman, CCR, and others, the Court in *Boumediene v. Bush* reaffirmed the rights of Guantánamo detainees to judicial review. This time, it held that they have not just a statutory right, as the Court had ruled in *Rasul*, but a constitutional right that could not be denied, even by Congress, short of a formal suspension of habeas corpus. Congress had in the interim repealed the habeas statute on which *Rasul* was based, so in *Boumediene* the Court, for the first time in its history, stood up to the executive and legislative branches acting together during wartime.[6] Ratner's quixotic effort to bring the rule of law and judicial review to Guantánamo had, against all odds, succeeded.

Notwithstanding the historic nature of these four decisions rejecting assertions of executive power in a time of war, the rulings did not formally require much of the Bush administration. *Rasul* and *Boumediene* concerned only the detainees' right to a day in court; they did not address the legality of the detentions themselves, nor order anyone's release. *Hamdan* rested on an interpretation of the Uniform Code of Military Justice, and the Court emphasized that Congress could allow the military commissions to proceed simply by amending that law, which Congress promptly did. *Hamdi* involved the rights of US citizens held as "enemy combatants," and only two US citizens were so held in the entire war on terror. Thus, while the decisions were symbolically important, they did not formally demand much from the Bush administration.[7]

Nonetheless, by the time Bush left office in 2009, he had significantly curtailed or modified many of his counterterrorism policies. When a secret Justice Department memorandum authorizing the CIA to use waterboarding and other forms of torture and cruelty on Al Qaeda suspects was leaked and published by the *Washington Post*, triggering widespread denunciations, the Bush administration rescinded it, leading the CIA to temporarily suspend its interrogation program. When civil society groups, legal experts, and the *New York Times*'s William Safire condemned the absence of judicial review of military commission decisions, then–White House Counsel Alberto Gonzales tried to limit the damage by publishing an op-ed claiming that the president never actually meant to deny judicial review— despite having said exactly that in his original order. After the CIA's secret prisons, or "black sites," were disclosed in the media, Bush moved all the CIA's detainees to Guantánamo Bay prison, where the International Committee for the Red Cross (ICRC) was for the first time granted access to them. When civil society groups, European governments, and others condemned the practice of abducting terror suspects and delivering or "rendering" them to third countries that use torture to interrogate, such "extraordinary renditions" ceased. After the *New York Times* revealed the National Security Agency's (NSA) warrantless wiretapping program and the ACLU and CCR challenged the program's legality in court, the administration agreed to subject the surveillance to judicial oversight. None of these reforms was compelled by a court or Congress.[8]

Bush also introduced many reforms at Guantánamo Bay, the vast majority of which were likewise not mandated by a court or Congress. The administration initially maintained that the men there deserved no hearings, and were "the worst of the worst." It subjected them to abusive interrogation tactics only slightly less extreme than those employed by the CIA in its secret prisons. Yet by the time Bush left office, he had freed more than five hundred of Guantánamo's 779 detainees, ended abusive interrogations, improved prison conditions, and offered "combatant status review" hearings to each detainee, albeit with inadequate procedures—all without judicial compulsion. By the end of Bush's second term, the former legal black hole of Guantánamo operated under legal limits and judicial oversight.[9]

The Bush administration did not make these changes because it independently realized the error of its ways. As their memoirs underscore, Bush and Vice President Dick Cheney are entirely unapologetic about the tactics they authorized in the war on terror—up to and including waterboarding. So why did Bush rein in so many measures that he had instituted and defended as necessary to keep America safe? The Supreme Court's four "enemy combatant" decisions—*Rasul, Hamdi, Hamdan,* and *Boumediene*—similarly demand explanation. Why did the Court break from its history of virtually complete deference to executive power in wartime and rule against the president in all four cases?[10]

The traditional answers would point to formal checks and balances and the force of constitutional doctrine. But as we have seen, no legal order or mandate drove the Bush administration to change course as it did. Nor did legal precedent dictate the results in the Supreme Court's four decisions against Bush. On the contrary, *Johnson v. Eisentrager* offered strong support for the Bush administration in *Rasul* and *Boumediene*. And a second World War II precedent, *Ex parte Quirin,* supported Bush's position in *Hamdan*, the military commissions case. *Quirin* had upheld military commission trials—and executions—of several Nazi saboteurs captured in the United States during World War II.

Bush's order creating the military tribunal was modeled directly on the Roosevelt order upheld in *Quirin*.[11]

In *Rasul* and *Hamdan*, moreover, the most important arguments the Court eventually adopted were barely advanced by the parties' lawyers. In *Rasul*, Justice Stevens distinguished *Eisentrager* by pointing to a subsequent Supreme Court decision, *Braden v. 30th Judicial Circuit Court of Kentucky*, which had changed the interpretation of the habeas corpus statute's rules regarding who can be sued. When Stevens asked Rasul's counsel, John Gibbons, a former federal appeals judge, about this at oral argument, Gibbons attempted to deflect the question; he didn't realize that Stevens was trying to find a way to rule in his favor. Rasul's brief cited *Braden* only twice, both times in passing and only in footnotes. Stevens effectively developed the prevailing argument on his own.[12]

Similarly, in *Hamdan*, the military commission case, the Court reached out unnecessarily to address the application of the Geneva Conventions to Al Qaeda detainees, a determination that proved to be the decision's primary legacy. The Court's principal ruling was that the military commissions were not authorized by Congress, because they impermissibly departed from statutorily authorized court-martial procedures. The Court could have stopped there, as this was a sufficient basis to invalidate the commissions and rule for Hamdan. But it went on to hold that Common Article 3 of the Geneva Conventions, a bill of rights for prisoners of war, protected Al Qaeda detainees, rejecting Bush's opposite conclusion from several years earlier. As in *Rasul*, Hamdan's lawyer, Neal Katyal, barely pressed the issue. His only discussion of Common Article 3 came in the last three pages of his fifty-page principal brief, and Katyal never argued, as the Court ultimately held, that Common Article 3 applied because the conflict with Al Qaeda was a non-international armed conflict.[13]

Finally, the results cannot be attributed to judicial hostility to Bush. The Rehnquist Court that decided *Rasul* and *Hamdi* had put Bush in office when it decided *Bush v. Gore* following the disputed 2000 election. The Roberts Court, with Bush appointees John Roberts and Samuel Alito as recent members, decided *Hamdan* and *Boumediene*. Both were conservative courts, and conservatives tend to support executive power. Neither the Rehnquist Court nor the Roberts Court could be accused of being overly protective of civil liberties. In every respect, then, these decisions run decidedly against the grain.

Michael Ratner, CCR, and the many lawyers and organizations involved in the enemy combatant cases were far more successful than they—or anyone else—anticipated. So how did they prevail? Something other than the force of legal precedent, the arguments of the advocates, or the political inclinations of the justices caused the Court to rule as it did. And something other than formal judicial or congressional mandates compelled Bush to curtail many of his counterterrorism measures. If we are to account for these developments, we must look elsewhere. The place to begin is not 9/11, but World War II.

13

Korematsu's Legacy

WHEN FRED KOREMATSU, AN AMERICAN CITIZEN OF JAPANESE DESCENT, REFUSED TO report for internment during World War II, he could not have known that his case would reach the Supreme Court, much less that it would eventually play a part in the treatment of executive power after the terrorist attacks of September 11, 2001. Korematsu lost his case in the Supreme Court in 1944, when the Court ruled that the president was justified in treating all persons of Japanese descent as suspect simply because of their race and ethnicity, without individualized evidence that any of them posed a threat. But Korematsu did not accept the Court's word as final. Eventually, he and his supporters prevailed in the judgment of history. The story of Korematsu's long struggle for justice leads, ultimately, to the case Michael Ratner and his co-counsel filed against President Bush for detentions without trial at Guantánamo. When the Guantánamo case came before the Supreme Court, Fred Korematsu filed an amicus brief urging the Court not to repeat its mistakes. It is almost certainly the most important amicus brief filed in the case—not so much because of its content, but because of who submitted it, and the history he represented.

It was far from inevitable that the Supreme Court's decision upholding Korematsu's wartime conviction would come to be seen as a shameful mistake. It was certainly not viewed as such at the time it was decided. President Franklin Roosevelt issued Executive Order 9066 in February 1942, directing that all persons of Japanese descent be excluded from the West Coast, and establishing internment camps for over 110,000 people. Shortly thereafter, Congress ratified the president's action by enacting a statute making it a crime to disobey the exclusion order. During the war, the ACLU was a lonely critic of internment, and even its objections were muted. The ACLU's national board sent a letter to Roosevelt in March 1942 expressing concerns over the constitutionality of his executive order. But many board members had close ties to the Roosevelt administration, and they attempted without success to dissuade the ACLU's two California chapters from challenging the internment in court.

Other groups that one might have expected to object did not. Most conspicuously, the Japanese American Citizens League (JACL), not wanting to reinforce suspicions that the Japanese community was hostile to the war effort, advocated cooperation with the order. It specifically distanced itself from the few Japanese-Americans, such as Korematsu, who resisted internment, saying "National Headquarters is unalterably opposed to test cases . . . at this time." The National Lawyers Guild, a progressive bar association, similarly declined to criticize the initiative.[1]

Fred Korematsu resisted. The son of Japanese immigrants who ran a plant nursery, Korematsu tried to enlist when war broke out, but was turned away. When he learned of Roosevelt's order, he refused to report for internment and attempted to pass as non-Japanese. But in 1942, he was arrested and charged with evading the exclusion order. The ACLU agreed to represent him, and challenged the internment order as racial and ethnic discrimination. The Supreme Court acknowledged that the order expressly discriminated on the basis of race and ethnicity, but found that doing so was justified by compelling concerns that some within the Japanese and Japanese American community might be spies or saboteurs. The Court accepted the Roosevelt administration's argument that it was not possible to distinguish the guilty from the innocent on an individualized basis, necessitating mass internment. To this day, the *Korematsu* decision remains the only case in which the Court has upheld official race-based action not deemed necessary to remedy past discrimination or to pursue affirmative action. Three justices—Owen Roberts, Frank Murphy, and Robert Jackson—dissented. Only Murphy, however, called the program what it most assuredly was: government conduct that "goes over 'the very brink of constitutional power' and falls into the ugly abyss of racism."[2]

Over time, Murphy's dissenting accusation became the prevailing view. But this transformation was not inevitable. Civil liberties and Japanese American organizations took it upon themselves to challenge internment long after the practice (and the war) had ended. Their challenges began modestly, but grew over time. The JACL initially requested only compensation for those who had lost property while interned. In 1948, Congress provided such compensation. The ACLU was more aggressive, but its challenges were also initially tangential to the main issue. It successfully sued to restore citizenship to the many Japanese Americans who had been coerced into renouncing citizenship while interned; by 1969, 4,987 of 5,766 such people had regained American citizenship.[3]

In the 1960s, Japanese Americans campaigned to repeal the Emergency Detention Act, a 1950s law that authorized the preventive detention of persons suspected of espionage or sabotage in the event of invasion, war, or insurrection. Although the law had been passed after World War II, and thus had not been the basis for their particular mistreatment, the Japanese American community understood its dangers only too well. In 1971, Congress passed the Non-Detention Act, which not only repealed the Emergency Detention Act, but expressly forbade preventive detention except where specifically authorized by Congress.[4]

It wasn't until 1970, however, that the JACL adopted a resolution expressly seeking redress for internment itself, mounting a direct challenge to the practice's legality. In the late 1970s, the movement for reparations grew, as the JACL was joined by the National Coalition for Redress/Reparations and the National Council for Japanese American Redress. The cause received support beyond the Japanese community as well, from such groups as the Veterans of Foreign Wars and the Western Baptist State Convention, and from the leader of the American Jewish Committee.[5]

In 1976, responding to these calls, President Gerald Ford issued a proclamation condemning the internment. In 1980, Congress created the Commission on Wartime Relocation and Internment of Civilians to study the issue. Three years later, and nearly forty years after the *Korematsu* decision, the Commission unequivocally denounced the internment and called for an official apology and reparations. Still, both the Reagan administration and the *New York Times* opposed the Commission's recommendation for reparations.

The validity of the *Korematsu* decision was also undermined by legal scholar Peter Irons's discovery, during research for a book on the internment, that Justice Department lawyers had intentionally kept from the Supreme Court information that would have undermined the government's case. Roosevelt had relied upon a report by Lieutenant General John DeWitt that the Japanese community on the West Coast posed a military threat. The report specifically cited their use of radio signals to communicate with Japanese submarines in the Pacific Ocean. But the FBI and the FCC had contemporaneously reported that they found no evidence of such signaling, or that the community posed a threat. Initial drafts of the government's Supreme Court brief included the FBI and FCC findings in a footnote, but the footnote was deleted in the final version filed with the Court. On the basis of this discovery, Korematsu in 1983 asked a federal court to vacate his conviction. Government lawyers, embarrassed by the revelations, offered Korematsu a pardon, but he declined, contending that the government should be seeking a pardon, not him. In November 1983, a federal judge vacated Korematsu's conviction.[6]

Korematsu then joined the National Coalition for Redress/Reparations and traveled to Washington to demand an apology and reparations from Congress. In 1988, Congress passed and Reagan signed the Civil Liberties Act, which provided $20,000 for each interned Japanese American, and contained an extraordinary official apology: "For these fundamental violations of the basic civil liberties and constitutional rights of these individuals of Japanese ancestry, the

Congress apologizes on behalf of the Nation." Ten years later, in 1998, President Clinton awarded Fred Korematsu the Presidential Medal of Freedom, the highest honor the United States can bestow on a civilian. Over the course of half a century, Fred Korematsu had gone from a subversive to a hero in the nation's eyes.[7]

Korematsu's amicus brief in the Guantánamo cases, drafted by University of Chicago Professor Geoffrey Stone and NYU Law Professor Stephen Schulhofer, warned the justices not to repeat their predecessors' mistake. It noted that time and again, the nation had sacrificed its constitutional ideals in the name of national security in a perceived crisis, only to regret it after the fact. Speaking from his own personal experience, Korematsu urged the Court not to defer uncritically to executive claims of national security prerogative.

The Court did not cite Korematsu's brief in its decision; it didn't have to. The *Korematsu* decision's legacy has become so much a part of the legal culture that the Guantánamo cases could not be decided without reflecting that history. To accept Bush's position that he had unchecked authority to detain without judicial oversight would have looked dangerously like the excessive deference employed in *Korematsu*. And even though the Court has never had the opportunity to overturn *Korematsu*, eight of the nine justices on the Supreme Court at the time of *Rasul* had stated that it was wrongly decided. By the time *Rasul* came before the Supreme Court, the nation's understanding of *Korematsu*, and therefore of the proper role of the Court, had dramatically changed.[8]

This development, like the other instances of constitutional change recounted here, was not the result of an abstract set of legal arguments. It took the courage and persistence of Fred Korematsu and forty years of concerted advocacy by multiple civil society organizations to achieve what was in effect a popular reversal of a Supreme Court decision. The consequences were not merely retrospective, setting the historical record straight and acknowledging a grievous wrong. The altered understanding of *Korematsu* had prospective effects as well, framing future conflicts between executive authority and basic constitutional principle during wartime—including those presented by Shafiq Rasul and his fellow detainees.

14

At Home Abroad

ONE OF THE MOST DAUNTING CHALLENGES THAT DEFENDERS OF CIVIL LIBERTIES AND human rights in the war on terror face is the fact that so many of the victims of government overreach are not US citizens. Even if liberty lies in the hearts of men and women, it often lies there principally for the benefit of themselves and others like them. As long as the excesses of the war on terror sacrificed the liberties of foreigners for the security of Americans, the public was unlikely to raise an alarm.

The prison at Guantánamo Bay Naval Base, for example, is for foreign nationals only. Its 779 detainees hailed from 42 different nations. With one very temporary exception, none has been a US citizen. When authorities learned in early 2002 that one of the first prisoners brought to the base, Yaser Hamdi, was a US citizen by birth, they swiftly spirited him off to a military brig in South Carolina. The notion that the United States could pick up its own citizens and hold them indefinitely on an island beyond the law would have been a hard sell. Limiting the prison to foreigners, made it less likely to arouse domestic opposition.[1]

Vice President Cheney invoked this double standard in defending President Bush's military commission order: "Somebody who comes into the United States of America illegally, who conducts a terrorist operation killing thousands of innocent Americans—men, women, and children—is not a lawful combatant. . . . They don't deserve the same guarantees and safeguards that would be used for American citizens going through the normal judicial process."[2] Even today, after numerous reforms, military commissions—the ad hoc military courts with diminished procedural protections in which some Guantánamo detainees have been tried—apply only to foreign nationals, not US citizens. William Lietzau, a Defense Department official who served under both Bush and Obama, told me he thinks this is wrong. But when he proposed internally in 2009 that the commissions should apply equally to citizens and noncitizens, Cabinet officials, including Secretary of State Hillary Clinton, overruled him—in his view, for the illegitimate reason that it would be easier to defend the ad hoc tribunals if the government could say to its people, "your rights are not threatened." Lietzau faced a similar reception from the Senate when, in 2006, as legal advisor to the Supreme Allied Commander Europe James L. Jones, he urged elimination of the citizen/noncitizen distinction in the law governing military commissions.[3]

Torture and cruel interrogation techniques were also to be used only against foreign nationals. Indeed, the Bush administration justified its coercive interrogation practices by arguing that the international law bar against cruel, inhuman, and degrading treatment did not apply to foreign nationals held outside US borders. The CIA similarly abducted and rendered many foreign nationals—but no US citizens— to foreign countries for purposes of having them tortured there.[4]

This double standard permeates surveillance as well. While the NSA has engaged in dragnet collection of Americans' telephone metadata—the records showing who one has called, when, and for how long—it insists that it does not target the content of Americans' calls absent a warrant. By contrast, the NSA can listen to and read the contents of phone calls, emails, and all other electronic communications of any target it believes to be a foreigner outside the United States. It need have no suspicion that the individual is involved in terrorism or any other criminal conduct, and no warrant. The public has in a sense ratified this double standard. Americans have expressed much greater concern about the NSA collecting their phone metadata than about it listening to the contents of foreigners' calls. In June 2015, Congress passed the aptly titled USA Freedom Act, which ended the NSA's dragnet or "bulk" collection of Americans' phone metadata, but imposed no limits whatsoever on the much more expansive authorities the NSA wields against foreigners abroad.[5]

The same selective concern is evident with respect to targeted killing. The Obama administration has used drones to kill several thousand foreign nationals by remote control, many of them far from any battlefield. But American concern was most exercised by the use of a drone to kill an American citizen, Anwar al-Awlaki, in Yemen, in September 2011. In March 2013, Senator Rand Paul conducted a thirteen-hour filibuster on the Senate floor over the exceedingly unlikely potential use of drones to kill Americans on US soil. No filibusters have been held about the drone killing of foreigners, even manifestly innocent ones. In 2015, when a drone strike at an Al Qaeda residence in Pakistan accidentally killed an American and an Italian being held as hostages there, Obama held a press conference to apologize. Yet despite many credible reports that other US drone strikes have accidentally killed dozens and possibly hundreds of foreign innocent civilians, the administration has never even admitted the fact, much less apologized for the loss of those lives.[6]

It is evidently easier to avoid domestic criticism if aggressive policies are restricted to foreigners. This is especially true when the targets are predominantly Arab or Muslim foreigners, broadly associated in the public eye with "the enemy." Human rights and civil liberties groups after 9/11 accordingly confronted a very basic question: how can one effectively advocate for foreigners' rights in a time of crisis?

One solution was to look beyond US borders. Activists reasoned that the plight of foreign nationals would garner more sympathy in their home countries. That sympathy could perhaps be turned into pressure on the United States to reform its practices. The rise of international human rights law after World War II, the substance of which often overlaps with constitutional rights, made such advocacy possible. It afforded a common language for bringing foreign criticism to bear on US actions. The United States played a central part in the initial recognition of international human rights many decades ago, and both international treaties and the US Constitution protect such rights as liberty, privacy, fair trials, and equality. A British citizen or official may feel ill-equipped to assess claims about American constitutional law, but human rights law speaks a universal language. Thus, where marriage equality and gun rights advocates turned to state law, civil liberties advocates turned to human rights and foreign audiences to create pressure for constitutional reform.

As a BRITISH NATIONAL who is also a US citizen, Clive Stafford Smith has a natural affinity for the plight of the foreigner. He is a tall, gangly man with an accent that reveals his privileged upbringing, a dry, characteristically English sense of humor, and an irrepressible sparkle in his eyes. Born in Cambridge, England, educated at an exclusive boarding school, Radley College, Stafford Smith turned down an offer of admission to Cambridge University in order to attend college and law school in the United States because he was interested in fighting the death penalty. Upon graduating from Columbia Law School, he worked for the Southern Center for Human Rights, one of the nation's preeminent capital punishment defense organizations, and then founded and directed the Louisiana Capital Assistance Center. He has defended some three hundred people facing the death penalty. Soon after 9/11, he began working with Michael Ratner and his friend and fellow Southern Center for Human Rights alumnus Joe Margulies on the initial strategy for the Guantánamo habeas cases.

But Stafford Smith never thought the Guantánamo detainees would be saved by the courts alone. He had learned early on, working with legendary criminal defense lawyers Millard Farmer and Stephen Bright, that a lawyer must defend his client not only in the courtroom but in the court of public opinion. And Stafford Smith's forte is the latter. He has an acute sense for what will generate publicity for his cause and bring embarrassment and political pressure to bear on the forces arrayed against him. He also has a sense of humor that he is not afraid to wield against his adversaries. In 2007, he achieved widespread notoriety when he released to the media an exchange of letters with the Guantánamo Bay commander regarding the military's allegation that Stafford Smith may have smuggled what the military called "Under Armor" underwear and a Speedo swimsuit to one of his clients. Stafford Smith replied that he was certainly not the source, as the military should have known since it searched him before every visit and videotaped all his meetings with clients. Moreover, he added:

> I had never heard of "Under Armor briefs" until you mentioned them, and my internet research has advanced my knowledge in two ways— first, Under Armour apparently sports a "U" in its name, which is significant only because it helps with the research.
>
> Second, and rather more important, this line of underpants are very popular among the military. . . . It would be worth checking whether this lingerie was purchased from the NEX [Navy Exchange store] there in GTMO, since the internet again leads one to suspect that the NEX would be purveyors of Under Armour. . . . Perhaps you might check the label to see whether these are "tactical" underwear, as this is apparently something Under Armour has created specially for the military.[7]

As one of his British colleagues, the noted defense attorney Gareth Pierce, told me, "Clive is a very fine lawyer, but he is, above all, a campaigner par excellence."

Stafford Smith believed early on that the natural audience for public campaigns about Guantánamo was outside the United States. The Guantánamo detainees were all foreigners, so it was to their home nations' citizens, media, and governments that he turned his attention. Working in tandem with Ratner and Margulies, Stafford Smith became the foreign minister of the Guantánamo bar. He had a special connection, needless to say, to the United Kingdom. Shortly before 9/11, he had founded a charity there, Reprieve, initially to facilitate work by young Britons who wanted to volunteer on behalf of death row inmates in the United States, as Stafford Smith himself had done. After 9/11,

Reprieve became one of the most significant and successful defenders of human rights in the war on terror. That it was located in London rather than the United States turned out to be a benefit, not a burden, as it was able to bring diplomatic pressure to bear from abroad on the abusive practices of the United States.

Through Reprieve, Stafford Smith has represented about eighty-five detainees at Guantánamo. He has filed habeas cases for them, and won the release of more than seventy—but not a single one by virtue of a court order. How has he done it? I asked him that one spring morning in Dorchester in 2013, at a café near his home. He explained that even though US public opinion was important, he felt that given the image the government had painted of his clients, he had to start elsewhere:

> How do we get allies? First thing you do is get their country to intervene. I traveled around to all sorts of exotic places. I apologized for the policies of George Bush, Tony Blair, too. That got everyone on our side. We often went over the government's head. Every country I went to, the first thing I'd do is hold a press conference, apologize for America's response to 9/11, say it wasn't the American people, it was the government, and then have the detainee's family members tell their stories.

Stafford Smith repeated this routine all over the world—including in Bahrain, Mauritania, Morocco, Egypt, Yemen, and Jordan. His interventions were designed to incite foreign audiences to demand respect for the rights of their countrymen, which, he hoped, would in turn induce the detainee's government to press the United States for its citizen's release. Borrowing a term from English football, Stafford Smith said, "in most countries, it was totally onside. The governments were bending over backwards to be helpful." Such foreign pressure did not translate into immediate release, of course. But with the assistance of world opinion, Stafford Smith parlayed resentments among foreign populations about how the United States was treating their countrymen into pressure on their own governments and ultimately on that of the United States to send the detainees home.

Stafford Smith first used this approach in his home country, Great Britain, alongside Gareth Peirce, and in coordination with Ratner, Margulies, and CCR. There were nine British nationals held at Guantánamo, as well as five nationals of other countries who had been granted residency in Great Britain. The much-vaunted "special relationship" between the United Kingdom and the United States, and especially Prime Minister Tony Blair's support of the US invasion of Iraq, meant that 10 Downing Street had a particularly influential voice with the Bush administration. But Blair's ties with Bush, and the British intelligence services' close connections with the CIA, meant that Blair was initially very reluctant to press for his own citizens' release, much less for the transfer of detainees who were foreign citizens and merely UK residents. Moreover, the United Kingdom was allegedly complicit with the United States in some of the captures and interrogations of the detainees, further limiting the government's interest in bringing the detainees home.

As we have seen, Gareth Peirce was the initial point of contact for several of the British detainees, including Shafiq Rasul. I spoke with Peirce in 2013 about her role. We met at her office, tucked away in a ramshackle house that had been converted into a warren of offices in Camden Town, a neighborhood better known for tattooed teens, dance clubs, and fringe clothing stores than for law offices. Like Stafford Smith, Peirce is a product of elite English education. She was schooled at Cheltenham Ladies' College, Oxford, and the London School of Economics. Best known for overturning the wrongful murder convictions of several IRA activists, including the Birmingham Six and the Guilford Four, she is widely respected for her courageous commitment to the most unpopular clients. At age seventy-five, she continues to maintain an active legal practice defending some of England's most renowned political dissidents. She served tea and biscuits as she recounted her role in winning the first prisoner releases from Guantánamo.

At first, Peirce explained, the British Guantánamo detainees attracted little support from the British public or media, and the Blair government refused to request their release. Public opinion began to change as details emerged about the men's treatment. The first protests were sparked by photos released by the US military showing hooded and shackled men in orange jumpsuits kneeling before armed guards. The photos prompted expressions of concern from Amnesty International, members of Parliament, the ICRC, senior clergy, and the UN High Commissioner for Human Rights, among others. In response, the British Foreign Office stated that consular officials had visited the men at Guantánamo, and that the detainees had "no substantial complaints."[8]

Media and public criticism mounted when Bush announced in February 2002 that Guantánamo detainees were not protected by the Geneva Conventions. Human rights groups pointed out that Bush was invoking wartime detention authority, yet refused to be restrained by the laws that govern wartime powers. But the Blair government supported Bush's decision.[9]

Peirce, Stafford Smith, and others filed suits in the British courts, alleging UK complicity in the British citizens' detention and seeking to compel the United Kingdom to intervene on the detainees' behalf or to disclose any exculpatory information it had about them. One of the detainees, Feroz Abbasi, requested a writ of habeas corpus from the British courts. The Court of Appeal for England and Wales denied the writ, finding that it lacked power to order the United States to release Abbasi. But the court expressed grave reservations about Abbasi's predicament, in effect urging US courts to intervene. After noting the ancient roots of habeas corpus as the fundamental protection of liberty in British as well as American law, the court stated that "what appears to us to be objectionable is that Mr. Abbasi should be subject to indefinite detention in territory over which the United States has exclusive control with no opportunity to challenge the legitimacy of his detention before any court or tribunal. It is important to record that the position may change when the appellate courts in the United States consider the matter."[10]

According to both Stafford Smith and Peirce, the biggest breakthrough in British public opinion came when the United States announced in June 2003 that it intended to try Abbasi and another British detainee, Moazzam Begg, in a military tribunal. The possibility that

British nationals would face the death penalty in such an ad hoc court sparked widespread objections. The *Times* cited "near-universal condemnation this week of the recent American proposals to try two British citizens detained at Guantánamo Bay by a military tribunal." The Blair administration at first requested only that the trials be fair. But within a week, "Tony Blair caved in . . . to mounting pressure over the two British terrorist suspects . . . and appealed for their repatriation."[11]

Following a meeting with Blair, Bush suspended the proceedings against Begg and Abbasi. The UK attorney general, Lord Goldsmith, then conducted a series of meetings in Washington and secured several concessions: the death penalty was taken off the table; the detainees would be given representation by a US lawyer of their choosing, as well as a British lawyer; the trials would be as public as security would allow; and any term of imprisonment could be served in the United Kingdom. Public calls for repatriation continued, however, especially after the press reported claims that the detainees had given false confessions under coercion and torture.[12]

In November 2003, Lord Steyn, an eminent retired British Law Lord—the equivalent of a former US Supreme Court justice—described Guantánamo as "a monstrous failure of justice" and condemned the military tribunals as "kangaroo courts." The next month, the UK Law Society, a professional lawyers' association, demanded that the government either repatriate the British detainees or get them a trial in civilian court in the United States. And in January 2004, 175 members of Parliament filed a friend-of-the-court brief in support of Shafiq Rasul in his Supreme Court case. It was the first time in history that members of Parliament filed a brief in the US Supreme Court. Counsel on the brief included Anthony Lester and David Pannick of Blackstone Chambers, two of the nation's leading barristers.[13]

Bowing to this pressure, in March 2004, Bush transferred five of the British citizens—Ruhal Ahmed, Tarek Dergoul, Jamal Udeen Al-Harith, Asif Iqbal, and Shafiq Rasul—to the United Kingdom. Within two days of their return, the detainees began speaking out about conditions at Guantánamo. Al-Harith claimed that prisoners had been subjected to beatings, chained for twelve hours at a time, and forced to violate their Muslim faith by watching naked prostitutes touching themselves. Peirce swiftly produced a booklet describing in detail the men's harsh treatment, backed by graphic illustrations. The *Guardian* ran a major two-part article ("How we survived jail hell") featuring an interview with the "Tipton Three" (Rasul, Iqbal, and Ahmed). It recounted the rough conditions of the men's capture and transfer to Guantánamo, described their abusive interrogations, and cited experts who opined that "this system seems almost calculated to produce fantastical accounts."[14]

In April 2004, photographs of prisoner abuse from the Abu Ghraib prison in Iraq were broadcast by *60 Minutes II* and published in the *New Yorker*. As one British newspaper put it, "previous allegations [from former detainees] were dismissed by the U.S. embassy in London, but after two weeks in which America has been convulsed by images of torture and humiliation, [the detainees'] latest challenge looked set to receive a more serious hearing." Rasul and Iqbal sent an open letter to Bush, claiming that the abuse they had suffered was similar to the treatment documented at Abu Ghraib. The letter cited assaults, naked shackling in stress positions, loud music, dogs, and religiously offensive exposure to women.[15]

The Abu Ghraib photos changed the conversation about the remaining four British detainees. Until that point, Blair seemed comfortable not repatriating the remaining detainees, and he continued to defend prisoner treatment at Guantánamo Bay. But the parallels between the released Guantánamo detainees' accounts of how they were treated and the Abu Ghraib photographs transformed the detainees' allegations into accepted fact for many Britons. It was now untenable that any British detainee be held at Guantánamo, regardless of the procedures used in military commissions. In June 2004, the *Times* reported that Blair "personally asked George Bush" for the repatriation of the remaining British detainees.[16]

The UK Foreign and Commonwealth Office's annual human rights report, released in November 2004, included "stinging criticism" of Guantánamo, a marked shift from the previous year's report, which had not even mentioned the prison. Around the same time, a confidential report of the ICRC, leaked to the *New York Times*, offered further corroboration of detainee abuse, charging that treatment of the Guantánamo prisoners was "tantamount to torture."[17]

In early October 2004, a letter from Moazzam Begg to his family made it out of Guantánamo uncensored. Clive Stafford Smith got it to the newspapers, which publicized Begg's description of "pernicious threats of torture, actual vindictive torture and death threats—amongst other coercively employed interrogation techniques." Later that year, Stafford Smith transcribed a thirty-page statement from Begg describing his mistreatment at Guantánamo. Stafford Smith then drafted a letter to Tony Blair regarding Begg's allegations and tried to include the statement. American military censors blocked the entirety of Begg's statement. Stafford Smith informed the press about the military's action, prompting further stories and public outcry. Responding to the pressure, the United States returned the remaining British detainees on January 26, 2005. None had been ordered released by a court. They had instead found freedom through the public advocacy of Peirce, Stafford Smith, and Reprieve.[18]

WINNING RELEASE OF THE detainees who were merely British residents, not citizens, was more challenging. The British public's sympathy for them was more muted, and the UK government asserted that it had no obligation or standing to advocate for them, as they were foreign nationals. But as stories of abuse at Guantánamo multiplied, public opinion began to shift even as to these detainees. In May 2006, Lord Goldsmith declared that "the existence of Guantánamo Bay remains unacceptable." In August 2007, the British government formally requested return of all five British residents. In December of that year, three of the five were released, leaving only two detainees with any British ties of residency: Binyam Mohamed and Shaker Aamer.[19]

The story of Binyam Mohamed is a particularly good example of the power of transnational advocacy. An Ethiopian national who had resided in Great Britain since 1994, Mohamed was captured in Pakistan and then reportedly transported by US agents to Morocco, where he was detained for a year and a half and claims to have suffered brutal torture, including razor cuts to his genitals. In January 2004, US agents took him to Afghanistan, where he claims he endured still more torture. In September of that year he arrived at Guantánamo. The United States was plainly reluctant to let Mohamed go; he was one of the few to be charged with war crimes in a military commission, and was said to have been part of a plot to detonate a radioactive "dirty bomb" in the United States.

Stafford Smith, who began representing Mohamed in April 2005, said that being charged in the military commission was "the best thing that ever happened to" Mohamed, as it greatly increased the critical attention of the British public. In May 2008, as the military commission proceedings wore on, Stafford Smith filed suit in England requesting that the Foreign Office be directed to produce any evidence in its possession relating to Mohamed's rendition and torture. He claimed that British officials had been complicit in Mohamed's mistreatment, and were obligated under British law to assist him. Stafford Smith saw Mohamed's UK case as an opportunity to build pressure on the British government to push for Mohamed's release. The case drew substantial media attention. Stafford Smith himself wrote an op-ed for the *Independent* on May 30, 2008, titled, "Why has the Government forsaken Binyam Mohamed?" The same day, the UK press reported on a letter Mohamed had written to Prime Minister Gordon Brown stating that he had been contemplating suicide, and seeking Brown's intervention.[20]

In June 2008, the UK Foreign Office admitted that earlier assertions that it did not have evidence regarding Mohamed's treatment were erroneous, and that it would provide Stafford Smith the information in its possession after review by the US authorities. On June 16, Daniel Bethlehem, the legal advisor to the Foreign Office, provided the information to US officials and again requested Mohamed's return. On August 21, 2008, the High Court ruled in the case Stafford Smith had filed on Mohamed's behalf that "the relationship of the United Kingdom Government to the United States authorities in connection with [Mohamed] was far beyond that of a bystander or witness to the alleged wrongdoing." It ordered the United Kingdom to disclose any evidence it had concerning his rendition, his treatment, the United Kingdom's involvement therein, and "any evidence that the United Kingdom has failed to provide [Mohamed] with assistance that should have been provided." [21]

The British government objected, maintaining that to reveal the information requested would undermine the UK-US intelligence relationship. The court reacted skeptically, ordering the government to reconsider its assertion "in the light of the allegations made by [Mohamed and] the abhorrence and condemnation accorded to torture and cruel, inhuman or degrading treatment."[22]

In October 2008, the United States dropped all military commission charges against Mohamed, but stated that it expected to bring new charges. The *New York Times* reported that the "dismissal was a retreat by the government facing an aggressive defense in the case." The UK proceedings continued, however, and later that month the court issued another opinion, finding "a clear evidential basis" for Mohamed's allegations that the United States dismissed the charges to avoid disclosure of Mohamed's treatment because "torturers do not readily hand over evidence of their conduct." The court expressed concern that US officials in the habeas case had disclosed only seven of the forty-two documents the UK court had seen; that even those documents had been heavily redacted, and that Mohamed's long detention had already had substantial negative effects on his mental health and the interests of justice. It concluded its opinion with the admonition that "we have found the events set out in this judgment deeply disturbing. This matter must be brought to a just conclusion as soon as possible."[23]

Stafford Smith's tactic of playing the United Kingdom against the United States and shaming UK authorities into advocating for his clients was clearly working. As the *New York Times* reported on October 31, 2008, Mohamed's case "has drawn international attention and been at the center of diplomatic tensions between the United States and Britain. . . . The tension between the governments has intensified in recent weeks after the Pentagon dropped war crimes charges against

Mr. Mohamed and the Justice Department said it would no longer rely on its dirty-bomb claims as a justification for holding him."[24]

Meanwhile, the US habeas court, having been alerted by the UK court that US officials had withheld exculpatory evidence in response to its earlier orders, issued an expanded discovery order, including a requirement that the agents responsible for Mohamed's interrogation submit to depositions by Stafford Smith and his co-counsel.[25]

Pressure for Mohamed's release continued to mount. Stafford Smith invited the British press to intervene formally in Mohamed's UK case over the issue of whether six paragraphs of the High Court's judgment, redacted at the request of the UK government, should be made public. The High Court acknowledged that disclosure was ultimately up to the United States, but made little secret of its view on the matter: "If the information in the redacted paragraphs which we consider so important to the rule of law, free speech and democratic accountability is to be put into the public domain, it must now be for the United States Government to consider changing its position or itself putting that information into the public domain." Finally, on February 22, 2009, the United States returned Mohamed to England. He was one of the first to be released by Barack Obama's new administration.[26]

Stafford Smith, Peirce, and Reprieve won release for these and other clients through a kind of guerrilla transnational advocacy, encouraging the British public and courts to bring pressure on the UK government, and ultimately, the United States. They brought to public attention abuses of a range of human rights, including the right not to be tortured, the right to a fair trial, the right to exculpatory evidence, and prohibitions on the death penalty. They appealed to British citizens' concern for their own nationals, but also to fundamental principles of human dignity and fairness common to both the British and American legal systems. And they exploited each incremental victory along the way to build momentum for their clients' release. Had they limited their advocacy to US courts, the British detainees might still be languishing at Guantánamo.

Did Stafford Smith, Peirce, and Reprieve change American constitutional law? Not in any formal way, to be sure. They achieved no

Supreme Court opinion vindicating their clients' rights. But they prevailed over executive prerogative, and won their clients' freedom. And as we shall see, the Tipton Three's allegations of abuse at Guantánamo, published shortly before the Supreme Court's oral arguments in the "enemy combatant" cases, may well have affected the course of those cases. In addition, the UK Court of Appeal's harsh assessment in *Abbasi*, expressing grave reservations about the possibility of unreviewable indefinite detention at Guantánamo, contributed to the pressure on the US Supreme Court to provide judicial review. From a broader perspective, the British advocacy played a formative role in the world's growing criticism of Guantánamo. Lord Steyn's comments were repeated the world over. The image of a prison beyond the law, repeated often in the British press, added still more pressure on the Supreme Court to grant Guantánamo detainees habeas corpus, on the Bush administration to release many more detainees, and on President Obama to commit to closing the prison.

OTHER FOREIGN VOICES ALSO played a part in cajoling the United States to comply with fundamental human rights. European institutions, governments, and organizations, for example, condemned the practice of "extraordinary renditions," in which the United States abducted suspected terrorists and delivered them to countries known for using torture and other cruel interrogation methods. Amrit Singh, a lawyer with the Open Society Justice Initiative (OSJI), has worked with human rights organizations in Eastern Europe to file human rights suits against various countries for their complicity in the CIA's renditions, disappearances, and torture. Thus far, the European Court of Human Rights has held Poland responsible for allowing the CIA to operate a secret prison on its soil, and has held Macedonia responsible for its role in the CIA's abduction from Macedonia of Khaled el-Masri, a German citizen, and his subsequent torture in a CIA prison in Afghanistan. In February 2013, the OSJI published a report naming fifty-four nations as complicit in the CIA's detention, interrogation, and rendition program, shaming not only each of those countries, but the United States itself. And numerous attempts have been made to bring criminal actions against US officials involved in rendition and torture under the principle of universal jurisdiction, which authorizes trial of certain egregious crimes, including torture, regardless of where the crime took place.[27]

Several former Bush administration officials report that foreign pressure had a significant impact on the curtailment of its counterterrorism measures. Matthew Waxman, who worked on detainee issues in the Bush administration's National Security Council, Department of Defense, and State Department, cited in particular the Blair government's advocacy on behalf of British detainees at Guantánamo. But the phenomenon was not limited to Britain, he stressed. The terrorist threat was transnational, and counterterrorism policy could succeed only if the United States could rely on the cooperation of many nations. That meant that global criticism stung in ways that it otherwise might not have.[28]

Few people observed the effect of foreign attitudes toward the United States more closely than Daniel Fried, a longtime foreign service officer who worked in the Clinton, Bush, and Obama administrations. Under Bush, Fried was in charge of European and Eurasian Affairs, first at the National Security Council and then at the State Department. Obama later tapped him to oversee the closure of Guantánamo. When I asked Fried in 2012 how he explained the Bush administration's retreat on so many counterterrorism initiatives, he cited foreign government pressure as an important factor. "We were getting beaten up for our unilateral policies all over the world, especially on Guantánamo," Fried said. "We were taking shots every day." He added that by 2003 "the criticism [from Europe] was terribly damaging. It got in the way of getting anything done." The opposition to Guantánamo and Iraq "made it harder for any European government to help us out in any endeavor, from missile defense to alternative energy policy. We were getting killed by this."[29]

Richard Fontaine, a senior staff advisor to Senator John McCain on foreign policy issues, agreed that one of the forces pushing the Bush administration to dial back its controversial measures was that "we were making it harder for our allies to work with us, because of political and legal concerns of complicity."[30]

John Bellinger, who served as legal advisor to Condoleezza Rice, first when she headed the National Security Council and later at the State Department, also confirmed that international criticism played an important part. As he put it, "we were getting a lot of criticism for this, as a country and as an administration, and it was hurting us." The administration's concerns were "driven less by the human rights groups than by international criticism," he said, although he acknowledged that "the two are related." Some members of the administration, he recalled, dismissed foreign criticism as inevitable, and even saw it as "a badge of honor." But others, including Bellinger and Rice, pushed to rein in the policies for which the administration was receiving widespread criticism, such as interrogation, detainee treatment, and rendition. In the second term, they gained the upper hand, in part because of the criticism the United States was receiving abroad and at home.

While civil liberties and human rights advocates did not have available the state "laboratories of experiment" that marriage equality and gun rights advocates used so effectively, they found alternative forums outside the United States. The fact that we tend to care more about our own rights than about foreigners' rights made advocacy in the United States difficult, but simultaneously opened up opportunities for advocacy abroad. In the age of the Internet, communication and coordination across borders are easier than ever. And the development of a language and law of international human rights in the post–World War II period meant that foreign audiences had a ready moral and legal compass by which to assess and criticize US practices that ran roughshod over such rights.

Some Americans might consider foreign criticism an improper intrusion into our domestic affairs. But the constitutional rights at stake in the war on terror, including liberty, privacy, fair trials, and freedom from torture, are also protected by international human rights treaties that the United States has signed and ratified. And nations frequently complain about other nations' violations of human rights, especially when their own nationals are the victims. The US State Department issues country-specific human rights reports on every nation every year, whether or not Americans are affected, as does the US-based Human Rights Watch. If it is appropriate for our government and our civil society organizations to attempt to influence other countries' human rights behavior, why shouldn't other countries similarly try to influence ours? In the war on terror, international criticism, much of it prompted and encouraged by civil society actors such as Stafford Smith and Peirce, played a crucial role in persuading the Bush administration to moderate its counterterrorism policy and practice.

But foreign criticism would not be enough in itself. It was equally important to develop credible criticism at home. Here, too, civil liberties and human rights groups played an essential part in the arc of the US post-9/11 response.

15

Messages and Messengers

"**E**ITHER YOU ARE WITH US, OR YOU ARE WITH THE TERRORISTS." THAT'S HOW PRESIDENT Bush framed the "war on terror," as he called it, in an address to Congress on September 20, 2001. For civil liberties and human rights advocates, that was a preemptive strike. A few months later, Attorney General John Ashcroft made the point even more explicitly in testimony to the Senate Judiciary Committee. Addressing "those who scare peace-loving people with phantoms of lost liberty," Ashcroft warned, "your tactics only aid terrorists—for they erode our national unity and diminish our resolve. They give ammunition to America's enemies, and pause to America's friends." If civil liberties and human rights groups were to make any headway in their opposition to many of Bush's counterterrorism initiatives, they would have to devise a competing frame of their own. Like marriage equality proponents, they would have to learn how to talk about their principles and goals in a way that did not prove counterproductive. But they faced a more daunting challenge: the president of the United States has unparalleled authority to set the agenda and define issues through the bully pulpit, perhaps never more so than when the nation is at war. Human rights groups had to beat Bush on his field of strength. Remarkably, they did.

They found their message in "the rule of law." Bush's assertions of executive power, they argued, were in effect a challenge to law itself. Guantánamo was a "law-free zone"; the administration was using the tools of war without abiding by the laws of war; Bush placed himself above the law by claiming power immune to checks from Congress or the Court. Far from being traitors, civil liberties advocates insisted, they were defending a central element of the American constitutional tradition: a government of laws, not of men.

The Bush administration's penchant for evading legal limits played into civil liberties advocates' hands. Time and again, the administration seemed to resist any oversight or constraint. It objected to judicial oversight at Guantánamo, held suspects incommunicado in secret prisons, rounded up thousands of Arabs and Muslims in the United States, held hundreds of immigration proceedings behind closed doors, and authorized secret and warrantless wiretapping. It argued that the Geneva Conventions and the Constitution were inapplicable to foreign detainees in the war on terror, and asserted that the president as commander-in-chief had power to ignore the laws Congress had set down. In response, civil liberties and human rights groups portrayed the administration's counterterrorism policy as lawless.[1]

The label stuck. By the time the first set of enemy combatant cases (*Rasul* and *Hamdi*) reached the Supreme Court in 2004, civil society groups had succeeded in framing the Court's choice as one between the rule of law and "law-free zones." Because of the transnational advocacy led by Clive Stafford Smith, Gareth Peirce, and other activists and civil society organizations, this frame had taken hold around the world. In 2002 alone, a special rapporteur for the UN's Commission on Human Rights wrote that the Guantánamo detentions "offend . . . the first principle of the rule of law"; in response to a human rights complaint filed by CCR, the Inter-American Commission on Human Rights found that the detainees at Guantánamo faced a risk of irreparable harm to their human rights; the ICRC expressed concern that the detainees were being held "beyond the law"; and as we have seen, a British Court of Appeal, ruling on the fate of Guantánamo detainee Feroz Abbasi, had declared its "deep concern that, in apparent contravention of fundamental principles of law, Mr. Abbasi may be subject to indefinite detention in territory over which the United States has exclusive control with no opportunity to challenge the legitimacy of his detention before any court or tribunal." Shirin Ebadi, the 2003 Nobel Peace Prize winner, denounced Guantánamo in her acceptance speech as contrary to fundamental human rights. And in a public lecture in November of that year, Lord Steyn, the retired British law lord, called Guantánamo a "legal black hole."[2]

As Douglass Cassel, a human rights lawyer who helped craft the amicus brief strategy in *Rasul*, explained, "the posture of the cases in the lower courts was 'the terrorists versus the government.' In the Supreme Court we tried to change the narrative to 'the rule of law v. the government.'" The lawyers and organizations in all four enemy combatant cases succeeded in recruiting amicus support from a wide range of civil society institutions and voices to highlight that theme, including the American Bar Association, over one hundred members of Parliament, former federal judges, retired US military officers, eminent legal scholars, and a broad range of non-governmental organizations.[3]

International human rights groups, such as Human Rights Watch, Human Rights First, and Amnesty International, mounted a critique founded not just on constitutional norms, but on international human rights principles more easily comprehended by foreign audiences. In the end, the frame advanced by civil society—the rule of law versus lawlessness—was more compelling than the frame advanced by the Bush administration.[4]

By the time *Rasul* and *Hamdi* reached the Supreme Court, it was not the terrorists against the government, nor was it CCR against the government. Rather, it was the mainstream American, British, and international legal communities against the US government. When one looks back at prior cases in which the Supreme Court was asked to review executive actions infringing on constitutional rights during wartime, such as the World War I speech cases or the World War II internment cases, there was no similar marshalling of professional opinion. Indeed, most of the civil society groups that participated in the enemy combatant cases did not even exist until after World War II.

The Bush administration did not, of course, concede its challengers' frame, nor was it inevitable that this frame would prevail. The administration insisted that the president's actions were fully authorized by law—by the Constitution, which makes the president commander-in-chief; Congress's formal Authorization for Use of Military Force, which empowered the president to wage war against Al Qaeda and the Taliban, and therefore to detain and try those fighting for the enemy; and, in *Boumediene*, the Detainee Treatment Act, which had repealed habeas corpus and substituted limited appellate court review for detainees at Guantánamo. The administration portrayed its actions as controlled and historically unexceptional responses to a dire national security threat. From its perspective, the petitioners were trying to elevate unprecedented notions of novel rights—in three of the four cases, foreign nationals' rights—over the compelling security needs of the nation. The administration stressed the importance of affording the commander-in-chief broad leeway in managing the war effort, and noted that the Court had consistently done just that in the past.

In some forums, the administration's perspective won out. When Lee Gelernt, an ACLU attorney, stood up to argue in the US Court of Appeals for the Third Circuit in 2002, he expected to be asked tough questions. He was representing the North Jersey Media Group in a challenge to a post-9/11 Justice Department practice of holding behind closed doors all immigration proceedings involving people "of interest" to the September 11 investigation. Hundreds of immigrants were designated as "of interest" to the investigation, often on little more than the fact that they were Arab or Muslim. None had any connection to 9/11, and all were eventually cleared. Yet the administration conducted their immigration hearings in secret, even where no classified information was involved. Gelernt and the ACLU argued that the First Amendment required the proceedings to be public absent specific showings that particular parts of the proceedings needed to be closed. As Gelernt began his argument, Judge Morton Greenberg interrupted, proclaiming, "people may die, lots of people, if we're wrong. You want us to run that risk. How can we do that?" Judge Greenberg went on to recall that he was working from home on September 11, 2001, when his wife told him to turn on the television after the first plane had hit the World Trade Center. "I can't erase the second hit from my mind," he told Gelernt. Most judges were not so candid, but similar thoughts no doubt ran through many judges' minds in national security cases after 9/11.[5]

Yet in the enemy combatant cases, the Supreme Court rejected the executive's frame and instead chose the challengers'. In each decision, it insisted that constitutional, statutory, or international law— and as an institutional matter, the courts—have a role in regulating and constraining the nation's response to terrorism. As Justice Sandra Day O'Connor put it in *Hamdi*, "a state of war is not a blank check for the President when it comes to the rights of the Nation's citizens." In that case, the Court rejected the executive's call for extraordinarily deferential review and held that Hamdi must be given a meaningful opportunity to confront the government's case for detention. In *Boumediene*, Justice Kennedy sounded a similar theme: "the laws and Constitution are designed to survive, and remain in force, in extraordinary times. Liberty and security can be reconciled, and in our system they are reconciled within the framework of the law." The Court in *Rasul* applied the habeas corpus statute, a touchstone of the rule of law. And in *Hamdan*, by finding the Geneva Conventions applicable to Al Qaeda, the Court ensured that the law of war would govern the treatment of Al Qaeda detainees. In all four enemy combatant cases, the Court insisted, as the civil liberties and human rights community had urged all along, that the president's war on terror must be subject to judicially enforceable legal limits. The Supreme Court's decisions, siding strongly with the rule of law, in turn lent even more legitimacy to the criticisms human rights and civil liberties groups had long been making.[6]

The power (and limits) of the law versus lawlessness frame are further illustrated by the cases civil liberties groups lost. When the government could not be portrayed as asserting authority to act beyond the law, challenges to its actions were generally unsuccessful. In 2004, the Supreme Court ruled that Jose Padilla, the second US citizen held as an enemy combatant, had filed his habeas challenge in the wrong forum; he could obtain review, but only by filing in another court. In 2009, it found that immigration detainees "of interest" to the 9/11 investigation failed to allege sufficient facts to link Attorney General John Ashcroft to their mistreatment. In 2010, in a case I argued, the Court upheld against a First Amendment challenge a statute that makes "material support" to terrorist organizations a crime, even where the support consists only of speech advocating peace and human rights. In 2011, it granted Ashcroft "qualified immunity" with respect to the detention of a Muslim man as a "material witness" who was never called to testify, finding that Ashcroft had violated no clearly established right. And in 2013, it ruled that Amnesty International and other plaintiffs lacked standing to challenge a statute authorizing the NSA to conduct surveillance of foreigners overseas, where none of the plaintiffs could show that they had actually been subject to the surveillance. Unlike the four enemy combatant cases, these cases did not fit easily into the law versus lawlessness frame. The government did not assert that the Constitution did not apply, or that courts had no role. Instead, the cases posed standard questions of the application of constitutional law. They illustrate the limits of the law versus lawlessness frame; so long as the administration adopted a more modest position, it seems, the Supreme Court was willing to defer.[7]

As MARRIAGE EQUALITY PROPONENTS found, a successful campaign also requires credible messengers. Gay rights advocates found that the best messengers were straight people—the more conservative, religious, and elderly, the better. So, too, the most persuasive voices for human rights and civil liberties were individuals the public identified with security above all. Who better than a retired four-star general to advance a message of respect for human rights?

One weekday morning in the summer of 2014, I found myself in a conference room at the offices of Human Rights First, sitting with men who had risen to the highest levels of America's armed forces: Leif Hendrickson, a retired brigadier general in the Marine Corps who had served as commanding officer at the Marine Corps training base at Quantico, Virginia; David Irvine, a retired US Army strategic intelligence officer and former Republican state legislator from Utah; retired Rear Admiral John D. Hutson, former judge advocate general of the Navy and dean of University of New Hampshire Law School; Charles Otstott, a legendary Army lieutenant general who had graduated from West Point in 1960 as the president of his class, the first captain, the ranking cadet, and the valedictorian, and who later served as deputy chairman of the North Atlantic Treaty Organization (NATO) Military Committee, the highest military office in NATO; and retired Brigadier General John Adams, who had also served as the NATO Committee's deputy chairman, and had been at the Pentagon when the plane struck on September 11, 2001.

As Hutson explained, "if you'd asked any of us, before we'd retired, are you going to be involved with Human Rights First or the ACLU, we would have said, 'What are you, nuts?'" They were trained not to question authority in public. Otstott said, "all of us grew up in a culture where you may disagree strongly behind closed doors, but we execute lawful orders after a decision by higher authority." Yet they had all chosen to become involved in an ad hoc group, sponsored by Human Rights First (HRF), that challenged human rights violations in the war on terror. They acted out of a sense of obligation. Adams put it most directly: "Don't we have a duty, even out of military uniform, to continue to support the Constitution? A legal duty, as citizens?"[8]

For all but one of them, the catalyst to their involvement with HRF was Abu Ghraib. Irvine, who taught prisoner-of-war interrogation for eighteen years at the Sixth US Army Intelligence School, recalled that when he first saw the pictures, "I was shocked. Nothing we have ever taught or preached squared with any of that stuff." Hutson came to the cause even earlier. In the first year after 9/11, he appeared on a National Public Radio show to defend military commissions. Elisa Massimino, then HRF's Washington director, now its president, was on the other side. Hutson recalls: "After twenty to thirty minutes, I started to realize she was right, and I was wrong. Now I'm in this moral quandary. Do I turn coat right there on NPR? After that I reached out to Elisa, and we connected." Hutson eventually joined HRF's board, and helped organize a group of retired military officers to urge adherence to the law of war and the Constitution in fighting terrorism.

Massimino, the daughter of a nuclear submarine commander, recognizes the importance of enlisting powerful allies. A philosophy professor turned lawyer, she is a persuasive advocate with a rigorous analytical mind, an unwavering commitment to principle, and perhaps most important, the pragmatic sense that it takes more than an airtight argument to move the political branches of government on human rights. As she put it, "criticism of torture by Human Rights First would be one thing; criticism by a group of respected retired generals and admirals would be something else entirely." With Hutson's assistance, HRF hosted an initial meeting of retired generals in the summer of 2004, shortly after the Abu Ghraib photos were released. A larger meeting followed in 2005, with fifty to sixty retired military officers attending.

By all accounts, the most revered man in the room at the 2005 meeting was General John W. "Jack" Vessey, a World War II hero and former chair of the Joint Chiefs of Staff who had devoted forty-six years to military service before retiring in 1985. As Irvine recalls, Vessey, then eighty-three years old, "picked up a really old raggedy manual and said, 'listen up, I have to tell you something.'" The manual was an *Officer's Guide*, published around 1950. According to Irvine, it "looked like he'd been carrying it ever since." Vessey read from the guide: "the law of the US follows the flag. We do not tolerate murder, rape, pillaging, criminal conduct. A commander who winks at this kind of behavior by his men is no different than if he had done it himself." Vessey then looked up at the group and said, "that's the gold standard, and we've got to get back to it."

The generals began by writing letters—to President Bush, individual members of Congress, the full Senate. The letters maintained that torture and cruel treatment are illegal, counterproductive, and inconsistent with American values. The content of these critiques was not new. But they carried significantly greater weight when articulated by men who had spent decades leading our national defense. Precisely because they were not "the usual suspects," the generals were more likely to cause others to take notice and listen, and were able to remind Americans of the power of our fundamental values—respect for dignity, humane treatment, and commitment to the rule of law.[9]

Among other things, the generals requested an independent commission to investigate allegations of torture and other abuse; urged the Senate Judiciary Committee to question Alberto Gonzales upon his nomination to become attorney general about his role in authorizing torture and cruel treatment; supported the provision of habeas corpus review to Guantánamo detainees; called for the closure of Guantánamo; and pressed the Senate Select Committee on Intelligence to release publicly its report on the CIA detention and interrogation program.

The retired generals met privately with most of the 2008 presidential candidates—including Hillary Clinton, Barack Obama, Joe Biden, Dennis Kucinich, John Edwards, Mike Huckabee, and Bill Richardson—to urge them to oppose torture and mistreatment of prisoners, to support the Geneva Conventions, and to close Guantánamo. (They didn't need to meet with John McCain, already a staunch ally.) Several of the candidates referred to these meetings during the campaign. When Mike Huckabee was asked about Guantánamo and waterboarding on *FOX News Sunday with Chris Wallace* in January 2008, he replied:

> I spent a couple of hours with 12 different general officers from the Navy and the Army and the Marine Corps. It was a very fascinating discussion. I share the same view that Colin Powell does, that every general officer that I know in the military shares, and that is that when you engage in torture, you do two things. First, you do not get the information that you are really seeking because it's rarely reliable. And the second thing is that you do something to the people who carry out the torture, and I'm not sure we want to do, and that is that we ask them to violate the very code that we teach them when they're going through the military.[10]

When Tim Russert asked the presidential candidates in a Democratic debate whether they would authorize torture in exceptional circumstances, both Joe Biden and Hillary Clinton cited their meetings with the generals. Biden said he would not, noting:

> Seventeen of our four-star, three-star generals said, Biden, will you make a commitment you will never use torture? It does not work. It is part of the reason why we got the faulty information on Iraq in the first place is because it was engaged in by one person who gave whatever answer they thought they were going to give in order to stop being tortured. It doesn't work. It should be no part of our policy ever—ever.

Clinton's answer also relied on the generals: "As a matter of policy it cannot be American policy, period. I met with those same three- and four-star retired generals, and their principal point—in addition to the values that are so important for our country to exhibit—is that there is very little evidence that it works."[11]

When former CIA Director George Tenet defended the agency's interrogation tactics in his memoir, the co-chairs of the generals' group, Joseph Hoar and Charles Krulak, wrote an op-ed in the *Washington Post* rejecting torture on principled and pragmatic grounds:

> The torture methods that Tenet defends have nurtured the recuperative power of the enemy. This war will be won or lost not on the battlefield but in the minds of potential supporters who have not yet thrown in their lot with the enemy. If we forfeit our values by signaling that they are negotiable in situations of grave or imminent danger, we drive those undecideds into the arms of the enemy. This way lies defeat, and we are well down the road to it.[12]

And when President Obama signed executive orders to close the CIA's secret prisons, ban enhanced interrogation techniques, and close Guantánamo within a year, he invited the generals to the Oval Office to stand behind him. Their presence made it more difficult to dismiss his orders as the actions of a liberal lacking sufficient commitment to the nation's security.

The generals' and HRF's most significant accomplishment came in 2005, when they helped persuade Congress to pass legislation that forbade the use of any "cruel, inhuman, or degrading" treatment against foreign detainees. The provision, sponsored by Senator John McCain and known as "the McCain Amendment," was sparked by the disclosure that the Justice Department had interpreted the Torture Convention's prohibition on cruel, inhuman, and degrading treatment as not protecting foreigners held by US forces outside our borders. The Torture Convention is a human rights treaty, designed to protect all human beings, and contains no nationality-based limitations. When McCain, himself a POW and a torture victim during the Vietnam War, learned of the Justice Department's interpretation, he was dismayed, and began working closely with HRF's Massimino and Tom Malinowski of Human Rights Watch to make clear that the treaty meant what it said, and protected all human beings everywhere from such abuse.

The generals supported McCain at every turn. They wrote letters to Congress, met with individual members, wrote op-eds, and voiced their support in the media. A letter to the Senate was signed by twenty-eight former military officers, including General John Shalikashvili, who had led peacekeeping operations in Iraq after the Gulf War and had been chairman of the Joint Chiefs of Staff, and General Joseph Hoar, of the Marine Corps, who had directed US Central Command. Their endorsement in turn encouraged General Colin Powell, who had been Bush's secretary of state, to add his support, breaking with his former boss.

McCain often invoked the generals' support in defending his amendment. In one meeting, he reportedly responded to Vice President Cheney's claim that the tough interrogation tactics were necessary by taking from his pocket the generals' letter supporting the amendment, and putting it down on the table between them, saying, "this is what I've got. What do you have?" In a press release, McCain prominently featured the generals' views, saying:

> That's not just my opinion, but that of many more distinguished
> military minds than mine, including General Colin Powell, General

Joseph Hoar, General John Shalikashvili, RADM John Hutson, and RADM Don Guter. These and other distinguished officers believe that the abuses at Abu Ghraib, Guantánamo and elsewhere took place in part because our soldiers received ambiguous instructions, which in some cases authorized treatment that went beyond what the Field Manual allows, and that, had the Manual been followed across the board, we could have avoided the prisoner abuse scandal.[13]

Richard Fontaine, McCain's foreign policy advisor at the time, told me that the generals' support was critical because "they helped frame it as a military security issue, not just a moral issue."[14]

In October 2005, the Senate approved McCain's amendment by a stunning 90–9 margin, handing Bush his most dramatic defeat in the Senate in eight years. When, six months later, the Supreme Court ruled in *Hamdan* that the Geneva Conventions protect Al Qaeda detainees, the administration had suffered defeats on the issue of detainee treatment in both of the other branches of the federal government—an exceedingly rare occurrence during wartime.[15]

In September 2006, Bush announced that he had transferred all detainees held in secret CIA prisons to Guantánamo Bay, where for the first time they would have access to lawyers and the courts. While the CIA's black sites technically remained open, and coercive interrogation techniques were still formally authorized, the Bush administration never again brought a detainee to a CIA secret prison, and reports of torture and cruel interrogation largely ceased.[16]

The administration's retreat on secret prisons and torture took place without a formal court order or a binding requirement from Congress. As we have seen, the Supreme Court's *Hamdan* decision held that the Geneva Conventions apply to Al Qaeda, but the Court did not mention, much less issue a ruling on, torture, cruel treatment, or disappearances. The federal courts have dismissed every case seeking to challenge the torture, cruel treatment, or disappearance of Al Qaeda suspects, and the Supreme Court has repeatedly declined review. And while the McCain Amendment affirmed the Torture Convention's ban on cruel, inhuman, and degrading treatment, it provided no mechanism for victims to enforce it. Meanwhile, the administration had drafted secret memos interpreting both the Geneva Conventions and the Torture Convention to permit the CIA to continue to use harsh interrogation tactics.[17]

What prompted the administration, then, to pull back from its aggressive detention and interrogation program, even as its lawyers wrote memos saying it could continue the program? No doubt multiple factors contributed to the decision. But any account of those factors would have to include the successful efforts of human rights and civil liberties groups to frame the Bush administration's war on terror as presenting a stark choice between the rule of law and lawlessness. And it would also have to include the efforts of Elisa Massimino, John Hutson, and HRF in harnessing the credibility of retired generals and admirals. Just as with marriage equality, both the message and the messengers—inside and outside the courtroom—were crucial elements in the campaign to preserve civil liberties and human rights in the war on terror.

Still, no matter how effective their message and how credible their messengers, human rights groups could not challenge what they could not see. And in the field of national security, unlike, say, marriage equality or gun rights, secrecy is endemic. An effective campaign to uphold human rights in the war on terror, therefore, required yet another element—a strategy for encouraging or forcing transparency.

16

Transformative Transparency

I N OCTOBER 2003, AS RUMORS OF ABUSE OF DETAINEES HELD BY THE US ABROAD BEGAN to appear in the media, Jameel Jaffer and Amrit Singh, then relatively recent additions to the ACLU legal team, filed a Freedom of Information Act (FOIA) request for government documents concerning detainee treatment in the war on terror. The government would divulge nothing voluntarily, so shortly thereafter, they filed suit to enforce the request. As with Ratner's filing of the *Rasul* case, no one expected much to come of the FOIA litigation. One ACLU colleague offered to pay a dollar for every page they received; another teasingly asked Singh if she'd cleared off enough shelf space for the government's response. Jaffer later told me that in his most optimistic moments, he hoped that the government's predictable refusal to disclose information might bring some critical attention to the issue.[1]

In retrospect, the FOIA litigation has been the centerpiece of civil society's transparency campaign on torture. Over the course of more than a decade, the lawsuit has pried loose nearly six thousand documents, totaling about 130,000 pages, from the Department of Defense, Justice Department, State Department, White House, Office of the Director of National Intelligence, and the CIA. Some of the earliest disclosures were firsthand accounts by FBI agents who described Guantánamo interrogation tactics as "torture techniques." Disclosure of those documents, which revealed that detainee abuse was not limited to a few "bad apples" at Abu Ghraib but was also occurring at Guantánamo, prompted major investigations by both the Justice Department and the Department of Defense.[2]

A FOIA response in 2006 revealed that President Bush had signed a secret memo in the first few days after 9/11 authorizing the CIA to conduct secret detentions and interrogations. Other disclosed documents included a memo showing that special forces threatened military personnel who reported on detainee abuse; complaints from Guantánamo prisoners that interrogators had defecated on the Qur'an; directives authorizing sensory deprivation of Iraqi detainees; and autopsy reports of prisoners who had died after being subjected to harsh interrogation. The documents came in dribs and drabs, often prompted by court rulings finding prior responses inadequate. Each time the ACLU received a new batch of materials, it would extract the most newsworthy details and issue a press release, often leading to major media coverage. As a result, Jaffer and Singh's case triggered a steady stream of news stories about torture over more than a decade, ensuring that the torture program was never long out of the public eye.[3]

Two of the most significant revelations came in 2009, after President Obama had taken office. In April of that year, the government released the full set of Justice Department memos authorizing the CIA's "enhanced interrogation techniques," all but two of which had remained classified until then. The memos showed Bush administration lawyers adopting ever more strained legal interpretations to ensure that the CIA had a green light to torture. In August 2009, the government released a redacted CIA inspector general's report that detailed abuses of CIA black site detainees well beyond those authorized by the Justice Department, including threats to kill detainees' family members, and pointing a gun and an electric drill at a detainee's head. Again, the disclosures prompted widespread media coverage and condemnation of the CIA's tactics.[4]

In addition to providing information to the media, Jaffer and Singh published a 456-page book collecting the most important of the documents they had retrieved.[5] The ACLU also created a searchable online database containing all of the documents, while another online resource, also published as a book in 2012, used the documents to construct a detailed narrative of the Bush administration's descent into torture.[6]

PEN American Center and the ACLU produced a script consisting of selected excerpts from the documents, and put on public readings in New York and Washington, DC, and at the Sundance Film Festival in Park City, Utah, among other places. The readers included Robert Redford, America Ferrera, Ellen Barkin, Art Spiegelman, Don DeLillo, Susanna Moore, Eve Ensler, A. M. Holmes, George Saunders, Paul Auster, Aasif Mandvi, Alice McDermott, Marilynne Robinson, Naomi Wolf, Annie Proulx, and Congressmen John Conyers, Keith Ellison, and Bobby Scott. They also put the script online and encouraged community groups to perform it themselves.[7]

One advantage of FOIA litigation is that the relative modesty of the relief requested—disclosure—may make it easier for courts to exercise some review of national security measures. Courts have been reluctant to address lawsuits that pose direct challenges to the US rendition, detention, and interrogation program. Enjoining an ongoing operation, or awarding damages based on a finding of illegality, is a grave step. The ACLU's FOIA lawsuit, by contrast, did not require the court to challenge the government's interrogation tactics directly, but simply to find that documents about the program should be made public. By shedding light on the government's abuses, however, the FOIA court contributed to their demise, because the practices were impossible to sustain in the light of day. Thus, transparency, while an end in itself, also became a crucial aspect of the overall strategy for ratcheting back questionable tactics in the war on terror.[8]

JAMES MADISON FAMOUSLY WROTE that "popular Government, without popular information, or the means of acquiring it, is but a Prologue to a

Farce or a Tragedy; or, perhaps both. Knowledge will forever govern ignorance: And a people who mean to be their own Governors, must arm themselves with the power which knowledge gives." "Popular information," it turns out, is critical not only to self-government, but to the protection of constitutional and human rights. The stigma attached to measures that violate such rights can be evaded if the measures are kept under wraps. Revealing the existence of such measures may be sufficient to rein them in. The Bush administration often retreated or modified its programs after they became public; its actions were sustainable only as long as they remained unknown. Thus, it rescinded the first Justice Department memo authorizing torture shortly after the memo was leaked to the *Washington Post*. It ended warrantless surveillance and subjected its surveillance to court oversight after the *New York Times* reported on the program. The CIA's black sites and interrogation program came to an end after many of the details appeared on the front pages of the nation's newspapers. The administration introduced significant reforms to Guantánamo only after a measure of transparency was brought to bear, through the reports of released detainees, FBI observers, and the lawyers who gained access to the prison through habeas litigation. This pattern has continued under Obama; the NSA's electronic surveillance practices were curtailed only after Edward Snowden disclosed their existence. When government officials are engaged in clandestine conduct that cannot be defended in public, transparency has a transformative power all its own.[9]

Officials charged with protecting national security invariably contend that their effectiveness is compromised by transparency. Secrecy prerogatives, unquestionably necessary in some circumstances, are notoriously prone to overuse. On matters of national security, therefore, the disclosure of improperly withheld information often must be forced, and almost always by civil society—through litigation, requests for information under the FOIA, and the media's publication of leaks. From Abu Ghraib to Snowden, disclosures of counterterrorism programs have time and again reshaped the nature of public debate. And in virtually every instance, the result has been the introduction of new restraints.[10]

TRANSPARENCY ABOUT PRISONER ABUSE may also have contributed to the results in the Supreme Court's four enemy combatant cases, by concretely underscoring the risks of accepting the president's claims of unreviewable authority over detainees. By the time the Supreme Court heard oral argument in the *Rasul* and *Hamdi* cases in 2004, reports of abusive interrogations at Guantánamo had already surfaced, thanks to the efforts of Gareth Peirce and Clive Stafford Smith to publicize the stories of the first men released from Guantánamo. These accounts were covered extensively by the British press in March 2004, just one month before the first Supreme Court oral arguments in the enemy combatant cases. At the argument in *Hamdi*, both Justices John Paul Stevens and Ruth Bader Ginsburg asked Deputy Solicitor General Paul Clement whether there were any legal limits on the government's interrogation of military detainees—even though that issue was not before the Court. Clement answered by pointing to the Torture Convention, and then added, with emphasis: "It's also the judgment of those involved in this process that the last thing you want to do is torture somebody or try to do something along those lines." In the second argument that day, *Padilla v. Rumsfeld*, involving only the technical question of whether a detainee's suit had been filed in the proper court, Ginsburg again asked Clement about torture. Clement's answer was even more emphatic: "our executive doesn't do that."[11]

That night, CBS's *60 Minutes II* first broadcast photographs of the now infamous abuse of prisoners at the Abu Ghraib military prison in Iraq. Two days later, the *New Yorker* published a story by Seymour Hersh, illustrated with many of the photographs. Clement's assurances could hardly have been more dramatically and dispositively refuted. The images underscored the inadequacy of the administration's assurances that the Court should "trust us." More than any legal argument, the graphic images of brutality toward helpless prisoners established the necessity of judicial oversight and legal limits.[12]

When Joe Margulies and Michael Ratner were initially planning the Guantánamo habeas litigation, Margulies predicted that "if we open it up, they will close it down." That was overly optimistic, to be sure. But Margulies was right that bringing lawyers to the island,

and thereby increasing visibility and awareness of what was going on there, would be an important step in that direction. For example, two Guantánamo habeas lawyers, Mark and Joshua Denbeaux, used records that resulted from the opening up of Guantánamo to cast serious doubt on the administration's claims that the detainees were "the worst of the worst." In a report issued in February 2006, based on records from Combatant Status Review Tribunals (CSRT) set up by the government in the wake of *Rasul*, the Denbeaux brothers showed that, according to the government's own findings, a mere 8 percent of the detainees were "fighters" for Al Qaeda, and only 16 percent were "fighters" for the Taliban; 40 percent of the detainees were not affiliated with Al Qaeda and 18 percent were not affiliated with either Al Qaeda or the Taliban. More than half the detainees had not committed any hostile act against the United States or coalition forces. The report received widespread media coverage, and directly contradicted the picture the Bush administration had painted of the detainees.[13]

Another Denbeaux report, similarly based on CSRT records, revealed that in the hearings, detainees were not informed of the evidence against them, much of which was classified. They were assisted by "personal representatives" from the US military, not lawyers, who in most instances had barely met them and often presented no defense. The detainees' requests to call exculpatory witnesses were almost always denied. When the *Boumediene* case reached the Supreme Court, the detainees' lawyers cited the Denbeaux study repeatedly in support of their argument that the CSRT procedures were an inadequate substitute for habeas corpus. The Court agreed.[14]

Transparency also may have influenced the Supreme Court's decision to address the application of the Geneva Conventions in *Hamdan v. Rumsfeld*, an issue that, as we have seen, was unnecessary to reach to resolve the case. The ACLU and Human Rights First each filed amicus briefs in *Hamdan* pointing to the abuse of Guantánamo detainees revealed in documents produced through the ACLU's FOIA litigation. The case formally concerned only the validity of Bush's military commission procedures, but the Court's determination that the Geneva Conventions applied to Al Qaeda made it illegal to deny the detainees

humane treatment. Within days of the Court's decision, Deputy Secretary of Defense Gordon England issued a memorandum to all de-
partments notifying them that, per the Supreme Court, the Geneva
Conventions now protected Al Qaeda detainees. One week later, the
administration rescinded part of a February 2002 executive order that
had rejected Geneva Convention protections. And in September 2006,
Bush cited the *Hamdan* decision in announcing his decision to transfer
all detainees from the CIA's secret prisons to Guantánamo.[15]

SECRECY HAS BEEN AN extraordinary obstacle for civil society advocates
in the war on terror, as it denies to them—and to the public at large—
the ability to evaluate the government's conduct. But where gay rights
and gun rights groups had to transform the content of constitutional
rights, civil liberties and human rights groups in many instances did
not. Torture, rendition, arbitrary detention, and warrantless wiretapping were already illegal; if advocates could bring these practices to
light, they could rely on the stigma attached to them to create pressure
for change. The strategy of transparency led the Bush administration to
modify or abandon several counterterrorism measures once they were
exposed to the light of day, and may well have spurred the Supreme
Court's decisions in the enemy combatant cases. Like Ratner before
them, Jaffer and Singh succeeded beyond all expectations.

17

The Obama Difference

W HEN PRESIDENT BARACK OBAMA WAS ELECTED IN 2008, HUMAN RIGHTS AND civil liberties advocates had every reason to celebrate—but, as it turns out, no reason to rest. As a candidate, Obama had harshly criticized many of the Bush administration's tactics in the war on terror. He was a constitutional law professor, a believer in checks and balances and individual rights. His very first acts as president were to close the CIA's secret prisons, restrict interrogation methods to those specifically authorized noncoercive techniques set forth in the Army Field Manual, and promise to close the military prison at Guantánamo Bay within the year. Since then, he has not brought a single additional detainee to Guantánamo, and has released more than one hundred. He has tried and convicted several alleged Al Qaeda terrorists captured abroad in ordinary criminal trials, rather than holding them indefinitely as accused "enemy combatants" or trying them in military commissions. He rescinded and made public previously secret Justice Department memos authorizing the CIA to engage in coercive interrogations, saying that he did so "to ensure that the actions described within them never take place again."[1]

Where Bush tried to thrust the law aside, Obama promised that his counterterrorism policies would be constrained by it. In what is very likely a first for any president, the Obama administration even argued that the courts had given the executive too much power. When a three-judge panel of the US Court of Appeals for the DC Circuit ruled in January 2010 that the president's authority to detain enemy combatants was not limited by the laws of war, the Obama administration objected, arguing that the president's authority is indeed so constrained. In response, the "en banc" court of appeals, comprised of all active judges on the DC Circuit, rejected the panel's prior reasoning as unnecessary to the result, denying it any precedential authority.[2]

Obama also appointed human rights advocates to key posts in his administration. Harold Koh, former dean of Yale Law School and an outspoken critic of the Bush administration's war on terror, became legal advisor to the State Department. Michael Posner, the founder of Human Rights First, became the assistant secretary of state for democracy, human rights, and labor. Samantha Power, founding director of Harvard's Carr Center for Human Rights Policy, became the National Security Council's director for multilateral affairs and human rights. Rosa Brooks, a Georgetown law professor and critic of Bush's counterterrorism policy, headed up a new office in the Pentagon devoted to rule of law and humanitarian policy. Sarah Cleveland, a Columbia law professor with strong human rights ties, went to the State Department legal advisor's office with Harold Koh. David Barron and Martin Lederman, law professors at Harvard and Georgetown, respectively, who had coauthored a major two-part article in the *Harvard Law Review* asserting the limits of the executive commander-in-chief power, went to the Office of Legal Counsel, which advises the executive branch on the constitutional limits of its powers.

Yet according to Ken Roth, executive director of Human Rights Watch, the Obama administration has been a huge disappointment on human rights. And Roth is not alone; most civil liberties and human rights advocates with whom I spoke said the same. They pointed to the fact that well into his second term, Obama had still not made good on his promise to close the prison at Guantánamo Bay. He dramatically increased the controversial use of drones to kill suspected Al Qaeda members, often far from the battlefield. He opposed accountability for CIA torture. And he continued to use flawed military commissions to try at least some Al Qaeda members for war crimes, including Khalid Sheikh Mohammed, charged as mastermind of the 9/11 attacks.[3]

The frustration of human rights and civil liberties groups is in one sense predictable. Such groups are unlikely to be satisfied by any executive branch's national security policy. A president's first obligation is to protect the security of the nation, and thus he is likely to prioritize security when it clashes with liberty. By contrast, human rights and civil liberties organizations by design prioritize liberty. It would be extraordinary, then, if the ACLU and Human Rights Watch were not protesting the president's decisions—whoever the president is. By virtue of his position, Ken Roth will never be satisfied. Nor should he be.

Civil liberties and human rights groups could not and did not close up shop when Obama was elected. But fighting for liberties under the new administration presented distinct challenges as well as new avenues for reform. In a perverse sense, Bush and Cheney were good for business. They inspired fear and concern about governmental overreaching, and motivated individuals and foundations to increase their support to groups like the ACLU and CCR, both of which grew exponentially in the Bush years. Once Obama was elected, these groups no longer had Cheney and Bush to rally against. Reports in April 2015 disclosed that the ACLU, which had doubled in size in the years after 9/11, had operated at an average $15 million deficit for the first five years of the Obama administration; in early 2015, it laid off 7 percent of its staff. And although much of the shortfall was due to the loss of a single, very generous donor, the shift was nonetheless emblematic. The Center for Constitutional Rights went through a similar experience; its annual revenues more than tripled between 2001 and 2009, to $9 million, but were back below $7 million in 2014.[4]

For similar reasons, it was also more difficult to motivate the courts, Congress, and foreign governments to challenge a president who was widely seen as a less serious threat to human rights. Against Bush, civil liberties groups won the support of foreign peoples and governments;

the backing of significant and influential voices at home; and, partially as a result, prevailed in four Supreme Court cases. Against Obama, they have won none. Yet threats to fundamental rights persist, and the work of human rights organizations continues to be essential. It may be necessary, however, for human rights and civil liberties groups to adjust tactics with a friend rather than a foe in office.

THE CIVIL LIBERTIES FIGHT against Bush had been by necessity almost exclusively an outside game. The aim was to change the opinions of others so that they would bring pressure to bear on Bush. With human rights advocates in key posts in the Obama administration, there was the possibility of an "inside track." Koh, the State Department legal advisor, for example, advocated internally for many reforms favored by human rights groups. He fought for more transparency about the US drone strike program—and over time the program became more public. He argued that the US should reverse its long-held position that the International Covenant on Civil and Political Rights and the Convention Against Torture, major international human rights treaties, do not apply to US actions abroad. In November 2014, the administration told the UN Committee against Torture that it now took the view that the Convention does apply abroad in some instances, and also applies in times of war. According to credible reports, Koh argued strongly, although without success, against the resumption of military tribunals. He urged the administration to limit the charges it would pursue through military tribunals in lieu of ordinary civilian courts. He pressed Obama not to waver on his commitment to closing Guantánamo at a time when others were insisting that the goal was unrealistic. He battled with the Defense Department over the terms delineating who could be detained as an enemy combatant, or targeted for a drone strike.[5]

Koh was often vastly outnumbered in the government's inner circles. As he recalled, "for every one voice expressing human rights concerns at a meeting on a national security issue, there were fifteen to thirty representatives of the national security side." The vast majority of the officials involved in national security decision making will not consider human rights a primary responsibility, under any administration. Still, when a more sympathetic administration is in office, civil liberties advocates must consider not only what they can achieve from outside, but also what progress is possible from within, and what they can do to assist such internal efforts.[6]

In the view of some human rights advocates, Koh compromised his principles while in the administration. In Koh's view, some human rights groups forfeited an opportunity to be more influential within the Obama administration by maintaining an unrealistic and overly aggressive stance, insisting on changes that were impractical. Both may have been right; compromise is essential to getting things done in a bureaucracy, and external advocates may have failed to grasp the constraints that Koh and other internal human rights advocates faced. The human rights advocacy Koh criticized as too extreme may have been a carryover from eight years of battle with the Bush administration, when there was little inside game to be played. But Koh believes such uncompromising views led some potential allies within the administration to dismiss human rights groups' concerns. "Some felt that these groups would never be satisfied, and therefore there was little or nothing to be gained by attempting to take their concerns seriously. They weren't interested in compromise, and would attack us regardless of the outcome." Koh's predecessor under Bush as State Department legal advisor, John Bellinger, one of the few in that administration who had met with human rights groups, felt similarly. In both men's experience, advocates who understood the need to compromise were more effective in prompting internal reform than their counterparts who assumed a more pure—and impractical—position.[7]

These are, of course, the views of insiders. Advocates seeking to work with administration insiders do need to be open to compromise. But insiders may also have their hand strengthened by advocates who take a more hard-line tone outside the administration. The more nuanced arguments necessary for effective internal reforms are often less likely to inspire broad public support, and internal reformers may be

taken more seriously if public critiques generate broad concern. In
the end, the combination of external pressure and internal advocacy
worked to bring about human rights reform under Obama.

CONSIDER, FOR EXAMPLE, OBAMA'S most controversial national security initiative—the use of remote-controlled unmanned airplanes, or
drones, for targeted killing far from the battlefield. Obama began his
presidency refusing even to acknowledge that the United States was
conducting drone strikes on human targets. Throughout his tenure,
however, human rights groups objected to the secrecy surrounding
the program, the reportedly large numbers of innocent civilians killed,
and the rising number of drone strikes. In response to these external
criticisms and pressure from human rights allies within, the administration's policy evolved, too slowly and insufficiently for many critics,
but nonetheless in significant ways.

The drone strike program was covert because both Pakistan and
Yemen apparently agreed to allow the United States to conduct such
strikes within their borders on the condition that it not admit that it
was doing so. But one cannot repeatedly kill people with explosives
dropped from the sky and keep it a secret. Civil society organizations
in this country and abroad tracked drone strikes, issued reports, and
demanded transparency and accountability, neither of which were
possible so long as the program remained covert. Reports by the
Washington-based New America Foundation and the London-based
Bureau of Investigative Journalism, tallying significant numbers of civilian casualties, fueled criticism of the program, directly challenged
the administration's silence, and increased pressure on Obama and his
deputies to publicly defend and rein in their actions.

Many human rights groups issued reports and position papers
about drone strikes, often focusing on their impact on innocent civilians, both those accidentally killed or injured, and those who live
in constant fear of an attack from the sky. In October 2013, Reprieve
and the Foundation for Fundamental Rights, a Pakistani human rights

group, brought nine-year-old Nibila ur Rehman from Pakistan to testify before Congress about a drone strike that killed her grandmother.
In June 2014, the Stimson Center issued the report of a blue-ribbon
panel comprising, among others, former senior officials from the CIA,
the Department of Defense, and the Department of State, calling for
greater transparency and accountability for US drone policy.[8]

International institutions and officials also weighed in. In June
2010, the UN special rapporteur on extrajudicial executions, Philip
Alston, issued a report based on six years of research, criticizing the expansion of authority to kill and the absence of adequate accountability
mechanisms. In February 2014, another UN special rapporteur, Ben
Emmerson, also issued a critical report, dwelling in particular on the
failure to account for civilian casualties.[9]

The media have paid substantial attention to the subject of drone
strikes. In May 2012, for example, the *New York Times* published a front-
page story detailing the bizarre and seemingly ad hoc process by which
the administration developed its list of targets to be killed. The account
described conference calls to review the kill list with as many as one
hundred government participants. In his 2012 book, *Kill or Capture*,
Dan Klaidman detailed the debates within the Obama administration
over the use of drones. These revelations prompted still further criticism and calls for reform.[10]

The notion that the United States was asserting the power to kill its
enemies in secret by remote control, deploying technology over which,
for the time being anyway, it had a virtual monopoly, led many people around the world to condemn the program. Surely, critics noted,
the United States would not tolerate other nations using armed drones
to kill their enemies within US borders. And as with the transnational
campaigns under Bush, these objections began to take root at home. In
August 2011, Dennis Blair, a retired admiral who had been director of
national intelligence in 2009 and 2010, wrote an op-ed in the *New York
Times* arguing that drone strikes in Pakistan had become counterproductive, and should be halted. As he put it, "our reliance on high-tech strikes
that pose no risk to our soldiers is bitterly resented in a country that
cannot duplicate such feats of warfare without cost to its own troops."[11]

Concerns escalated when, in 2010, the *New York Daily News* reported that the Obama administration had placed a US citizen, Anwar al-Awlaki, on its "kill list." In August of that year, the ACLU and CCR jointly sued on Awlaki's father's behalf, arguing that to kill Awlaki far from any battlefield without charges or a trial would violate his constitutional rights. The suit, even more of a long shot than CCR's initial habeas filing on behalf of Guantánamo detainees, requested an injunction barring the intended attack. The district court dismissed the case, finding that the president's decision to kill an asserted enemy in an armed conflict could not be reviewed by a court. The lawsuit nonetheless brought more media attention, and helped raise the profile of the drone question.[12]

On September 30, 2011, a US drone killed Awlaki. In March 2013, Senator Rand Paul conducted a thirteen-hour filibuster on the Senate floor to object to the (exceedingly unlikely) potential use of a drone to kill a US citizen on US soil. A Gallup poll found that 70 percent of Americans agreed that drone strikes at home are unacceptable, and that a majority also opposed the use of drones to kill US-citizen terror suspects abroad.[13]

As criticism mounted, the Obama administration gradually responded. Koh first broke the administration's silence. In May 2010, he delivered a speech at the American Society of International Law annual meeting that defended the use of armed drones against Al Qaeda. He responded to four specific arguments that had been made by human rights critics: that targeting particular individuals to kill was illegal; that the use of drones was illegal; that the strikes constituted extrajudicial killings prohibited by international law; and that the strikes violated a domestic law ban on assassinations. Koh later told me that many national security officials objected to even this very general public discussion of the program.[14]

Over the next several years, civil society groups continued to criticize the program, and the administration responded by authorizing more officials to make public speeches defending its actions, each time providing a little more detail. White House National Security Advisor John Brennan, Attorney General Eric Holder, and Defense Department General Counsels Jeh Johnson and Stephen Preston all gave speeches defending the program, each time responding to criticisms that had been voiced by civil society groups and advocates.[15]

In May 2013, Obama himself directly addressed the issue. In a speech at the National Defense University, and formalized in a Presidential Policy Guidance, he announced new limitations on the use of targeted killing. He stated that he would authorize such killings outside a traditional battlefield only where (1) they are necessary to respond to individuals who pose a "continuing and imminent threat to the American people"; (2) capture is not feasible; (3) the host country is unwilling or unable to countermand the threat the individual poses; and (4) there is a "near certainty that no civilians will be killed or injured." This is a demanding standard, possibly even more demanding than the law of war, which does not require a near certainty that no civilians will be injured, but only that collateral damage be reasonably limited.[16]

Human rights advocates continued to raise questions about how the administration defines such key terms as "continuing but imminent threat" and "feasibility of capture," what process is used to make these assessments, and why there is no accountability or transparency with respect to individual strikes. In April 2014, in response to another FOIA suit filed by Jameel Jaffer and the ACLU, an appeals court in New York ordered the Obama administration to release a Justice Department memo authorizing the killing of Anwar al-Awlaki. The court reasoned that earlier disclosures, prompted by criticism of the killing, had already revealed substantial aspects of the administration's analysis, and there was no legitimate reason for continuing to withhold the memo itself.[17]

The administration did not just change its talking points in response to these pressures. As criticism mounted, the number of drone strikes and casualties fell dramatically. According to the Bureau of Investigative Journalism, for example, there were 471 total deaths by drone strikes in Pakistan in 2009, 751 in 2010, and 363 in 2011, but only 108 in 2013 and 35 in 2014. The number of estimated civilian casualties from strikes in Pakistan also dropped significantly over that time period, from a high of 100 in 2009 to zero in both 2013 and 2014.

The *Long War Journal* reported a similar trajectory counting drone strikes rather than resulting deaths. Drone strikes in Pakistan dropped from a high of 117 in 2010 to 24 in 2014 and 9 in 2015. Parallel trends are evident in Yemen. Evidently, as the program became less covert and more responsive to human rights politics, the Obama administration grew more restrained and selective in its targeting.[18]

Problems remain. In April 2015, Obama held a news conference to announce that in a drone strike in Pakistan in January, the United States had mistakenly killed two Western hostages: an American, Warren Weinstein, and an Italian, Giovanni Lo Porto. Civil society groups insisted that there can be no moral justification for apologizing only when the United States kills Western innocents and not civilians of other nationalities. The ACLU, CCR, HRW, HRF, Reprieve, the Open Society Foundations, and several other groups wrote Obama to urge him to adopt "the same approach for all other U.S. counterterrorism strikes in which civilians are killed or injured—regardless of their nationality." They appended a list of ten such strikes.[19]

In short, human rights groups have consistently pressed for restraint and reform of the drone program since Obama took office, and the administration has responded by providing some, although still insufficient, transparency; by announcing, at least in theory, stringent restraints on drone use; and by sharply reducing the number of drone strikes. It is highly unlikely that the CIA, which runs most of the drone program, would have countenanced such reforms were it not for the pressure created by human rights advocates within and outside the administration.

ONE COULD TELL SIMILAR stories about advocacy campaigns focused on Guantánamo, accountability for torture, and NSA spying. On each of those issues, some progress has been made, and in virtually all instances through external civil society advocacy and internal efforts by officials with human rights backgrounds or affinities. Reasonable people can and do differ about how compliant the Obama administration has been with human rights. But were human rights and civil liberties groups not engaged in the full range of advocacy—educating their members and the public at large, providing information and analysis to the press, reaching out to foreign audiences, filing lawsuits, conducting their own investigations, recruiting unexpected allies, and working with like-minded individuals within the administration—many of the reforms that did emerge under Obama might never have occurred. And just as with the gay rights and gun rights campaigns, most of the advocacy took place outside a federal courtroom, even if in the end the goal was to protect constitutional and human rights.

Civil liberties and human rights require sophisticated and committed watchdogs no matter who is in the Oval Office. Just as the security services must be ever vigilant against threats to our security, we as citizens must carefully guard against threats to our fundamental rights. The responsibility for vigilance lies with each of us, but is undertaken largely by the institutions of civil society. As with gay rights groups and the NRA, the work of human rights groups continues under every administration. The tactics may change, but active engagement remains essential.

The success of civil liberties and human rights groups in limiting infringements on basic rights after 9/11 was more qualified, to be sure, than that of the gay rights and gun rights campaigns. Human rights groups were more successful in compelling Bush to conform his counterterrorism practices to legal restraints than most would have predicted on 9/11. They have been less successful under Obama than many hoped when he was first elected. In both administrations, however, civil society groups consistently advocated for human rights and achieved significant victories.

As Tom Malinowski, a senior lawyer with HRW, told me in 2013, human rights groups "help define what legitimate and illegitimate government policy is." The ACLU's and CCR's institutional commitment to constitutional rights, like HRF's and HRW's commitment to human rights, meant that even when the tides of popular opinion were flowing strongly in the direction of deference to executive power and sacrifice of the individual rights of disfavored "outsiders," these groups resisted. Just as a constitution is designed to counter the political pressures of the moment in the name of commitment to larger and more enduring principles, so these groups of citizens, drawn together by shared values, checked the temptations of the majority to abandon their principles in times of fear. Without such groups, the laws that bind us would be far less effective. With such groups, fidelity to our ideals remains a struggle—but at least there is a struggle. After 9/11, it was civil society that defended the rule of law when the president, the Congress, the courts, and the people themselves were all too ready to look the other way.

Conclusion

I N ONE OF HIS LEGENDARY DEBATES WITH STEPHEN DOUGLAS, ABRAHAM LINCOLN SAID, "Public sentiment is everything. With public sentiment, nothing can fail; without it, nothing can succeed. Consequently he who molds public sentiment goes deeper than he who enacts statutes or pronounces decisions. He makes statutes and decisions possible or impossible to be executed." Lincoln was talking about the politics of slavery, but the stories of constitutional struggle recounted in this book illustrate that this is equally true of constitutional law. The campaigns for marriage equality, gun rights, and human rights in the "war on terror" were as much about molding public sentiment as shaping law, as much about working outside the courts as pressing a case within them.[1]

This is not to say that constitutional law merely reflects the whims of the public. The constitutional advocacy groups I've featured are not beholden to what the majority desires at a particular moment. They are defined by principled commitments to particular ideals, and they defend those ideals whether popular or not. In fact, they are most needed precisely when the rights they are designed to protect are under attack by our democratically elected representatives. When the majority of Americans opposed the recognition of same-sex marriage, Lambda

Legal Defense Fund, GLAD, and the ACLU, among a handful of others, fought for that recognition on principles of equal dignity and liberty. When conventional wisdom and judicial precedent held that the Constitution did not protect an individual right to bear arms, the NRA set to work to change that understanding. And when most Americans were content to sacrifice the rights of foreigners accused of terrorism, CCR, Reprieve, and the ACLU objected on constitutional and human rights grounds. If minority visions for our constitutional rights can become the new consensus, then the already widespread opposition to Donald Trump stands a chance of realizing its claims with much greater speed and impact than Evan Wolfson, Marion Hammer, and Michael Ratner ever expected for their own causes.

Campaigns for constitutional reform will always be with us. At the moment, advocates are working to end the death penalty, to limit the influence of money in politics, to expand property rights against government regulation, to establish a right to die with dignity, and to cut back on the right to terminate a pregnancy. Trump's election has spurred citizens from across the country to come together in defense of such basic values as the right to vote, women's rights, freedom of the press, and immigrants' rights. New groups have emerged to capture this energy, and organizations like the ACLU have seen unprecedented growth in membership and support. Every campaign to defend or advance constitutional liberty faces different challenges and will have to adopt different strategies. But the stories told here offer several important lessons about social change, political mobilization, and constitutional law. Each lesson has particular resonance for the struggle to defend liberty in the Trump era.

Liberty lives in, and depends on, us. As Margaret Mead reminded us, "Never underestimate the power of a small group of committed people to change the world. In fact, it is the only thing that ever has." Constitutional law, the guardian of our liberty, is not something that hovers in the sky above us, to be divined, intoned, and enforced exclusively by judges in robes seated behind the well in formal courtrooms. It is something that we can all take part in shaping and preserving. And indeed, through our participation in the struggle for liberty, we help ensure that constitutional law remains a vibrant and living force, and not a dead letter bequeathed to us two centuries ago by a small group of prominent white men. As citizens, we make and remake constitutional law in our own image, by fighting for it in association with our fellow citizens. If you care about our nation's fundamental values, the way forward should be clear: find or found associations of like-minded people, engage broadly and creatively, and do not leave constitutional law to the lawyers, much less the judges.

This is where, as a civil liberties lawyer, I found the most reason for hope in the early days of the Trump administration. While Trump poses unprecedented threats, the popular resistance that emerged after his election was remarkable. Never before had I seen such concerted and widespread activism. Every gathering I attended about how to defend liberty in the Trump era drew standing-room-only crowds. Citizens wanted to know what they could do. They were eager to act. The ACLU never before had as many volunteers offer their help. Across the country, citizens gathered in house parties and other events, formal and informal, inspired by the women's march, religious communities, colleges, nonprofit groups, and other grassroots endeavors. In a democracy, this is where power resides. Properly focused and deployed, the people will, I am confident, preserve liberty from its gravest threat.

Most of the work of defending and advancing liberty takes place outside the federal courts. Constitutional law, the guardian of our liberty, is conventionally understood as something judges, not ordinary citizens, do. Since very early in the nation's history, the courts have had the power to review the actions of the political branches and to declare them null and void if they violate constitutional provisions. To exercise that power, courts must interpret the Constitution, and by these acts of interpretation, constitutional law evolves. But as the campaigns here make clear, this conventional wisdom is wrong. Most of the work that goes into the defense and transformation of constitutional liberty takes place outside the federal courts, by actors who are not judges or lawyers, but ordinary citizens. Even if one's ultimate goal is to change constitutional law through a federal court decision, the principal venues for urging that reform lie beyond the courts. There are countless forums for defending liberty. Overlapping state, federal, and international legal systems offer multiple possibilities, whether in city councils, state legislatures, state courts, Congress, the executive branch, the United Nations, or other international bodies. And those are just the legal forums. Equally if not more important are nonlegal venues: the press, the academy, religious communities, social media, the workplace, and voluntary associations. In all these places, citizens can and do take part, and can press and have pressed successfully to defend and advance constitutional liberty.

The advocates featured here were opportunistic: they pursued their claims wherever a promising opportunity arose. Gay rights groups and the NRA looked principally to the states, deploying a federalist strategy in an attempt to establish principles in state statutory and constitutional law long before presenting the issue head-on in the federal courts. In both cases, constitutional reform was achieved incrementally, state by state, before it was ready for federal recognition.

The NRA also looked to the legal academy, and seeded and encouraged a major scholarly undertaking to unearth historical evidence to support its view that the Second Amendment was originally understood to protect an individual right to bear arms. By the time the Supreme Court addressed the question, the academy had helped pave the way, and its work informed the Court's decisions in both *Heller* and *McDonald*, as the Court cited and relied upon the evidence and arguments that NRA-supported scholars had been advancing for two decades.

In the war on terror, human rights groups directed much of their advocacy overseas, using the international language of human rights, and enlisting the aid of foreign populations and governments to pressure the US government to respect foreigners' rights. They also fed stories to the media, lobbied Congress and the executive branch, and pursued a strategy of transparency and shaming directed at the public at large, at home and abroad.

As with marriage, guns, and human rights, so with civil rights and civil liberties under President Trump: advocates must defend these values in multiple forums. This is an opportunity as much as a challenge. It means that even if the Republicans control all three branches of the federal government, there are other avenues for resistance. Here, again, the institutions of civil society have played a large part: the press, the academy, faith communities, and the nonprofit sector. Citizens understand this, and have shown their support—by creating new institutions, joining groups like the ACLU in record numbers, and offering support to institutions that they see as sites of resistance. With Trump in the White House, many have newfound appreciation for those who perform watchdog roles, including the media; subscriptions to the *New York Times* and *Washington Post* have skyrocketed. Citizens are engaging in political advocacy in astounding numbers, deploying new and old networks, religious and secular, local, regional, and national, to organize and express their objections to Trump's assaults. All these institutions play a critical part—at least as important as the courts—in defending constitutional freedoms.

Act locally, because small steps add up. The idea that any of us could possibly affect national politics, much less constitutional law, may seem hopelessly grandiose. What difference can one person possibly make? We tend to think of constitutional law as a law above all others, impervious to politics and enforced through the dictates of unelected judges. Constitutional law, we are taught, is distinct from federal statutory law, as well as from municipal and state law. We might be able to change some of these latter forms of law, but constitutional law stands against change. Under the American system, constitutional law, the safeguard of our liberties, is supreme over all other law.

Yet the campaigns recounted here illustrate that there is in fact much more continuity than difference between these various bodies of law—and between local and national politics. As a practical matter, that means that we all have opportunities to contribute to the defense and evolution of constitutional freedoms. State law developments foreshadowed and made possible the federal constitutional recognition of marriage equality and the right to bear arms. International human rights arguments in forums at home and abroad contributed to the extension of constitutional protections to "enemy combatants" and the curtailment of the Bush administration's extraconstitutional measures. Public protests against Trump's Muslim ban prompted state attorneys general to sue, and encouraged judges to stand up to the president. The Constitution's Bill of Rights overlaps substantially with rights recognized in state statutes and constitutions, with the International Covenant on Civil and Political Rights, and with our social norms and moral values. That means that each of these legal and extralegal settings offers a place to advance arguments that might eventually make their way into federal constitutional law as well.

The bulk of the work done by gay rights, gun rights, and human rights groups was not constitutional in the narrow sense. It involved electoral politics; lobbying city council members and state legislators; writing op-eds and blogs; speaking to family, friends, and coworkers; and, occasionally, marching in the streets. But all of this advocacy was constitutional in a broader and more important sense: it was in service of constitutional principle, and it buttressed the underlying liberties and rights in question.

Sometimes these efforts made formal resort to constitutional guarantees unnecessary. Even if gun rights advocates had lost in *Heller*, the NRA's efforts at the state level to protect gun owners would have assured the protection of an individual right to bear arms for most Americans. At the same time, the fact that the NRA had already succeeded in achieving extensive state law gun rights protections made it easier for the Supreme Court to recognize a federal constitutional right. Similarly, the federal courts never had to declare torture or cruel, inhuman, or degrading treatment of foreign prisoners unconstitutional; the moral opprobrium attached to the practice meant that the Bush administration was forced to curtail its controversial practices without a judicial decision ordering it to do so.

Thus, in operation, the Constitution's safeguards of liberty are less distinct from other forms of law than is conventionally understood— and more susceptible to the concerted actions of citizens than we generally think. Whether you seek to defend or change constitutional law, you can and must operate in multiple legal systems in order to have a chance at succeeding.

The battles for liberty under the Trump administration will similarly take place on multiple fronts, many of them far from the Supreme Court. Trump vowed, during his campaign, to criminalize abortion and "open up" libel laws. But both libel and abortion are primarily regulated by state law, so the struggle for the rights of reproductive choice and a free press will be fought at least in the first instance at the state and local levels. The same is true for voting rights. Trump's false claims that millions voted fraudulently have inspired increased efforts to enact voter identification laws, whose true purpose is not to counter non-existent voter fraud but to suppress the votes of poor and minority citizens, who are less likely to support Republican candidates. Trump supporters at the state level have been emboldened to seek new laws limiting abortion and restricting access to the ballot. The first line of defense in these struggles is not the Supreme Court, or the lower federal courts, but state government. State legislators and governors are bound to uphold the Constitution, and we as citizens must hold them to it. In just the first several weeks of the Trump administration, several state attorneys general filed or joined lawsuits challenging Trump's "Muslim ban," and many cities declared themselves "sanctuary cities," announcing that they would decline to participate in Trump's enhanced deportation efforts. Shortly after Trump's inauguration, the ACLU launched PeoplePower.org, an online initiative designed to encourage and facilitate offline citizen engagement at the local level. Its first campaign, "Freedom Cities," invited citizens to meet with their local police chiefs to ask them to respect immigrants' rights and decline to enforce federal immigration law.

The fact that much of the battle will be local should be empowering, as it takes a proportionally smaller group of citizens to have a measurable impact at the state and local levels. But citizens must be ready to engage in those arenas. We cannot passively rely on the Supreme Court or large protests in the nation's capital to alone defeat Trump's ambitions; we need to prepare the ground for the protection of liberty at every level of government. And this is a job that all of us can—and must—do.

Framing and messaging are as essential to the defense of liberty as formal legal argument. Each of the campaigns discussed here succeeded in part because it was able to advance a "frame" for understanding the issue that proved sympathetic. Gay rights groups learned that it was better not to speak in terms of rights when advocating for marriage equality. Appeals to "love and commitment" were more likely to reach those torn between a fidelity to traditional values and recognition of the right of same-sex couples to marry. Relatedly, from the outset marriage equality advocates stressed the similarities between same-sex and opposite-sex couples, invariably choosing as plaintiffs couples who had been together a long time, had families, and were upstanding members of their communities. For its part, the NRA framed the right to own a weapon as a check on tyranny, as a cornerstone of liberty, and as integral to the right and obligation to protect one's home and loved ones from danger. Human rights groups successfully supplanted President Bush's frame of "us vs. them" with "law vs. lawlessness."

The appeal of a message is a function not only of its content but also of who delivers it. Again, all three campaigns looked for effective messengers. The NRA stresses the number of women and police officers in its organization; gay rights groups recruited heterosexuals, the more straitlaced the better, to make their case; and human rights groups looked to military leaders and former government officials for support and legitimacy. All made an effort to identify unlikely spokespersons in order to expand their core of support.

The narrative that has already taken hold regarding the Trump administration sees the president as erratic, narcissistic, and impulsive, with little regard for basic constitutional norms and principles of democracy such as a free press and independent courts. In his first days in office, he was more obsessed with the disappointingly small crowds at his inauguration than with the work of governance—especially when millions came out the next day at the women's march to protest his taking office. His administration found itself mired in controversy over Russia's interference in the election, whether Trump campaign representatives colluded with Russian officials, and whether Trump illegally interfered in the investigation by urging FBI director James Comey to drop an investigation of Michael Flynn, Trump's national security adviser, and then firing Comey on pretextual grounds. His executive orders imposing a ban on admission from predominantly Muslim countries were widely condemned, and enjoined by the courts. Trump's impulsive tweets, filled with ALL CAPS and exclamation points, regularly made unsupported or false claims. As much as his base appeared to appreciate his antics, over time this image will increasingly drive other government actors to seek to distance themselves from him, and therefore to be more likely to check his abuses.

This image can help to rein in the president. Trump himself has of course fueled the narrative by his own actions. Calling the judge who first issued a nationwide injunction against his travel ban a "so-called judge," for example, did Trump no favors with the judiciary. Even his allies, including newly appointed Supreme Court Justice Neil Gorsuch and federal judge Jay Bybee, have criticized the president for his words. But to persuade those who may have initially voted for or supported Trump, it will be important to recruit unlikely allies and credible spokespeople to confirm the message: former national security officials and military leaders of both parties have already spoken out against him. As the gun rights, gay rights, and human rights campaigns recounted here illustrate, the messenger can be as important as the message.

The work of defending and advancing liberty is intensely political—and democratic. The Constitution's safeguards of liberty are designed to stand above ordinary politics and are not directly responsive to political pressure in the way that legislation or executive action can be. The justices' responsibility is not to represent their constituents but to enforce the Constitution, and they are afforded life tenure precisely so that they will be independent. But as these accounts of constitutional reform illustrate, public and elite opinion are nonetheless central to the process of defending and advancing liberty. A major feature of all three campaigns included appeals to politicians, and to the public at large, often conducted through traditional political channels.

The NRA has almost certainly done more to protect gun rights through its involvement in elections for public office than through federal court litigation. By grading every federal and state elected official or candidate on his or her respect for gun rights, and by supporting their friends and attacking their foes, the NRA ensures that the political process itself will be sensitive to gun rights. It has always been able to secure greater protection through the political process than through the courts. The key to the NRA's success is that it understands the democratic roots of constitutional rights.

Gay rights groups similarly engaged wholeheartedly and single-mindedly in electoral campaigns. They devoted millions of dollars and thousands of volunteers and paid staff to referendum campaigns. They spent at least as much time and energy on campaign ads as on legal analysis. They supported legislators who backed their cause, and campaigned against those who opposed their claims. Like the NRA, they understood that the route to a constitutional right ran through the people and their representatives at least as much as through the federal courts.

A political campaign requires the mobilization of supporters, and here, too, politics and constitutionalism converge. The NRA is dedicated to fostering a sense of identity in its members and supporters, so that they can be more easily mobilized to act in coordinated ways in the political arena—by voting, campaigning, or contacting or visiting their elected representatives. The NRA's success in this regard is the envy of every other nonprofit organization. Gay rights groups have similarly built a sense of community and identity among gay and lesbian Americans, and encouraged their supporters to press for marriage equality by volunteering for referendum and electoral campaigns, contacting their representatives, and speaking openly with their friends and family about the issue.

Human rights groups lack the natural constituency that gay rights and gun rights groups enjoy. But they, too, engaged in extensive political work to further their ends, lobbying foreign governments and international institutions, recruiting influential institutional allies (such as the American Bar Association), using the media to propound their "rule of law" message, advising presidential candidates, and pressing Congress and the executive branch for reform on such issues as torture, Guantánamo, NSA surveillance, and drone warfare.

All of this work could be described as ordinary politics, not constitutional law. Yet it all played a necessary role in the overall campaign of each group to advance its respective constitutional ideals. Political activism is integral to both the preservation and evolution of constitutional rights and liberties.

Supreme Court justices are less likely to change constitutional law of their own accord than to recognize that it has changed, through evolution in the country's constitutional understanding, as manifested in public opinion, state laws, the writings of scholars, and the views of the press, Congress, and the president. The justices will not admit that this is what they are doing. Once cases reach the Supreme Court, the convention is that the justices must decide them based on the controlling precedents. But as the accounts here illustrate, constitutional change starts long before a case reaches the Supreme Court, driven by the efforts of citizens acting together, politically and democratically.

Here, too, the eagerness of the citizenry to play an active part in resisting Trump's constitutional rights abuses is a significant reason for hope. Constitutional law is designed to put brakes on overreaching by the political branches, but as this book has shown, it works best when the citizenry are actively engaged in defending it. The extraordinary level of political activism triggered by Trump's election is therefore the most promising sign that constitutional principles will limit the damage Trump would otherwise do. The activism needs to be maintained and effectively channeled, as the next two points emphasize. But for many campaigns, the biggest challenge is motivating people to act; when it comes to defending liberty from Trump, motivation has thus far not proved to be a problem.

Constitutional reform can be slow and difficult—but that works to liberty's advantage. As Susan Murray told Beth Robinson in Vermont in the early days of the campaign for marriage equality, "It's a marathon, not a sprint." Constitutional law can sometimes seem to change overnight. The Supreme Court recognized the right of same-sex couples to marry on June 26, 2015; the right to bear arms on June 26, 2008; and the right of Guantánamo detainees to habeas corpus on June 12, 2008. Yet as we have seen, the processes that led to these decisions took years. Constitutional change generally occurs slowly, in incremental steps.

Take the fight for marriage equality. Evan Wolfson writes a paper exploring the concept at Harvard Law School; some progressive cities and firms extend limited domestic partnership benefits to same-sex partners of their employees; state family law evolves to afford same-sex couples parental rights analogous to those of opposite-sex couples; local non-discrimination laws are amended to include discrimination on the basis of sexual orientation; states begin to enact and then to expand domestic partnership laws to include same-sex partners; a state court requires civil unions as a matter of state law; another state court recognizes same-sex marriage, also as a matter of state law; marriage equality begins to win in legislatures and popular referenda; and then, and only then, the Supreme Court recognizes a constitutional right to marry. Appearances to the contrary, reform is generally slow and steady, not revolutionary.[2]

The slow pace of change can be frustrating. But the difficulty of achieving constitutional change should work to the advantage of those who seek to defend liberty in the age of Trump. The Constitution was designed to constrain overconfident and aggressive presidents, and its guarantees will limit what Trump can achieve. The Constitution supports those who seek to defend, rather than change, the liberties it safe-guards. Trump's first executive order targeting Muslims was enjoined almost immediately on constitutional grounds. And because changing constitutional law generally requires patient incrementalism, Trump is unlikely to be able to transform existing constitutional limits without an extended and painstaking strategy over years. Patient incremental-ism is not exactly Trump's strong suit. He is unlikely to have the ability, interest, or fortitude to see through the various changes to constitu-tional law that he seems to desire—especially if we resist.

Collective action is essential to the defense and progress of liberty. Perhaps the most important lesson of this book is that effective constitutional advocacy, whether in defense of existing liberties or in support of ex-panded rights, requires citizens to act together. In this sense, the First Amendment right of association plays a foundational part in protecting all of the liberties in the Constitution. It is the power of citizens, *united*, that moves constitutional law.

Only organizations devoted to protecting constitutional rights are likely to have the capacity, expertise, resources, and persistence nec-essary to commit to the long haul. None of the campaigns recounted here would have been feasible without institutions. Activists and aca-demics often talk loosely about the importance of "social movements," and in the marriage equality story in particular, progress is attribut-able not only to specific civil society institutions but to a broader social movement. But movements without a solid institutional base are less likely to succeed. Consider, for example, Occupy Wall Street, a move-ment that inspired debate and brought much-needed attention to the growing wealth gap in America, but that in the absence of strong insti-tutions faded away without achieving lasting reform. Behind any truly successful movement for liberty are the civil society organizations that speak for, lead, and enable the movement, and that have the capacity to press for change with laser-like focus over the long term.

The need for organized *collective* action in defense of liberty under-scores the central importance of associations and institutions. President

Trump's election caused many millions of Americans to harbor grave concerns about what his presidency might mean for the country's most basic values and norms. But if that civic concern is to translate into effective limits on what Trump would like to do, it will require that citizens create, join, and support institutions whose very purpose is the defense of those values. Liberty must lie in people's hearts and minds, Learned Hand warned. But it is civil society organizations committed to those values that ensure liberty's place in our political order.

ODDLY ENOUGH, OF ALL the people I interviewed for this book on American constitutionalism, perhaps no one captured the essence of citizen movements better than the renowned British defense lawyer Gareth Peirce. Peirce has taken on some of her country's most controversial and politically challenging criminal defense cases, including alleged IRA and Muslim terrorists. She operates in a legal system without a written constitution, but her words nonetheless ring as true here as in her own country: "You know how it is, campaigning. It's years and years of starvation, famine, and then suddenly, a feast for the suspect community. . . . And it may be dangerous to think that a campaign can achieve something without using absolutely every tool you might have, regardless of what the law is."[3]

The defense of liberty ultimately depends on such campaigns. We must be willing to stand up as citizens, in coordination with others, to fight, again and again, for our core values. To recognize the importance of such popular constitutional engagement is not to reject the role of courts and formal legal institutions, but to understand that courts are only part of the process of making rights real. My hope is that the stories I've recounted in this book will inspire continued participation and association in the struggle for justice, because that is the lifeblood of liberty.

The relationship between hope and action is often misunderstood. Many people assume that it is only those who have hope who get involved in struggles for justice. But as Cornel West and Roberto Unger have written, "Hope is more the consequence of action than its cause. As the experience of the spectator favors fatalism, so the action of the agent produces hope."[4] People are not born with a "hope" chromosome. One does not engage in activism because one is hopeful. The causation runs the other way. "The action of the agent produces hope." By providing avenues for action, civil society groups foster the hope that is essential to a vibrant, living, and lived Constitution.

Chronologies

237

Massachusetts adds sexual orientation to its statewide nondiscrimination law.

1990   Vermont adds animus against gays and lesbians to its hate crimes law.

1991   Same-sex couples denied marriage licenses in Hawaii file suit in state court, initiating *Baehr v. Lewin.*

Massachusetts adds animus against gays and lesbians to its hate crimes law.

1992   Vermont prohibits discrimination on the basis of sexual orientation in employment, housing, and public accommodations.

1993   *Baehr v. Lewin,* 852 P.2d 44 (Haw. 1993): Hawaii Supreme Court rules that denying same-sex marriage is sex discrimination under Hawaii Constitution, remands for state to attempt to justify the practice in lower court.

Massachusetts and Vermont Supreme Courts allow a lesbian to adopt her partner's child (second-parent adoption).

1994   Vermont becomes first state to offer health insurance benefits to same-sex domestic partners of all state employees.

1996   Congress enacts the Defense of Marriage Act (DOMA).

San Francisco enacts a domestic partnership ordinance.

Vermont legislature codifies second-parent adoptions.

Hawaii trial court rules on remand that same-sex marriage must be recognized under Hawaii Constitution, in the renamed case *Baehr v. Miike,* No. 91–1394, 1996 WL 694235 (Cir. Ct. Haw. Dec. 3, 1996).

1997   Same-sex couples denied marriage licenses in Vermont file suit in state court, initiating *Baker v. Vermont.*

1998   *Brause v. Bureau of Vital Statistics,* 1998 WL 88743 (Alaska Super. Ct. Feb. 27, 1998): Alaska trial court rules that denying recognition to same-sex marriage is sex discrimination in violation of Alaska Constitution.

Alaska and Hawaii amend their state constitutions by referendum to ban same-sex marriage.

1999   *Baker v. Vermont,* 744 A.2d 864 (Vt. 1999): Vermont Supreme Court rules that denying benefits associated with marriage to same-sex couples violates Vermont Constitution, gives legislature choice to extend marriage or civil unions to same-sex couples.

California enacts a limited state-wide domestic partnership benefits law.

Massachusetts governor extends same-sex domestic partnership benefits to state employees.

2000 California legislature adds the right to secure senior housing for same-sex couples to its domestic partnership law.

Vermont legislature extends civil unions to same-sex couples.

Nebraska amends its constitution to ban same-sex marriage.

2001 California legislature expands domestic partnership benefits to include a range of family rights.

Same-sex couples denied marriage licenses in Massachusetts file suit in state court, initiating *Goodridge v. Dept. of Public Health*.

2002 California legislature adds inheritance rights for domestic partners.

Nevada amends its constitution, banning same-sex marriage.

2003 *Lawrence v. Texas*, 539 U.S. 558, 577 (2003): Supreme Court reverses *Bowers*, holds unconstitutional a Texas law making homosexual sodomy a crime.

California legislature adopts comprehensive domestic partnership law, extending all rights associated with marriage to domestic partners.

Evan Wolfson founds Freedom to Marry.

Maine passes limited domestic partnership law.

Goodridge v. Dept. of Pub. Health, 798 N.E.2d 941 (Mass. 2003): Massachusetts Supreme Court rules that denial of marriage to same-sex couples violates state constitution.

2004 Mayor of San Francisco authorizes San Francisco's City Hall to issue marriage licenses to same-sex couples, but California Supreme Court rules those marriages are invalid.

Thirteen more states—Arkansas, Georgia, Kentucky, Louisiana, Michigan, Mississippi, Missouri, Montana, North Dakota, Ohio, Oklahoma, Oregon, and Utah—approve constitutional amendments banning same-sex marriage.

2005 Maine legislature bans discrimination on the basis of sexual orientation in employment, housing, and other government programs.

Kansas and Texas amend their constitutions, banning same-sex marriage.

2006 Alabama, Colorado, Idaho, South Carolina, South Dakota, Tennessee, Virginia, and Wisconsin approve constitutional amendments banning same-sex marriage.

2008 *In re Marriage Cases*, 183 P.3d 384, 400–01 (Cal. 2008): California Supreme Court rules state constitution requires recognition of same-sex marriage.

Kerrigan v. Commissioner of Public Health, 289 Conn. 135, 957 A.2d 407 (Conn. 2008): Connecticut Supreme Court rules that state constitution requires recognition of same-sex marriage.

California voters approve Proposition 8, amending its constitution to ban same-sex marriage.

Arizona and Florida also approve constitutional amendments banning same-sex marriage.

2009   Vermont legislature authorizes same-sex marriage, overriding governor's veto.

Iowa, New Hampshire, and the District of Columbia legalize same-sex marriage.

Challengers to Proposition 8 file suit in federal court, initiating *Perry v. Schwarzenegger.*

Maine voters overturn legislature's recognition of same-sex marriage by referendum.

2010   *Perry v. Schwarzenegger*, 704 F.Supp.2d 921 (N.D. Cal. 2010): Federal district court invalidates Proposition 8, becoming first court to rule that failing to recognize same-sex marriage violates US Constitution.

2011   Hawaii's legislature allows civil unions.

New York legislature legalizes same-sex marriage.

2012   US Court of Appeals for the Ninth Circuit affirms district court decision in *Perry v. Schwarzenegger*, in *Perry v. Brown*, 671 F.3d 1052 (9th Cir. 2012).

North Carolina amends its constitution to ban same-sex marriage.

Maine voters legalize same-sex marriage by ballot initiative.

Washington and Maryland legalize same-sex marriage by ballot initiative.

Minnesota voters reject a constitutional amendment that would ban same-sex marriage.

2013   Hawaii's legislature legalizes same-sex marriage.

United States v. Windsor, 133 S.Ct. 2675 (2013): Supreme Court declares unconstitutional provision of DOMA denying federal benefits to same-sex couples whose states have recognized their marriages.

Hollingsworth v. Perry, 133 S.Ct. 2652 (2013): Supreme Court dismisses appeal of *Perry v. Schwarzenegger* by Proposition 8 proponents.

Seven more states—Delaware, Hawaii, Illinois, Minnesota, New Jersey, New Mexico, and Rhode Island—legalize same-sex marriage.

2014   Multiple federal courts hold that failing to recognize same-sex marriage violates the US Constitution, legalizing same-sex marriage in Alaska, Arizona, Colorado, Idaho, Indiana, Kansas, Montana, Nevada, North Carolina, Oklahoma, Oregon, Pennsylvania, South Carolina, Utah, Virginia, West Virginia, Wisconsin, and Wyoming.

US Supreme Court grants review after US Court of Appeals for the Sixth Circuit upholds same-sex marriage bans in Michigan, Ohio, Kentucky, and Tennessee.

2015   *Obergefell v. Hodges*, 135 S.Ct. 2584 (2015): Supreme Court holds that the US Constitution requires recognition of same-sex marriage nationwide.

Freedom to Marry announces that, having achieved its objective, it will disband.

PART TWO: RIGHT TO BEAR ARMS

1871   National Rifle Association (NRA) founded.

1939   *United States v. Miller*, 307 U.S. 174 (1939): Supreme Court upholds federal ban on sawed-off shotguns, in a decision widely interpreted to hold that Second Amendment protects only the states' right to maintain militias, and not individual right to bear arms.

1968   Congress enacts Gun Control Act in wake of assassinations of John F. Kennedy, Robert Kennedy, Martin Luther King Jr., and Malcolm X.

1974   First national gun control organizations, Coalition to Ban Handguns and the National Council to Control Handguns, founded.

1975   NRA creates lobbying arm, the Institute for Legislative Action (NRA-ILA).

1976   Massachusetts referendum to ban handguns fails by wide margin.

1977   In "Cincinnati revolt," NRA members replace existing leadership and commit organization to defense of an individual right to bear arms.

1981   Gun rights advocates file several lawsuits challenging ban on handguns in Morton Grove, a Chicago suburb, including *Quilici v. Village of Morton Grove*.

Stephen Halbrook publishes his first article on an individual right to bear arms, "The Jurisprudence of the Second and Fourteenth Amendments," *George Mason University Law Review* 4 (1981): 1.

1982   *Quilici v. Village of Morton Grove*, 695 F.2d 261 (7th Cir. 1982): US Court of Appeals for the Seventh Circuit rejects challenge to Morton Grove handgun ban, holding that Second Amendment protects only arms related to state militias.

NRA prioritizes promoting "preemption" laws in states, which require all gun legislation to be passed at the state level, rather than by municipalities.

California gun control referendum fails by wide margin.

Senate Judiciary Committee's Subcommittee on the Constitution publishes report supporting "individual rights" view of Second Amendment.

1983   Donald Kates publishes an article advancing the individual-rights view, "Handgun Prohibition and the Original Meaning of the Second Amendment," *Michigan Law Review* 82 (1983): 204.

1985   NRA initiates campaign to promote "shall issue" concealed carry state laws, which require states to grant concealed carry permits unless applicant is prohibited by specific criteria.

1986   Congress passes Firearms Owners Protection Act, easing restrictions imposed by the 1968 Gun Control Act.

1987   Florida adopts a "shall-issue" concealed carry law.

1989   Sanford Levinson cites historical support for individual-rights view of Second Amendment in "The Embarrassing Second Amendment," *Yale Law Journal* 90 (1989): 637.

1990   Retired Supreme Court Chief Justice Warren Burger dismisses the notion that the Second Amendment protects an individual right to bear arms as fraudulent.

1993   Congress passes the Brady Bill, mandating waiting periods for gun purchases and requiring state and local police to conduct background checks.

1994   Congress passes ban on semi-automatic "assault weapons."

Democrats lose control of the House of Representatives in the midterm election; President Clinton and others attribute loss to the NRA campaigning against representatives who supported assault-weapon ban.

1996 Joyce Malcolm argues that English right to bear arms supports individual-rights view of Second Amendment in *To Keep and Bear Arms: The Origins of an Anglo-American Right* (Cambridge, MA: Harvard University Press, 1996).

1997 *Printz v. United States*, 521 U.S. 898 (1997): Supreme Court holds unconstitutional a federal law requiring local officials to conduct background checks for gun purchases.

2001 Attorney General John Ashcroft states in a letter to the NRA his view that the Second Amendment protects an individual right to bear arms.

      United States v. Emerson, 270 F.3d 203 (5th Cir. 2001): US Court of Appeals for the Fifth Circuit becomes first federal appeals court to adopt individual-rights view of the Second Amendment.

2002 Solicitor general files briefs with Supreme Court explaining the Justice Department now takes view that Second Amendment protects an individual right to bear arms.

      Gun rights advocates file federal court challenge to DC handgun ban, *Heller v. District of Columbia*.

2004 Justice Department's Office of Legal Counsel issues a 105-page formal opinion supporting individual-rights view of Second Amendment.

2005 Forty-five states have full or partial preemption laws as a result of the NRA's preemption campaign.

      Florida adopts the first "stand your ground" state law, expanding the right to self-defense outside the home.

      Congress passes the Protection of Lawful Commerce in Arms Act, blocking tort suits against gun manufacturers and featuring official congressional endorsement of individual-rights view of Second Amendment.

      Chief Justice John Roberts joins the Court, replacing William Rehnquist.

2006 Justice Samuel Alito joins the Court, replacing Sandra Day O'Connor.

2008 *District of Columbia v. Heller*, 554 U.S. 570 (2008): Supreme Court holds for the first time that the Second Amendment protects an individual right to bear arms, striking down a District of Columbia law banning possession of handguns.

2010   *McDonald v. City of Chicago*, 561 U.S. 472 (2010): Supreme Court rules that the Second Amendment's individual right to bear arms also binds the states.

2012   *Moore v. Madigan*, 702 F.3d 933 (2012): Seventh Circuit strikes down the last remaining state law prohibiting individuals from carrying concealed firearms.

2013   Illinois legislature passes a "concealed carry" law, becoming the fiftieth state to adopt such a law.

        After mass shooting at Sandy Hook Elementary School, Congress is unable to pass a bill to extend background checks for prospective gun buyers to gun shows and Internet sales.

PART THREE: HUMAN RIGHTS IN THE WAR ON TERROR

1942   President Franklin Delano Roosevelt issues Executive Order 9066, excluding all persons of Japanese descent from the West Coast, and effectively establishing internment.

1944   *Korematsu v. United States*, 323 U.S. 214 (1944): Supreme Court upholds internment of Japanese and Japanese Americans without any evidence of espionage or sabotage.

1948   Congress provides compensation for internees who had lost property as a result of the internment in response to appeal from the Japanese American Citizens League.

1950   *Johnson v. Eisentrager*, 339 U.S. 763, 768 (1950): Supreme Court dismisses habeas corpus petitions filed by German prisoners of war convicted for war crimes and detained abroad.

1971   Congress repeals Emergency Detention Act, which authorized preventive detention, and passes in its stead the Non-Detention Act, which forbids preventive detention except where specifically authorized by Congress, in response to campaign by Japanese Americans.

1976   President Gerald Ford issues presidential proclamation condemning the internment.

1983   Congressional Commission on Wartime Relocation and Internment of Civilians denounces internment and calls for an official apology and reparations.

1984   Federal district court in San Francisco vacates Fred Korematsu's conviction, on the basis of new evidence that Justice Department misrepresented facts to Supreme Court, in *Korematsu v. United States*, 584 F.Supp. 1406 (N.D. Cal. 1984).

1988   Congress passes Civil Liberties Act of 1988, formally apologizing to internees and paying $20,000 reparations to survivors.

1998   President Clinton awards Korematsu the Presidential Medal of Freedom, the country's highest civilian honor, for his courage in fighting for justice.

2001   Al Qaeda terrorists hijack planes and fly them into World Trade Center and Pentagon, killing nearly three thousand people.

Congress passes Authorization for Use of Military Force (AUMF) against Al Qaeda and those who harbor it, and the USA PA-TRIOT Act, expanding national security authorities.

President Bush issues "Presidential Order No. 1," an executive order establishing a military tribunal to try alleged war criminals without judicial review.

President Bush secretly authorizes the CIA to detain and interrogate detainees in "war on terror."

President Bush secretly authorizes the NSA to engage in warrantless electronic surveillance of communications between US citizens and persons overseas.

Bush administration secretly begins program of "extraordinary rendition," abducting and delivering detainees to countries with a history of using torture in interrogations.

2002   Bush administration announces that Al Qaeda detainees are not protected by the Geneva Conventions.

Al Qaeda detainees brought to military prison on Guantánamo Bay Naval Base, on land leased permanently to the United States from Cuba.

The Office of Legal Counsel authorizes the CIA to use harsh interrogation techniques, including waterboarding, on Al Qaeda detainees.

Center for Constitutional Rights files suit in federal court challenging detentions at Guantánamo of Shafiq Rasul, Asif Iqbal, David Hicks, Mamdouh Habib, and Ruhal Ahmed, initiating *Rasul v. Bush*.

The district court rules that foreigners detained outside of the United States have no right to habeas corpus, in *Rasul v. Bush*, 215 F. Supp.2d 55 (D.D.C. 2002).

CCR and the ACLU file lawsuits challenging the administration's practice of holding hundreds of immigration hearings in closed sessions.

CCR files suit on behalf of immigrants detained in connection with September 11 investigation, claiming violations of their due process and equal protection rights.

The Center for National Security Studies sues to challenge the administration's refusal to identify detainees.

2003   US Court of Appeals for the DC Circuit affirms the district court's dismissal in *Rasul v. Bush* in *Al Odah v. United States*, 321 F3d 1134 (D.C. Cir. 2003), and US Supreme Court grants review.

ACLU files Freedom of Information Act request and lawsuit to obtain documents relating to interrogation of detainees in war on terror.

US government announces it intends to try two British detainees, Moazzam Begg and Feroz Abbasi, in military tribunals.

2004   Several British detainees from Guantánamo are returned home after substantial pressure from the United Kingdom, and they immediately recount stories of abuse at hands of US captors.

Photographs of prisoner abuse from Abu Ghraib in Iraq are released and published.

Washington Post publishes leaked Office of Legal Counsel memo authorizing waterboarding and other harsh interrogation methods against Al Qaeda detainees.

Rasul v. Bush, 542 U.S. 466 (2004): Supreme Court holds that Guantánamo detainees can file habeas corpus petitions challenging the legality of their detentions.

Hamdi v. Rumsfeld, 542 U.S. 507 (2004): Supreme Court rules that a US citizen held as an "enemy combatant" has constitutional right to meaningful opportunity to defend himself in fair hearing.

Bush administration begins "Combatant Status Review Tribunals" at Guantánamo Bay to determine status of detainees.

2005   A group of retired generals and admirals publicly opposes torture and presses for limits on interrogation, an effort sponsored by Human Rights First.

Congress passes the McCain Amendment, which forbids the use of any "cruel, inhuman, or degrading" treatment against foreign detainees, despite intense opposition from Bush administration.

Washington Post publishes story disclosing existence of CIA secret prisons, into which CIA "disappears" and interrogates Al Qaeda detainees.

Remaining British nationals detained at Guantánamo are returned to the United Kingdom.

The *New York Times* publishes account of the Bush administration's warrantless wiretapping program.

2006   *Hamdan v. Rumsfeld*, 548 U.S. 557 (2006): Supreme Court declares President Bush's military commissions illegal, and rejects Bush administration's position that the Geneva Conventions do not apply to Al Qaeda detainees.

Bush administration rescinds part of prior executive order that had rejected Geneva Convention protections for Al Qaeda detainees.

Congress passes Military Commissions Act of 2006, authorizing military commissions to resume.

Bush announces that all detainees in CIA secret prisons, or "black sites," have been moved to Guantánamo Bay.

President Bush says he would like to close Guantánamo.

2007   Bush administration announces that it has subjected NSA electronic surveillance program to court supervision.

Congress passes Protect America Act, authorizing electronic surveillance of foreign nationals overseas.

2008   *Boumediene v. Bush*, 553 U.S. 723 (2008): Supreme Court holds that Guantánamo detainees have constitutional right to judicial review of detention that cannot be denied short of a formal suspension of the writ of habeas corpus.

2009   President Bush leaves office, having released more than five hundred Guantánamo detainees.

President Obama takes office, issues executive orders closing CIA secret prisons and banning torture and other cruel interrogation techniques; he promises to close Guantánamo within a year.

Congress enacts Military Commissions Act of 2009, barring the use of involuntary confessions, providing additional independent appellate review, and conforming military commissions more closely to the court-martial procedures used for trying American soldiers.

2010   The Obama administration escalates use of drone strikes in Pakistan, Yemen, and Somalia, while refusing to acknowledge it is doing so.

State Department legal advisor Harold Koh makes speech publicly defending drone strikes for first time, and responding to human rights critics.

2011   Obama administration uses a drone to kill an American citizen, Anwar al-Awlaki, in Yemen.

2012   John Brennan, chief counterterrorism advisor to President Obama, and Attorney General Eric Holder give public speeches describing and defending the US drone strike policy.

2013   President Obama gives speech at National Defense University setting forth a restrictive policy for drone strikes outside of traditional battlefields, and issues guidelines implementing those restrictions.

The number of drone strikes in Pakistan and Yemen begins to drop substantially.

Edward Snowden, a consultant to the NSA, discloses classified documents detailing extensive electronic surveillance by the NSA at home and abroad, stirring global criticism of the scope of the NSA's actions.

2014   President Obama announces that he will impose several reforms to rein in NSA electronic surveillance, adopting recommendations of an expert review group he appointed in the wake of Snowden revelations.

Obama administration tells UN Committee on Torture that it has reversed its longstanding position and now takes the view that the Convention Against Torture applies abroad in some instances, and in times of war.

2015   *ACLU v. Clapper*, No. 14–42, 2015 WL 4196833 (2d Cir. June 9, 2015): US Court of Appeals for the Second Circuit rules that the NSA domestic telephone metadata program was illegal, as it was not authorized by Congress.

Congress passes USA Freedom Act, ending NSA's bulk collection of telephone metadata, and marking the first federal law imposing restrictions on electronic surveillance since 9/11.

Acknowledgments

THIS BOOK COULD NOT HAVE BEEN WRITTEN WITHOUT THE GENEROUS INPUT OF MANY COMMITTED constitutional activists, lawyers, and scholars. For each of the rights campaigns I cover, I interviewed many of those who were directly involved. These interviews provided crucial perspective on each campaign's tactics and strategies, on what worked and what didn't work, and on the challenges of advocating for constitutional reform. All quotations were specifically approved for use by the speaker.

I am grateful to all who agreed to speak with me, including John Adams, James Baker, John Bellinger, Mary Bonauto, Kevin Cathcart, Matt Coles, Chris Cox, Greg Craig, Chuck Cunningham, Jackson Darling, Jennifer Daskal, Jon Davidson, James Esseks, Dave Fleischer, Richard Fontaine, Joan Garry, Steve Halbrook, Julia Hall, Marion Hammer, Leif Hendrickson, Nan Hunter, John Hutson, David Irvine, Rebecca Isaacs, Jameel Jaffer, Wolfgang Kaleck, David Keene, Kate Kendell, Harold Koh, Marty Lederman, David Lehman, Robert Levy, William Lietzau, Joyce Malcolm, Tom Malinowski, Joe Margulies, Joanne Mariner, Elisa Massimino, Moof Mayeda, Matt McTighe, Alberto Mora, Susan Murray, Charles Otstott, Katherine Peck, Gareth Peirce, Jennifer Pizer, Michael Ratner, Sarah Reece, Beth Robinson, Kayne Robinson, Chris Rogers, Anthony Romero, Marc Rotenberg, Brad Sears, Stephen Shapiro, Amy Simon, Betsy Smith, Clive Stafford Smith, Paul Smith, Jack Straw, Therese Stewart, Tim Sweeney, William Howard Taft IV, Linda Walker, Phyllis Watts, Matthew Waxman, Tobias Wolff, Evan Wolfson, and Doreena Wong.

The book also benefited from discussions with and comments on draft chapters from Ken Anderson, Leonard Bernado, William Eskridge, Ryan Goodman, Mort Halperin, Stephen Hubbell, Nan Hunter, Andrew Koppelman, Jules Lobel, Allegra McLeod, Aryeh Neier, Nina Pillard, Steve Rickard, Mike Seidman, Amanda Shanor, Stephen Shapiro, Amrit Singh, Sidney Tarrow, and Adam Winkler.

I had tremendous research assistance from Noah Baron, Alyssa Kaercher, Jacob Kenswil, T.J. McCarrick, Bill Margeson, Maggie Nivison, Aparna Krishnaswamy Patrie, Reid Rector, Bethany Rishell, and the fabulous research librarian staff at the Georgetown Law Library. My assistant, Sarah Naiman, worked tirelessly on the manuscript. And Betsy Kuhn did a very careful proofreading job.

My editor, Dan Gerstle, and my copyeditor, Karl Yambert, improved the book many times over. And my agent, Sam Stoloff of Frances Goldin Literary Agency, has been a sure and steady guide throughout.

I presented early versions of the ideas in this book at a variety of workshops, including at Georgetown Law, Yale Law School, the Open Society Foundations, University of Toronto Law School, NYU Law School, and the Center for Transnational Legal Studies in London.

I received generous financial support for my research from the Open Society Foundations, with which I had a fellowship in 2013–14, and from Georgetown University Law Center.

I have been personally involved in litigating for human rights and civil liberties in the "war on terror," often as co-counsel with lawyers from the Center for Constitutional Rights (CCR) and the American Civil Liberties Union (ACLU), including in several cases mentioned in the book. I began my career at CCR, and after becoming a law professor, continued to litigate cases as a cooperating attorney with CCR for more than two decades. Michael Ratner, who at various times has been legal director, board member, and president of CCR, and to whom this book is dedicated, was an inspiring mentor as I began my career, and helped shape my understanding of how constitutionalism works.

Finally, I am ever grateful to the love of my life, Nina Pillard, and to the two brightest stars in our firmament, Aidan and Sarah. They sustain me.

—*David Cole*
Washington, DC, October 2015

Notes

INTRODUCTION

1. In 2016 the PEN American Center changed its name to simply PEN America.

2. Learned Hand, "The Spirit of Liberty," speech at "I Am an American Day" ceremony, Central Park, New York, May 21, 1944.

3. David Cole, "Trump in Court," *New York Review of Books, NYR Daily*, February 10, 2017.

4. Evan Wolfson (founder, Freedom to Marry), interview with author, 2013; *Baker v. Nelson*, 291 Minn. 310 (1971), *appeal dismissed*, 409 U.S. 810 (1972); Michael J. Klarman, *From the Closet to the Altar: Courts, Backlash, and the Struggle for Same-Sex Marriage* (New York: Oxford University Press, 2013), 19–20; Michael Boucai, "Glorious Precedents: When Gay Marriage Was Radical," *Yale Journal of Law & the Humanities* 27 (2015): 1.

5. *Obergefell v. Hodges*, 135 S.Ct. 2584 (2015); Dara Lind, "What's Next for One Same-Sex Marriage Group? Nothing. They've Won.," *Vox*, June 25, 2015 (quoting Wolfson as saying Freedom to Marry will close "in months"); Evan Wolfson, "What's Next in the Fight for Gay Equality," *New York Times*, June 26, 2015.

6. Marion Hammer (former president, NRA), interview with author, 2014.

7. *United States v. Miller*, 307 U.S. 174 (1939); Warren Burger, "The Right to Bear Arms," *Parade*, January 14, 1990; "History and the Law: Debunking the NRA Myth," Sane Guns, http://www.saneguns.org/law/nramythquotes .html (quoting Warren Burger's statement on the MacNeil/Lehrer *NewsHour*, December 16, 1991); Robert H. Bork, *Slouching Towards Gomorrah: Modern Liberalism and American Decline* (New York: Regan Books/HarperCollins, 1996), 166; *District of Columbia v. Heller*, 554 U.S. 570 (2008).

8. Michael Ratner (president emeritus, CCR), interview with author, 2012; *Johnson v. Eisentrager*, 339 U.S. 763 (1950). In the interests of full disclosure, I began my legal career working with the Center for Constitutional Rights, continued to litigate cases pro bono for the center throughout my career, and served on its board from the early 1990s until 2013.

9. Thom Shanker and David E. Sanger, "New to Job, Gates Argued for Closing Guantánamo," *New York Times*, March 23, 2007 (noting that Bush, Rice, and Gates all wanted to close Guantánamo); Exec. Order No. 13,492 § 2(b), 3 C.F.R. § 13492 (2010) (stating that in the preceding seven years, over five hundred detainees were removed from Guantánamo). For most recent numbers see "The Guantánamo Docket," "The Detainees," *New York Times*, at https://www.nytimes.com/interactive/projects/guantanamo/detainees.

10. "Civil society" is a broad term that generally encompasses all nongovernmental institutions, including the press, the academy, religion, fraternal organizations, local community groups, and the like. My interest here is in the particular role played by groups that define themselves by their commitment to particular constitutional values. These organizations' very purpose is to affect constitutional law. Other civil society actors, including the press and the academy, often help to shape constitutional law as well, but generally in a more episodic way, as that is not their reason for being.

11. Richard Kluger, *Simple Justice: The History of* Brown v. Board of Education *and Black America's Struggle for Equality* (New York: Knopf, 1976).

12. Political scientists and sociologists have long recognized that there are important connections among public opinion, social movements, and constitutional law. But for the most part, they have tended to focus on broad movements and opinion trends rather than on advocacy organizations that seek to transform a particular aspect of constitutional law and practice. And social movement scholars have also paid less attention to the particular demands of constitutional change, as opposed to other sorts of reforms.

In recent years, legal scholars have also begun to pay more attention to how the Constitution operates outside the courts. "Popular constitutionalism" seeks to reorient constitutional theory away from the traditional focus on courts to a consideration of the role of the people, and of the political branches, in constitutional law. Some scholars are openly hostile to what they call "judicial supremacy," namely, the notion that the Supreme Court has the final say on constitutional questions. Mark Tushnet, for example, argues that the Supreme Court should not have the power to declare actions of the other branches unconstitutional, while Larry Kramer maintains that "we the people," not the Court, should have the final say on constitutional questions. Mark Tushnet, *Taking the Constitution Away from the Courts* (Princeton, NJ: Princeton University Press, 1999); Larry D. Kramer, *The People Themselves: Popular Constitutionalism and Judicial Review* (Oxford, England: Oxford University Press, 2004). They believe that the Court's final authority on constitutional issues has undermined democracy and civic participation on the most important issues of the day. For powerful refutations of these arguments for undermining judicial review see Larry Alexander and Lawrence B. Solum, "Popular? Constitutionalism?," *Harvard Law Review* 118 (2005): 1603 (reviewing Larry D. Kramer, *The People Themselves*); Erwin Chemerinsky, "In Defense of Judicial Review: The Perils of Popular Constitutionalism," *University of Illinois Law Review* 3 (2004): 673.

My own take is more consistent with what Robert Post and Reva Siegel have called "democratic constitutionalism." This approach is less critical of the courts than is popular constitutionalism but emphasizes the important dynamic interplay between judicial decisions on constitutional matters and social movements. See Robert Post and Reva Siegel, "Roe Rage: Democratic Constitutionalism and Backlash," *Harvard Civil Rights–Civil Liberties Law Review* 42 (2007): 373; Reva B. Siegel, "Dead or Alive: Originalism as Popular Constitutionalism in *Heller*," *Harvard Law Review* 122 (2008): 191; see also William N. Eskridge Jr., "Channeling: Identity-Based Social Movements and Public Law," *University of Pennsylvania Law Review* 150 (2001): 419.

For social science analysis of constitutional change see Nathaniel Persily, Jack Citrin, and Patrick J. Egan, *Public Opinion and Constitutional Controversy* (Oxford, England: Oxford University Press, 2008); see also Gerald Rosenberg, *The Hollow Hope: Can Courts Bring About Social Change?* 2d ed. (Chicago: University of Chicago Press, 2008). "Social movement" scholars also study the relationship between political action and social change, although they do not necessarily focus on the particular case of *constitutional* change, and they are often more interested in theorizing about movement dynamics at an abstract level than in examining the particular strategies of specific organizations within a movement. See, e.g., Sidney Tarrow, *Power in Movements and Contentious Politics*, 2d ed. (Cambridge, England: Cambridge University Press, 1998); Michael McCann, ed., *Law and Social Movements* (Burlington, VT: Ashgate, 2006); Doug McAdam, *Political Process and the Development of*

Black Insurgency, 1930–1970, 2d ed. (Chicago: University of Chicago Press, 1999). For an interesting application of these theories to legal change see Eskridge, "Channeling," 419.

In many of the above accounts, the precise mechanics of how the people help shape constitutional law are left vague. As David Pozen writes, "hardly any attention has been paid to questions of institutional design." David E. Pozen, "Judicial Elections as Popular Constitutionalism," *Columbia Law Review* 110 (2010): 2050. Pozen looks to the election of state judges; Kramer speaks of mob rule and jury nullification; Yale Law professor Jack Balkin and University of Texas law professor Sanford Levinson point to the confirmation process for federal judges. Jack M. Balkin and Sanford Levinson, "Understanding the Constitutional Revolution," *Virginia Law Review* 87 (2001): 1045. Balkin has also suggested that legal arguments once considered frivolous or hopeless can gain legitimacy if they are adopted by powerful constituencies—including intellectuals, social movements, political parties, or the public at large. Jack Balkin, "How Social Movements Change (or Fail to Change) the Constitution: The Case of the New Departure," *Suffolk Law Review* 39 (2005): 27; Jack Balkin, "From off the Wall to on the Wall: How the Mandate Challenge Went Mainstream," *Atlantic*, June 4, 2012.

These are important correctives to the all-too-often blindered focus of constitutional law teaching and scholarship on Supreme Court decisions. But most of them pay insufficient attention to the civil society organizations that actually do much of the work of constitutionalism. As the stories recounted here illustrate, the existence of robust judicial review has not, as Tushnet and Kramer fear, diminished political engagement in constitutional issues; it is alive and well in modern-day civil society organizations defined for precisely that purpose. Nonprofit groups committed to constitutionalism have never been more robust or active in American history. These groups' influence on the evolution of constitutional law is far more complex and multidimensional than the appointment of judges, although, as we shall see, judicial appointments are sometimes part of the story. While the Supreme Court plays an important role, to be sure, in articulating constitutional doctrine, I argue here that the bulk of constitutionalism actually takes place away from the Court altogether. And it is not enough to trace the evolution of ideas, "social movements," or public opinion. These are important aspects of the story, to be sure, but they are supplemented in important ways by the particular contributions made by civil society organizations devoted to constitutional rights. If one is interested in what one can *do* to effectuate constitutional change, surely the best place to look is to those organizations that have intentionally sought to do just that, and succeeded.

13. Some people, most notably the late Justice Antonin Scalia, dismiss the concept of a living Constitution and insist that the only legitimate way to interpret the document is to divine its "original meaning" at the time of the Framing. Antonin Scalia and Bryan A. Garner, *Reading Law: The Interpretation of Legal Texts* (St. Paul, MN: Thompson/West, 2012). In Scalia's "originalist" view, any other method of judicial interpretation invites unelected judges to impose their own personal values. The stories told here illustrate, however, that in fact constitutional law does evolve over time, and that its content is determined not by the views of long-dead Framers, or by justices' personal preferences, but by ongoing public debates, informed and often driven by organizations dedicated to constitutional principles. In *Planned Parenthood of Southeastern Pennsylvania v. Casey*, Justice Scalia expressed distress "about the 'political pressure' directed to the Court: the marches, the mail, the protests aimed at inducing us to change our opinions. How upsetting it is that so many of our citizens ... think that we Justices should properly take into account their views, as though we were engaged not in ascertaining an objective law, but in determining some kind of social consensus." *Planned Parenthood of Southeastern Pennsylvania v. Casey*, 505 U.S. 833, 999–1000 (1992) (Scalia, dissenting).

But the responsiveness of constitutional law to developing social norms is a historical fact—and given the open-ended character of many of the Constitution's guarantees, it is inevitable. However one might wish the Court to act, we have over two hundred years of evidence showing how it actually does act. The Court holds fast to our time-honored fundamental commitments but is also flexible enough to adapt them when, over a sustained period, the commitments themselves change. The original understanding offers a starting point; but especially when constitutional rights are broadly defined, as in "due process" or "equal protection," development over time is to be expected. This flexibility is a strength, not a weakness. It keeps the Constitution alive for each generation and ensures that it is not relegated to the dead hand of the past.

PART ONE: MARRIAGE EQUALITY

1. Jonathan Ned Katz, *Gay American History* (New York: Thomas Y. Crowell Co., 1976), 413.

2. Frank Kameny, "Government v. Gays: Two Sad Stories with Two Happy Endings, Civil Service Employment and Security Clearances," in *Creating Change: Sexuality, Public Policy, and Civil Rights*, ed. John D. Emilio et al. (New York: St. Martin's Press, 2000), 192.

3. William N. Eskridge Jr., *Equality Practice: Civil Unions and the Future of Gay Rights* (New York: Routledge, 2002), 1.

4. Matthew Coles (Deputy Legal Director and Director of Center for Equality, ACLU), interview with author, 2014. See, e.g., *Gay Students Organization of University of New Hampshire v. Bonner*, 509 F.2d 652 (1st Cir. 1974).

5. Randy Shilts, *And the Band Played On: Politics, People, and the AIDS Epidemic* (New York: St. Martin's Press, 2007).

6. Ibid.

7. In 1990, only about two dozen US corporations extended domestic partner benefits to same-sex partners. By 2000, Human Rights Campaign (HRC) reported that 3,572 private corporations, colleges and universities, and state and local governments provided such benefits. By 2005, the number was up to 9,370. Domestic partner benefits for same-sex couples began as an exception, but over time became the norm. Gerald N. Rosenberg, *The Hollow Hope: Can Courts Bring About Social Change?* (Chicago: University of Chicago Press, 2008), 410–411 (citing HRC reports).

In 2000, 1,708 private corporations, colleges and universities, and government employers had policies prohibiting discrimination on the basis of sexual orientation. By 2005, that number had jumped to 2,958. By 2006, 430 of the nation's Fortune 500 companies prohibited discrimination on the basis of sexual orientation. By 2014, twenty-one states and the District of Columbia prohibited discrimination on the basis of sexual orientation. Rosenberg, *The Hollow Hope*, 412–413 (citing HRC reports); "State Nondiscrimination Laws in the US," National Gay and Lesbian Task Force, http://www.thetaskforce.org/downloads/reports/issue_maps/non_discrimination_5_14_color.pdf.

8. Joan Garry (former Executive Director of GLAAD), interview with author, 2014. For a detailed examination of the cultural shifts that have affected gay rights, see William N. Eskridge Jr. and John Ferejohn, *Republic of Statutes: The New American Constitution* (New Haven: Yale University Press, 2010), 349–386.

CHAPTER 1: THE VISION

1. Michael Boucai, "Glorious Precedents: When Gay Marriage Was Radical," *Yale Journal of Law & the Humanities* 27 (2015): 1; see, e.g., *Slayton v. State*, 633 S.W.2d 934, 937 (1982) (stating that it is not possible in Texas for a marriage to exist between persons of the same sex); *Adams v. Howerton*, 486 F. Supp. 1119 (C.D. Cal. 1980) (rejecting the appeal of a California man attempting to marry an Australian man), *aff'd*, 673 F.2d 1036 (9th Cir. 1982); *Francis B. v. Mark B.*, 355 N.Y.S.2d 712, 716 (N.Y. Sup. Ct. 1974) (defining marriage in the state of New York as a union between one man and one

woman); *Baker v. Nelson*, 191 N.W. 2d 185 (Minn. 1971) (upholding Minnesota's refusal to grant same-sex marriage license), *aff'd on other grounds*, 409 U.S. 810 (1972); *McConnell v. Nooner*, 547 F.2d 54 (8th Cir. 1976) (upholding Veterans Administration denial of spousal education benefits to a veteran's same-sex partner); *Bowers v. Hardwick*, 478 U.S. 186 (1986) (upholding Georgia sodomy statute against a constitutional challenge).

2. Evan Wolfson, "Samesex Marriage and Morality: the Human Rights Vision of the Constitution" (student paper, Harvard Law School, 1983), 30.

3. Wolfson, "Samesex Marriage and Morality," 73; *Bowers*, 478 U.S. at 216 (1986) (Stevens, dissenting); *Lawrence v. Texas*, 539 U.S. 558, 577 (2003) (quoting Justice Stevens's dissent in *Bowers*).

4. Michael Klarman, *From the Closet to the Altar: Courts, Backlash, and the Struggle for Same-Sex Marriage* (Oxford, England: Oxford University Press, 2013), 48; Jon Davidson (National Legal Director, Lambda) and Jennifer Pizer (Law and Policy Project National Director, Lambda), interview with author, 2013.

5. Paula Ettelbrick and Tom Stoddard, "Gay Marriage: A Must or a Bust?" *Out/Look* 2 (1989): 8–17. For a nuanced account of the debate, and of the complex interrelationship between marriage and alternative forms of domestic partnerships, see Doug NeJaime, "Before Marriage: The Unexplored History of Nonmarital Recognition and Its Relationship to Marriage," *California Law Review* 102 (2014): 87.

6. Tom Stoddard, "Why Gay People Should Seek the Right to Marry," *Out/Look* 2 (1989): 9, 10–11.

7. One early exception was *Dean v. District of Columbia*, 653 A.2d 307 (D.C.1995), in which a gay couple advanced a federal constitutional argument as a basis for interpreting a DC statute to encompass same-sex marriage. When both the DC trial court and the DC Court of Appeals rejected their claims, however, Dean and his partner wisely did not seek Supreme Court review. Had they prevailed in the lower courts, their case could have been reviewed (and likely reversed) by the Supreme Court, because the couple advanced a federal constitutional claim.

8. *Baehr v. Lewin*, 852 P.2d 44 (Haw. 1993); Evan Wolfson (Founder and President, Freedom to Marry), interview with author, 2012.

9. Quoted in Klarman, *From the Closet*, 57.

10. Klarman, *From the Closet*, 58–59.

11. *Baehr v. Miike*, No. 91–1394, 1996 WL 694235 (Haw. Cir. Ct. Dec. 3, 1996); Wolfson, interview.

12. Wolfson, interview; Klarman, *From the Closet*, 55–73. For other accounts of *Baehr* and its aftermath, see Ellen Ann Anderson, *Out of the Closets and*

into the Courts: Legal Opportunity Structure and Gay Rights Litigation (Ann Arbor, MI: University of Michigan Press, 2004), 178–83; Michael D. Sant'Ambrogio and Sylvia A. Law, "Baehr v. Lewin and the Long Road to Marriage Equality," *University of Hawai'i Law Review* 33 (2011): 716–19.

13. *Brause v. Bureau of Vital Statistics*, 1998 WL 88743 (Alaska Super. Ct. Feb. 27, 1998; Klarman, *From the Closet*, 66-68.

14. See, e.g., Evan Wolfson, *Why Marriage Matters: America, Equality, and Gay People's Right to Marry* (New York: Simon & Schuster, 2004); Evan Wolfson, "Momentum 2012: The Freedom to Marry," *Tides: Momentum Magazine*, June 10, 2012; Evan Wolfson, "Obama Showed Moral Leadership with Gay Marriage Support," *U.S. News & World Report*, May 11, 2012; Evan Wolfson, "The Anti-Gay Base is Shrinking," *New York Times*, April 16, 2012; Evan Wolfson, "The Scary Work of Winning" (keynote address, Lavender Law, Minneapolis, MN, October 4, 2004).

15. Wolfson, interview, 2014; Mary Bonauto (director, Civil Rights Project, GLAD), interview with author, 2013; Matthew Coles (Deputy Legal Director and Director of Center for Equality, ACLU), interview with author, 2014. *Perez v. Sharp*, 198 P.2d 17 (Cal. 1948); *Loving v. Virginia*, 388 U.S. 1 (1967); see Nancy F. Cott, *Public Vows: A History of Marriage and the Nation* (Cambridge, MA: Harvard University Press, 2002), 98–100 (describing evolution of laws on miscegenation); Jonathan Grossman, "The Origin of the U.S. Department of Labor," Department of Labor, http://www.dol.gov/dol/aboutdol/history/dolorigabridge.htm (discussing the state-by-state strategy in the movement for a national Department of Labor). For a timeline of states granting women suffrage before the enactment of the Nineteenth Amendment, see National Constitution Center, Centuries of Citizenship: A Constitutional Timeline, Map: States grant women the right to vote, at http://constitutioncenter.org/timeline/html/cw08_12159.html. For an account of the political campaign for abortion rights before *Roe v. Wade*, see Linda Greenhouse and Reva B. Siegel, "Before (and After) Roe v. Wade: New Questions About Backlash," *Yale Law Journal* 120 (2011): 2028; Lawrence Lader, *Abortion II: Making the Revolution* (Beacon Press, 1973) 70, 116–118, 172. Prior to *Roe*, fourteen states had legalized abortion under some circumstances, and four had repealed all prohibitions. Sarah Kliff, "Thirteen Charts That Explain How *Roe v. Wade* Changed Abortion Rights," *Washington Post*, January 22, 2014. For a general discussion of the role that federalism plays in the development of constitutional rights, see Heather K. Gerken, "Federalism as the New Nationalism: An Overview," *Yale Law Journal* 123 (2013): 1889–1918; Heather K. Gerken, "The Loyal Opposition," *Yale Law Journal* 123 (2014): 1958–1994.

CHAPTER 2: A MARATHON, NOT A SPRINT: VERMONT

1. Beth Robinson (Associate Justice, Vermont Supreme Court) and Susan Murray (Attorney, Langrock, Sperry, and Wool), interview with the author, 2014. For a comprehensive account of the initial battle for marriage equality in Vermont, see Michael Mello, *Legalizing Gay Marriage: Vermont and the National Debate* (Philadelphia: Temple University Press, 2004).

2. Vt. Const. ch 1, art. 7; Robinson and Murray, interview.

3. Susan Murray, e-mail to author, August 20, 2014.

4. Robinson and Murray, interview.

5. See Kees Waaldijk, "Standard Sequences in the Legal Recognition of Homosexuality—Europe's Past Present and Future," *Australian Gay & Lesbian Law Journal* 4 (1994): 50, 51–52; Kees Waaldijk, "Towards the Recognition of Same-sex Partners in European Union Law: Expectations Based on Trends in National Law," and "Small Changes: How the Road to Same-Sex Marriage Got Paved in the Netherlands," in *Legal Recognition of Same-Sex Partnerships: A Study of National, European and International Law*, eds. Robert Wintemute and Mads Andenas (Oxford: Hart Publishing, 2001), 638–639, 437–464.

6. See William N. Eskridge Jr., *Equality Practice: Civil Unions and the Future of Gay Rights* (New York: Routledge, 2002), 45; Michael Klarman, *From the Closet to the Altar: Courts, Backlash, and the Struggle for Same-Sex Marriage* (New York: Oxford University Press, 2013), 75.

7. Vt. Const. ch. 2, art. 72.

8. Robinson and Murray, interview; Mary Bonauto (Director, Civil Rights Project, GLAD), interview with author, 2013.

9. Bonauto, interview.

10. *Baker v. Vermont*, 744 A.2d 864, 888 (Vt. 1999) (quoting Cass Sunstein, "Foreword: Leaving Things Undecided," *Harvard Law Review* 110 (1996): 101). The court was unanimous as to the constitutional violation, but Justice Johnson wrote separately regarding the remedy, maintaining that the plaintiffs should be given marriage licenses without any intervening legislative process.

11. Klarman, *From the Closet*, 79.

12. Adam Lisberg, "Panel Backs Gay Partnership," *Burlington Free Press*, Feb. 10, 2000, 1A.

13. Klarman, *From the Closet*, 79.

14. Thomas M. Keck, "Beyond Backlash: Assessing the Impact of Judicial Decisions on LGBT Rights," *Law and Society Review* 43 (2009): 162; Bonauto, interview.

15. Bonauto, interview; Robinson and Murray, interview.

CHAPTER 3: ONE STEP FORWARD, HOW MANY BACK? MASSACHUSETTS

1. Mary Bonauto, "*Goodridge* in Context," *Harvard Civil Rights–Civil Liberties Law Review* 40 (2005): 26–27.

2. *Goodridge v. Department of Public Health*, 798 N.E.2d 941, 960 (Mass. 2003).

3. *Goodridge*, 798 N.E.2d at 970; David Lampo, *A Fundamental Freedom: Why Republicans, Conservatives and Libertarians Should Support Gay Rights* (Lanham, MD: Rowman and Littlefield Publishers, 2012), 58 (Massachusetts was the sixth jurisdiction in the world to recognize same-sex marriage).

4. Mary Bonauto (Director, Civil Rights Project, GLAD), interview with author, 2013; Michael Klarman, *From the Closet to the Altar: Courts, Backlash, and the Struggle for Same-Sex Marriage* (New York: Oxford University Press, 2013), 89–118. For an excellent and detailed inside account of the Massachusetts battle that followed *Goodridge*, see Marc Solomon, *Winning Marriage: The Inside Story of How Same-Sex Couples Took on the Politicians and Pundits—and Won* (Lebanon, NH: ForeEdge, 2014), 3–146. Solomon was the director of MassEquality, and later became the national campaign director for Freedom to Marry.

5. Klarman, *From the Closet*, 95–97.

6. Gerald N. Rosenberg, "Courting Disaster: Looking for Change in All the Wrong Places," *Drake Law Review* 54 (2006): 812; Gerald N. Rosenberg, *The Hollow Hope: Can Courts Bring About Social Change?* (Chicago: University of Chicago Press, 2008), 343; Klarman, *From the Closet*, 105–106; John D'Emilio, "The Marriage Fight Is Setting Us Back," *Gay and Lesbian Review Worldwide* November-December (2006).

7. Thomas Keck, "Beyond Backlash: Assessing the Impact of Judicial Decisions on LGBT Rights," *Law & Society Review* 43 (2009): 153.

8. William N. Eskridge, Jr., "Backlash Politics: How Constitutional Litigation has Advanced Marriage Equality in the United States," *Boston University Law Review* 93 (2013): 282 ("For a minority whose members were socially disparaged and politically toxic, courts were virtually the only forums where minority group members can seek decent treatment from the state.")

9. Daniel Pinello, *America's Struggle for Same-Sex Marriage* (Cambridge, England: Cambridge University Press, 2006), 190–193; Keck, "Beyond Backlash," 158–159.

10. Evan Wolfson (Founder and President, Freedom to Marry), interview with author, 2014. See also Michael C. Dorf and Sidney Tarrow, "Strange Bedfellows: How an Anticipatory Countermovement Brought Same-Sex Marriage into the Public Arena," *Law & Social Inquiry* 39 (2014): 449–473. For a sophisticated exploration of the many ways that movements and coun-

termovements can interact and reinforce each other, see David S. Meyer and Suzanne Staggenborg, "Movements, Countermovements, and the Structure of Political Opportunity," *American Journal of Sociology* 101 (1996): 1628–1660.

11. *Winning Marriage: What We Need to Do*, June 21, 2005, on file with author. The group included Mary Bonauto, Rea Carey from the National Gay and Lesbian Task Force, Michael Adams from Lambda Legal, Toni Broaddus from the Equality Federation, Seth Kilbourn from Human Rights Campaign, Shannon Minter from the National Center for Lesbian Rights, Alexander Robinson from the National Black Justice Coalition, and Roey Thorpe from Basic Rights Oregon. The document is not generally available to the public, but was shared with me on background by more than one participant, on the condition that I could describe its content but not quote from it.

CHAPTER 4: A VICTORY LOST—AND REGAINED: CALIFORNIA

1. Jon Davidson (National Legal Director, Lambda) and Jennifer Pizer (Law and Policy Project National Director, Lambda), interview with author, 2013; Matthew Coles (Deputy Legal Director and Director of Center for Equality, ACLU), interview with author, 2014. See also Scott L. Cummings and Douglas NeJaime, "Lawyering for Marriage Equality," *UCLA Law Review* 57 (2010): 1253; ibid. at 1255 (quoting Pizer).

2. Cummings and NeJaime, "Lawyering for Marriage Equality," 1257; see also Douglas NeJaime, "Before Marriage: The Unexplored History of Nonmarriage Recognition and Its Relationship to Marriage," *California Law Review* 102 (2014): 87.

3. 2003 Cal. Legis. Serv. 2586, 2588 (West) (codified at Cal. Fam. Code § 297.5); see generally Cummings and NeJaime, "Lawyering for Marriage Equality," 1263–68.

4. Cummings and NeJaime, "Lawyering for Marriage Equality," 1270 (quoting Jon W. Davidson, "Memorandum on Amendment of the California Constitution to California Marriage Litigation Roundtable," Lambda Legal, December 16, 2002).

5. Kate Kendell (Executive Director, National Center for Lesbian Rights), interview with author, 2013.

6. Daniel R. Pinello, *America's Struggle for Same-Sex Marriage* (Cambridge, England: Cambridge University Press, 2006), 79 (quoting Molly McKay).

7. Kendell, interview; Therese Stewart (Chief Deputy City Attorney for the City and County of San Francisco), interview with author, 2013; *Lockyer v. City of San Francisco*, 2004 WL 473257 (Cal. S. Ct. Mar. 11, 2004).

8. Cummings and NeJaime, "Lawyering for Marriage Equality," 1284 (quoting telephone interview with Pizer).

9. *In re Marriage Cases*, 183 P.3d 384, 400–01 (Cal. 2008).

10. Marc Solomon, *Winning Marriage: The Inside Story of How Same-Sex Couples Took on the Politicians and Pundits—and Won* (Lebanon, NH: ForeEdge, 2014), 226–227; Dave Fleischer (Political Consultant, LA Gay and Lesbian Community Center), interview with author, 2013.

11. *Loving v. Virginia*, 388 U.S. 1 (1967); *Gideon v. Wainwright*, 372 U.S. 335 (1963); *Lawrence v. Texas*, 539 U.S. 558 (2003); see also Dale Carpenter, *Flagrant Conduct: The Story of Lawrence v. Texas* (New York: W.W. Norton, 2011), 183. Thirty-five states required appointment of counsel in non-capital criminal cases before *Gideon*. Brief for the State Government Amici Curiae, p. 10, *Gideon v. Wainwright*, 372 U.S. 335 (1963).

12. *Perry v. Schwarzenegger*, 704 F.Supp.2d 921 (N.D.Cal.2010).

13. See, e.g., *In re Marriage Cases*, 183 P.3d 384; *Kerrigan v. Commissioner of Public Health*, 957 A.2d 407 (Conn. 2008); *Baker v. Vermont*, 744 A.2d 864 (Vt. 1999); *Goodridge v. Department of Public Health*, 798 N.E.2d 941 (Mass. 2003); *Varnum v. Brien*, 763 N.W.2d 862 (Iowa 2009).

14. *Perry v. Schwarzenegger*, 628 F.3d 1191 (9th Cir. 2011).

15. *Hollingsworth v. Perry*, 133 S. Ct. 2653 (2013).

16. Jo Becker, *Forcing the Spring: Inside the Fight for Marriage Equality* (New York: Penguin, 2013), 3; David Boies and Ted Olson, *Redeeming the Dream: The Case for Marriage Equality* (New York: Viking, 2014).

CHAPTER 5: LOSING FORWARD: MAINE

1. Molly Ball, "How Gay Marriage Became a Constitutional Right," *Atlantic*, July 1, 2015. Arizona voters in 2006 narrowly rejected an amendment that would not only have banned same-sex marriages but any legal status affording rights or benefits to same-sex couples; the victory was short-lived, however, as two years later, Arizona voters approved a narrower referendum limiting marriage to the union of a man and a woman. Michael Klarman, *From the Closet to the Altar: Courts, Backlash, and the Struggle for Same-Sex Marriage* (Oxford, England: Oxford University Press, 2013), 115.

2. Betsy Smith (Executive Director, EqualityMaine), interview with author, 2013; Dave Fleischer (Political Consultant, LA Gay and Lesbian Community Center), interview with author, 2013.

3. Sarah Reece (Organizer, National LGBTQ Task Force), interview with author, 2015.

4. In the summer of 2015, the journal *Science* retracted a study it had pub-

lished in December 2014 claiming to have shown that short conversations could change voters' minds about marriage equality. Marcia McNutt, "Editorial Expression of Concern on LaCour and Green," *Science* 5 (June 2015): 1100. The paper, entitled "When contact changes minds: An experiment on transmission of support for gay equality," was written by Columbia University professor David Green and a graduate student, Michael LaCour. LaCour was responsible for gathering the data, but when questions arose about the data's validity, he was unable to produce it. Green agreed to the retraction. The findings noted in the text are those of advocates and campaigners, not social scientists. I spoke with several individuals, including door-to-door canvassers and their supervisors, who reported similar experiences with the kind of extended conversations Dave Fleischer pioneered. But the method remains to be tested by rigorous social science standards.

5. "Case Study: Marriage for Gay Couples," Third Way, http://www.thirdway.org/case-study/marriage-for-gay-couples; Marc Solomon, *Winning Marriage: The Inside Story of How Same-Sex Couples Took on the Politicians and Pundits—and Won* (Lebanon, NH: ForeEdge, 2014), 229–236; see Thalia Zepatos and Lanae Erickson Hatalsky, "The Marriage Movement's Secret Weapon: Radical Cooperation," *Huffington Post*, June 26, 2015.

6. Amy Simon (political pollster, Goodwin Simon Strategic Research), interview with author, 2014; Phyllis Watts (applied social psychologist), interview with author, 2014. The ads against Proposition 8 can be viewed on YouTube. See, e.g., https://www.youtube.com/watch?v=b9T7ux8M4Go.

7. "Knowing Someone Gay/Lesbian Affects Views of Gay Issues," Gallup, May 29, 2009, http://www.gallup.com/poll/118931/knowing-someone-gay-lesbian-affects-views-gay-issues.aspx.

8. Zepatos and Hatalsky, "The Marriage Movement's Secret Weapon."

9. William N. Eskridge Jr., *The Case for Same-Sex Marriage: From Sexual Liberty to Civilized Commitment* (New York: Free Press, 1996), 1; Evan Wolfson, *Why Marriage Matters: America, Equality, and Gay People's Right to Marry* (New York: Simon & Schuster, 2004), 6.

10. See "The Gardner Family—Why Marriage Matters Maine," at https://www.youtube.com/watch?v=gvJrmMK8Hl0.

11. Michael C. Dorf and Sidney Tarrow, "Strange Bedfellows: How an Anticipatory Countermovement Brought Same-Sex Marriage into the Public Arena," *Law & Social Inquiry* 39 (2014): 449–473.

CHAPTER 6: THE END GAME: *WINDSOR* AND *OBERGEFELL*

1. *United States v. Windsor*, 133 S. Ct. 2675 (2013).

2. Mary Bonauto (Director, Civil Rights Project, GLAD), interview with author, 2013; Evan Wolfson (Founder and President, Freedom to Marry), interview with author, 2014; Matthew Coles (Deputy Legal Director and Director of Center for Equality, ACLU), interview with author, 2014; James Esseks (Director, ACLU LGBT Rights Project), interview with author, 2015.

3. "Frequently Asked Questions: *Gill et al. v. Office of Personnel Manament et al.,*" GLAD, March 3, 2009, http://www.glad.org/uploads/docs/publications /gill-v-opm-faq.pdf, 3–4.

4. *Romer v. Evans,* 517 U.S. 620 (1996); Wolfson, interview; Bonauto, interview.

5. *United States v. Windsor,* 133 S. Ct. 2675, 2693 (2013) (quoting H.R. Rep. No. 104–664, 16).

6. *Lawrence v. Texas,* 539 U.S. 558, 577–78 (2003).

7. John Aravosis, "Obama defends DOMA in federal court. Says banning gay marriage is good for the federal budget. Invokes incest and marrying children," http://americablog.com/2009/06/obama-defends-doma-in-federal -court-says-banning-gay-marriage-is-good-for-the-federal-budget-invokes -incest-and-marrying-children.html; Editorial, "A Bad Call on Gay Rights," *New York Times,* June 16, 2009.

8. *Massachusetts v. U.S. Dep't of HHS,* 682 F.3d 1 (1st Cir. 2012); *Windsor v. United States,* 699 F.3d 169 (2d Cir. 2012).

9. *United States v. Windsor,* 133 S. Ct. 2675 (2013); Complaint in *Gill v. Office of Personnel Management,* Civ. Action No. 1:09-cv-10309 (D. Mass. filed July 31, 2009), available at http://www.glad.org/doma/documents/. Heather Gerken has argued that the *Windsor* decision's reliance on both states' rights and individual rights reasoning can be defended on the ground that the Court was "clearing the channels of political change" by striking down DOMA, thereby allowing the issue of same-sex marriage to continue to develop in the states. Heather Gerken, "*Windsor's* Mad Genius: The Interlocking Gears of Rights and Structure," *Boston University Law Review* 95 (2015): 587. It is true that our federalist system facilitated development of the marriage equality right in the states, as I have shown here. But it doesn't follow that *Windsor* cleared the channels for political change at the state level. DOMA, enacted in 1996, did not foreclose any state from recognizing same-sex marriage, as we have seen; indeed, twelve states and the District of Columbia had done so by the time *Windsor* was decided. Thus, *Windsor* did not clear the channels; they were already clear. DOMA or no DOMA, the way was open for states to develop the constitutional claim of marriage equality—and they did just that.

10. "Marriage Rulings in the Courts," Freedom to Marry, updated March 2, 2015, http://www.freedomtomarry.org/pages/marriage-rulings-in-the-courts?

(stating that there have been sixty-five victories for same-sex marriage since *Windsor* in 2013).

11. Robert Barnes, "Supreme Court Declines to Review Same-Sex Marriage Cases, Allowing Unions in 5 States," *Washington Post*, October 6, 2014.

12. *DeBoer v. Snyder*, 772 F.3d 388 (6th Cir. 2014), *cert. granted by Tanco v. Haslam*, 135 S. Ct. 1040 (2015).

13. *Obergefell v. Hodges*, No. 14–556, Transcript of Oral Argument, Apr. 28, 2015, 39–41, at http://www.supremecourt.gov/oral_arguments/argument _transcript/2014.

14. *Loving v. Virginia*, 388 U.S. 1 (1967) (right to marry person of another race); *Turner v. Safley*, 482 U.S. 78 (1987) (right to marry of prisoners); *Zablocki v. Redhail*, 434 U.S. 374 (1978) (right to marry of fathers who are behind on child custody payments); *Pierce v. Society of Sisters*, 268 U.S. 510 (1925) (right to decide how to educate one's children); *Lawrence v. Texas*, 539 U.S. 558 (2003) (right of consenting adults to sexual intimacy); *Griswold v. Connecticut*, 381 U.S. 479 (1965) (right to use contraception); *Roe v. Wade*, 410 U.S. 113 (1973) (right to abortion)

15. *Obergefell v. Hodges*, 135 S. Ct. 2584 (2015).

16. Ibid. at 2627, 2628, 2630 n. 22, 2631 (Scalia, dissenting); ibid. at 2626 (Roberts, dissenting).

17. *Obergefell*, 135 S. Ct. at 2621–22 (Roberts, dissenting); see also William Baude, "Is Polygamy Next?" *New York Times*, July 21, 2015.

18. *Baker v. Nelson*, 409 U.S. 810 (1972).

19. *Obergefell*, 135 S. Ct. at 2626 (Roberts, dissenting); id. at 2602, 2590 (majority opinion).

PART TWO: RIGHT TO BEAR ARMS

1. *Silveira v. Lockyer*, 312 F.3d 1052, 1063 (9th Cir. 2002) (quoting Warren Burger, "The Right to Bear Arms," *Parade*, January 14, 1990, 4); *District of Columbia v. Heller*, 554 U.S. 570 (2008); *United States v. Miller*, 307 U.S. 174 (1939).

2. See *Heller*, 554 U.S. at 636 (Stevens, dissenting). Justice Breyer wrote a separate dissent, joined by Justices Stevens, Ginsburg, and Souter, which maintained, again largely on originalist grounds, that even if the Second Amendment protected an individual right to bear arms, the DC gun regulation should be upheld, because it was similar to gun regulations that existed at the time of the Second Amendment's adoption. Ibid. at 681 (Breyer, dissenting).

3. John Houston Craige, *The Practical Book of American Guns* (New York, NY: Bramhall House, 1950), 84–93.

4. Josh Sugarmann, *National Rifle Association: Money, Firepower, and Fear* (Washington, DC: National Press Books, 1992), 27 (quoting the NRA's magazine, *Arms and the Man*).

5. Ibid. at 30.

6. *United States v. Tot*, 131 F.2d 261, 266 (3d Cir. 1942), *rev'd on other grounds*, 319 U.S. 463 (1943).

7. *Stevens v. United States*, 440 F.2d 144, 149 (6th Cir. 1971); *United States v. Nelsen*, 859 F.2d 1318, 1320 (8th Cir. 1988).

CHAPTER 7: ONE STATE AT A TIME

1. "Congress Threshes Out Gun Law Issue," *American Rifleman*, November 1968, 22–25. In 2001, *Fortune* named the NRA the most powerful lobbying group in Washington, ahead of even the AARP. See Joel Achenbach, Scott Higham, and Sari Horwitz, "How NRA's True Believers Converted a Marksmanship Group into a Mighty Gun Lobby," *Washington Post*, January 12, 2013 (calling it "arguably the most powerful lobbying organization in the nation's capital, and certainly one of the most feared"). In 2014, the Pew Research Center described the NRA as "one of the most politically powerful advocacy groups in the U.S." Pew Research Center, "5 Facts about the NRA and Gun Control," Pew Research Center, http://www.pewresearch.org/fact-tank/2014/04/24/5 -facts-about-the-nra-and-guns-in-america/. For an excellent general overview of the NRA's political activities, see Michael Waldman, *The Second Amendment: A Biography* (New York: Simon & Schuster, 2014), 87–137.

2. Joseph Tartaro, *Revolt at Cincinnati* (Buffalo, NY: Hawkeye Publishing, 1981), 17–18.

3. Ibid. at 36. After the revolt, the *American Rifleman*, the NRA's flagship magazine, described the NRA as follows: "The NRA, the foremost guardian of the traditional American right to 'keep and bear arms,' believes that every law-abiding citizen is entitled to the ownership and legal use of firearms, and that every reputable gun owner should be an NRA member." Scott Melzer, *Gun Crusaders: The NRA's Culture War* (New York: New York University Press, 2009), 89.

4. Ronald G. Shaiko and Marc A. Wallace, "Going Hunting Where the Ducks Are: The National Rifle Association and the Grassroots," in *The Changing Politics of Gun Control*, eds. John M. Bruce and Clyde Wilcox (Lanham, MD: Rowman & Littlefield, 1998), 155, 157–158. The NRA's budget varies from year to year, but according to the NRA's 990 tax report for 2013, 12 percent of the organization's expenditures were for legislative services.

5. *Quilici v. Village of Morton Grove*, 695 F.2d 261, 270 (7th Cir. 1982).

6. Dave Kopel, "Against All Odds," NRA, http://www.davekopel .org/2A/Mags/A1F/Against-all-odds.html; "Guns, Marriage, and the Constitution," Open Society Foundations, January 23, 2013, http://www.open societyfoundations.org/events/guns-marriage-and-the-constitution.

7. Michael C. Bender, "Pistol-Packing Grandma Helps NRA Push State Pro-Gun Laws," *Bloomberg*, May 11, 2012 (quoting Richard Feldman).

8. Marion Hammer (former President, NRA), interview with author, 2013.

9. Darwin Farrar, "In Defense of Home Rule: California's Preemption of Local Firearms Regulation," *Stanford Law & Policy Review* 7 (1996): 54 (quoting Institute for Legislative Action, NRA, NRA-ILA State Legislative Issue Brief, 1986); Kristin A. Goss, *Disarmed: The Missing Movement for Gun Control in America* (Princeton, NJ: Princeton University Press, 2006), 163–165; Alexander DeConde, *Gun Violence in America: The Struggle for Control* (Boston: Northeastern University Press, 2001), 217 (discussing the invalidation of a 1982 San Francisco ordinance enacted after the assassination of Harvey Milk on preemption grounds).

10. *District of Columbia v. Heller*, 554 U.S. 570, 601–03 (2008) (quoting state constitutional provisions); Nicholas J. Johnson, "A Second Amendment Moment: The Constitutional Politics of Gun Control," *Brooklyn Law Review* 71 (2005–2006): 735–739.

11. For discussion of concealed carry laws, see DeConde, *Gun Violence in America*, 230. Hammer, interview.

12. David McDowall, Colin Loftin, and Brian Wiersema, "Easing Concealed Firearms Laws: Effects on Homicide in Three States," *Journal of Criminal Law & Criminology* 86 (1995): 194; Bender, "Pistol-Packing Grandma"; *Moore v. Madigan*, 702 F.3d 933 (7th Cir. 2012); David Heinzmann, Monique Garcia, and Jeremy Gorner, "How Gun Law Works: Likely 2014 Before Permits Issued," *Chicago Tribune*, July 10, 2013.

13. The NRA has conducted this campaign with the assistance of American Legislative Exchange Council (ALEC), a conservative partnership that develops and advocates for model legislation in state assemblies. Adam Weinstein, "How the NRA and Its Allies Helped Spread a Radical Gun Law Nationwide," *Mother Jones*, June 7, 2012. Cynthia V. Ward, "'Stand Your Ground' and Self-Defense," *American Journal of Criminal Law* 42 (forthcoming 2015); "'Stand Your Ground' Policy Summary," Law Center to Prevent Gun Violence, http://smartgunlaws.org/stand-your -ground-policy-summary/; Erica Goode, "N.R.A.'s Influence Seen in Expansion of Self-Defense Laws," *New York Times*, April 12, 2013.

14. Chuck Cunningham (Director of Political Affairs, NRA-ILA) interview with author, 2014; Dave Kopel, "Against All Odds"; Johnson, "A Second

Amendment Moment," 778–779; DeConde, *Gun Violence in America*, 221. The NRA obtained subsequent victories on similar measures in New Hampshire and Nevada. California's gun control ballot initiative was winning by a two-to-one margin at the outset of the campaign. DeConde, *Gun Violence in America*, 221–222.

15. Those states are Alabama, Alaska, Arizona, Arkansas, Colorado, Delaware, Florida, Georgia, Idaho, Indiana, Kansas, Kentucky, Louisiana, Maine, Michigan, Mississippi, Missouri, Montana, Nebraska, Nevada, New Hampshire, North Carolina, North Dakota, Ohio, Oklahoma, Pennsylvania, South Carolina, South Dakota, Tennessee, Texas, Utah, Virginia, Washington, and West Virginia. See "Gun Industry Immunity Policy Summary," Law Center to Prevent Gun Violence, http://smartgunlaws.org/gun-industry-immunity-policy-summary/.

16. David Lehman, e-mail to author, March 26, 2015; Chris Cox (Executive Director, NRA-ILA), interview with author, 2015; Memorandum from Wes Anderson and Kayla Dunlap to NRA Leadership, NRA National Survey—Counting the Votes, July 27, 2015 (on file with author). For a list of the NRA's state associations, see http://clubs.nra.org/state-associations.aspx.

17. Goss, *Disarmed*; Osha Gray Davidson, *Under Fire: The NRA and the Battle for Gun Control* (Iowa City, IA: University of Iowa Press, 1998), 65–66, 80–81.

18. Cox, interview.

19. Cunningham, interview.

20. Cunningham, interview; "Guns, Marriage, and the Constitution," Open Society Foundations (quoting David Keene); David A. Fahrenthold, "NRA's Support Helped Put Sanders in Congress," *Washington Post*, July 20, 2015, A1.

21. Scott Higham and Sari Harowitz, "NRA Tactics: Take No Prisoners," *Washington Post*, May 18, 2013.

22. Cunningham, interview.

23. For, example, when the Supreme Court ruled that police may conduct arrests for suspected felonies in public places without first obtaining a warrant, it cited that practice at the time of the Founding as justification for its decision. *United States v. Watson*, 423 U.S. 411, 418–420 (1976).

24. As Heather Gerken has argued: "National movements rarely begin as national movements. They start small and grow. Leaders of social movements have long used states and localities as sites for organizing and as testing grounds for their ideas. These local platforms don't just facilitate early mobilization, but also help connect nascent movements to the large and powerful policymaking networks that fuel national politics. . . . As with a clock, you need movement from lots of small, interlocking gears to move a bigger one."

Heather K. Gerken, "*Windsor*'s Mad Genius: The Interlocking Gears of Rights and Structure," *Boston University Law Review* 95 (2015): 597.

CHAPTER 8: REVISIONIST HISTORY

1. Stephen Halbrook (gun rights scholar and attorney), interview with author, 2013.

2. Halbrook, interview; Robert Elias, Abu Shanab, and Stephen P. Halbrook, *Social Philosophy: From Plato to Che* (Dubuque, IA: Kendall Hunt Publishing, 1972).

3. Halbrook, interview; Carl T. Bogus, "The History and Politics of Second Amendment Scholarship: A Primer," *Chicago-Kent Law Review* 76 (2000–2001): 8–10. Stephen P. Halbrook, "The Jurisprudence of the Second and Fourteenth Amendments," *George Mason University Law Review* 4 (1981): 1. For a full listing of Halbrook's gun rights scholarship, see http://www.stephenhalbrook.com/articles.html.

4. Don B. Kates Jr., "Handgun Prohibition and the Original Meaning of the Second Amendment," *Michigan Law Review* 82 (1983): 204.

5. Bogus, "The History and Politics of Second Amendment Scholarship," 8–10.

6. See, e.g., Kates, "Handgun Prohibitions"; Stephen P. Halbrook, *The Founders' Second Amendment: Origins of the Right to Bear Arms* (Chicago: Independent Institute, 2008); Stephen P. Halbrook, *That Every Man Be Armed: The Evolution of a Constitutional Right* (Albuquerque, NM: University of New Mexico Press, 1984).

7. Garry Wills, "To Keep and Bear Arms," *New York Review of Books*, September 21, 1995; *District of Columbia v. Heller*, 554 U.S. 570, 636 (2008) (Stevens, dissenting); Michael Waldman, *The Second Amendment: A Biography* (New York: Simon & Schuster, 2014), 3–84; Paul Finkelman, "'A Well Regulated Militia': The Second Amendment in Historical Perspective," in *The Second Amendment in Law and History*, ed. Carl T. Bogus (New York: New Press, 2000), 117.

8. Glenn Harlan Reynolds, "A Critical Guide to the Second Amendment," *Tennessee Law Review* 62 (1995): 461.

9. *McDonald v. City of Chicago*, 561 U.S. 742 (2010); Brief for 55 Members of the United States Senate, et al., as Amici Curiae in Support of Respondent, *District of Columbia v. Heller*, 554 U.S. 570 (2008) (No. 07–290).

10. Bogus, "The History and Politics of Second Amendment Scholarship," 8–9 and n. 28.

11. Joyce Malcolm (Patrick Henry Professor of Constitutional Law and the Second Amendment, George Mason University School of Law), interview

with author, 2015; Joyce Lee Malcolm, *To Keep and Bear Arms: The Origins of an Anglo-American Right* (Cambridge, MA: Harvard University Press, 1996); Joyce Lee Malcolm, "The Right of the People to Keep and Bear Arms," *Hastings Constitutional Law Quarterly* 10 (1983): 303.

12. *Heller*, 554 U.S. at 593–94 (quoting William Blackstone, *Commentaries on the Laws of England* (1769)).

13. Sanford Levinson, "The Embarrassing Second Amendment," *Yale Law Journal* 90 (1989): 637.

14. Bogus, "The History and Politics of Second Amendment Scholarship," 14.

15. Akhil Reed Amar, *The Bill of Rights* (New Haven, CT: Yale University Press, 1998), 257–268 (arguing that Fourteenth Amendment incorporated a personal right to bear arms); William Van Alstyne, "The Second Amendment and the Personal Right to Arms," *Duke Law Journal* 43 (1994): 1236; Leonard W. Levy, *Origins of the Bill of Rights* (New Haven, CT: Yale University Press, 1999), 133; Laurence H. Tribe, *American Constitutional Law* 898–92 n.213 (St. Paul, MN: Foundation Press, 3d ed., 2000); Amitai Etzioni, "Are Liberal Scholars Acting Irresponsibly on Gun Control?" *Chronicle of Higher Education*, April 6, 2001.

16. Malcolm, interview.

17. For an excellent overview of the broader social and political developments that contributed to the result in *Heller*, see Reva Siegel, "Dead or Alive: Originalism as Popular Constitutionalism in *Heller*," *Harvard Law Review* 122 (2008): 191.

CHAPTER 9: FEDERAL FORUMS

1. Glenn Kessler, "Update: Obama Claim on Background Checks Moved from 'Verdict Pending' to 2 Pinocchios," *Washington Post*, January 25, 2013; "April 2013 Post-ABC Poll–Economy, Gun Control and Immigration Issues," *Washington Post*, April 16, 2013; Robert A. Levy, "A Libertarian Case for Expanding Gun Background Checks," *New York Times*, April 26, 2013.

2. Ben Jacobs, "Gun Control Push Fails to Materialize in Congress after Charleston Shooting," *Guardian*, June 24, 2015; Richard Fausset and Alan Blinder, "South Carolina Settles Its Decades-Old Dispute over a Confederate Flag," *New York Times*, July 9, 2015.

3. Subcomm. on the Const. of S. Judiciary Comm., 97th Cong., Rep. on The Right to Keep and Bear Arms (Comm. Print 1982).

4. Ibid. at 12 and appendices. The first essay is by David Hardy, whose appended biography identifies him as a member of the NRA and of the "Legal Advisory Board" of the Second Amendment Foundation. In an earlier article,

Hardy described himself as a consultant to the NRA. David T. Hardy, "Firearms Ownership and Regulation: Tackling an Old Problem with Renewed Vigor," *William & Mary Law Review* 20 (1978): 235. In his Senate submission, Hardy expressly thanked Bob Dowlut, of the NRA's general counsel office, for his assistance. The second essay is by Steve Halbrook, the NRA's go-to lawyer and scholar. And the third is by three attorneys from the NRA's general counsel office.

5. Michael Barone and Grant Ujifusa, *The Almanac of American Politics: 1984* (Washington, DC: National Journal, 1984), 1190.

6. Firearms Owners' Protection Act, Pub. L. No. 99–308, § 1(b) (1986).

7. *Printz v. United States*, 521 U.S. 898 (1997); ibid. at 938 (Thomas, concurring).

8. Adam Winkler, *Gunfight: The Battle over the Right to Bear Arms in America* (New York: W.W. Norton, 2011), 38–39.

9. Ibid.; Carl Bogus, "How Gun Control Got Murdered," *American Prospect*, August 30, 2011; Doug Mataconis, "Bill Clinton Warns Democrats Against Overreaching On Gun Debate," *Outside the Beltway*, January 20, 2013; Bill Clinton, *My Life* (New York: Knopf, 2004), 629.

10. Chris Cox (Executive Director, NRA-ILA) interview with author, 2015; Joe Conason, "The Salon Interview: Bill Clinton," *Salon*, June 25, 2004; Michael Waldman, *The Second Amendment: A Biography* (New York: Simon & Schuster, 2014), 118. For NRA expenditures in support of George W. Bush and against Al Gore in 2000, see "Influence Explorer: Data," The Sunlight Foundation, http://data.influenceexplorer.com/ (looking at all types of contributions made by the NRA for and against the presidential candidates during the 1999–2000 cycle). See also Winkler, *Gunfight*, 46.

11. *Whose Right to Keep And Bear Arms? The Second Amendment as a Source of Individual Rights:* Hearing Before the Subcomm. on the Constitution, Federalism, and Property Rights of the S. Comm. on the Judiciary, 105th Cong. 2d Sess. 18 (1998); Hearing on United States Dep't of Justice before the H. Judiciary Comm., 107th Cong. 1st Sess. 60–62 (2001) (reproducing Att'y Gen. John Ashcroft, Letter to James J. Baker, May 17, 2001). For Halbrook's analysis, see Stephen P. Halbrook, "Attorney General Ashcroft & the Second Amendment," NRA-ILA, https://www.nraila.org/articles/20040701/attorney-general-ashcroft-the-second-1.

12. *United States v. Emerson*, 270 F.3d 203 (5th Cir. 2001), *cert. denied*, 536 U.S. 907 (2002); Linda Greenhouse, "U.S., in a Shift, Tells Justices Citizens Have a Right to Guns," *New York Times*, May 8, 2002; Brief for the United States in Opposition to Petition for Certiorari, *Emerson*, 536 U.S. 907 (2002) (No. 01–8780). The brief appended Ashcroft's letter to federal prosecutors, and included the following statement: "In its brief to the court of appeals, the

government argued that the Second Amendment protects only such acts of firearm possession as are reasonably related to the preservation or efficiency of the militia. The current position of the United States, however, is that the Second Amendment more broadly protects the rights of individuals, including persons who are not members of any militia or engaged in active military service or training, to possess and bear their own firearms, subject to reasonable restrictions designed to prevent possession by unfit persons or to restrict the possession of types of firearms that are particularly suited to criminal misuse."

13. *Whether the Second Amendment Secures an Individual Right*, Opinion of the Office of Legal Counsel (Aug. 24, 2004).

14. The act begins by finding that the Second Amendment "protects the rights of individuals, including those who are not members of a militia or engaged in military service or training, to keep and bear arms." Protection of Lawful Commerce in Arms Act, Pub. L. No. 109–92, 119 Stat. 2095, § 2(a) (2) (2005).

CHAPTER 10: SUPREME RECOGNITION

1. Robert Levy (Chairman of the Board, Cato Institute), interview with author, 2013; Adam Winkler, *Gunfight: The Battle over the Right to Bear Arms in America* (New York: W.W. Norton, 2011), 45–55.

2. Chris Cox (Executive Director, NRA-ILA), interview with author, 2015; Levy, interview; "Guns, Marriage, and the Constitution," Open Society Foundations, January 23, 2014, http://www.opensocietyfoundations.org /events/guns-marriage-and-constitution.

3. Levy, interview; *Parker v. District of Columbia*, 478 F.3d 370 (D.C. Cir. 2007); Winkler, *Gunfight*, 91–92.

4. Levy, interview; Winkler, *Gunfight*, 127–129.

5. Brief for the National Rifle Association and the NRA Civil Rights Defense Fund as Amici Curiae in Support of Respondent, *District of Columbia v. Heller*, 554 U.S. 570 (2008) (No. 07–290); Brief for 55 Members of the United States Senate, et al., as Amici Curiae in Support of Respondent, *District of Columbia v. Heller*, 554 U.S. 570 (2008) (No. 07–290).

6. For NRA expenditures in support of Bush and against Kerry in 2004, see "Influence Explorer: Data," The Sunlight Foundation, http://data .influenceexplorer.com/ (looking at all types of contributions made by the NRA for and against the presidential candidates during the 2003–2004 cycle).

7. Cox, interview.

8. *National Rifle Association v. City of Chicago*, 567 F.3d 856 (7th Cir. 2009) (appealing three consolidated cases).

9. *McDonald v. City of Chicago*, 561 U.S. 742 (2010). Brief for Amicus Cur-

iae Senator Kay Bailey Hutchison, et al. in Support of Petitioners, *McDonald v. City of Chicago*, 561 U.S. 742 (2010) (No. 08–1521).

10. Winkler, *Gunfight*, 291 (quoting Henigan).

11. Some courts have agreed with the NRA's First Amendment analogy, at least in principle. See, e.g., *United States v. Marzzarella*, 614 F.3d 85, 96–97 (3d Cir. 2010) ("The right to free speech, an undeniably enumerated fundamental right, is susceptible to several standards of scrutiny, depending upon the type of law challenged and the type of speech at issue. We see no reason why the Second Amendment would be any different" [citation omitted].) Most courts have been more deferential. See, e.g., *United States v. Rene E.*, 583 F.3d 8 (1st Cir. 2009) (upholding prohibition on possession of handguns by minors); *United States v. Masciandaro*, 638 F.3d 458 (4th Cir. 2011) (upholding prohibition of carrying loaded handgun in national park, as applied to defendant); *National Rifle Association of America, Inc. v. Bureau of Alcohol, Tobacco, Firearms, and Explosives*, 700 F.3d 185 (5th Cir. 2012) (upholding statute that prohibited otherwise licensed dealers from selling handguns to individuals under the age of twenty-one); *United States v. Skoien*, 614 F.3d 638 (7th Cir. 2010) (upholding statute prohibiting those convicted for domestic violence misdemeanors from carrying arms); *United States v. Henry*, 688 F.3d 637 (9th Cir. 2012) (upholding prohibition on possession of homemade machine gun); *People v. Jason K.*, 116 Cal. Rptr. 3d 443, 450, 453 (Cal. Ct. App. 2010) (upholding confiscation of firearm from person who was involuntarily committed to a psychiatric hospital under state law requiring such confiscation for five years); *DiGiacinto v. Rector & Visitors of George Mason University*, 704 S.E.2d 365, 369–70 (Va. 2011) (upholding regulation prohibiting the possession of firearms on a university campus). See generally Benjamin H. Weissman, "Regulating the Militia Well: Evaluating Choices for State and Municipal Regulators Post-*Heller*," *Fordham Law Review* 82 (2014): 3504–3509 (describing case law post-*Heller*); Jeff Golimowski, "Pulling the Trigger: Evaluating Criminal Gun Laws in a Post-*Heller* World," *American Criminal Law Review* 49 (2012): 1599–1622 (same).

CHAPTER 11: PEOPLE POWER

1. NRA's IRS Form 990, 2013.

2. David Lehman (Deputy Executive Director and General Counsel, NRA), interview with author, 2013.

3. The NRA-ILA staff numbers as of March 2015 were Executive Affairs (7); Federal Affairs (10); State & Local Affairs (25); Public Affairs (3); Grassroots (11); Finance (8); Research & Information (8); Conservation, Wildlife & Natural Resources (1); and Office of Legislative Counsel (5). Wendy Martin (Executive

Assistant, NRA-ILA State and Local Affairs), e-mail to author, March 23, 2015; see also NRA's IRS Form 990 for 2013 (reporting 785 employees and 150,000 volunteers).

4. "Blood Money: How the Gun Industry Bankrolls the NRA," Violence Policy Center, April 2011, www.vpc.org/studies/bloodmoney.pdf.

5. Chris Cox (Executive Director, NRA-ILA), interview with author, 2015; "Guns, Marriage, and the Constitution," Open Society Foundations, January 23, 2013, http://www.opensocietyfoundations.org/events/guns-marriage-and-constitution.

6. Osha Gray Davidson, *Under Fire: The NRA and the Battle for Gun Control* (Iowa City, IA: University of Iowa Press, 1998), 80–81. According to Gregg Lee Carter, editor of *Guns in American Society* (2nd ed., Santa Barbara, CA: ABC-CLIO), "The issue is not so much how much the NRA gives any senator or member of the House, it's how they can make their lives miserable. And how they make their lives miserable is they e-mail 'em, they call 'em, they fax 'em, they show up at meetings. The typical person who is for gun control is very different from the [pro-gun] person calling you or being right there, being an annoyance, hassling you personally. They're much more activist than the other side and that's what really produces their gains." Quoted in Alan Berlow and Gordon Witkin, "Gun lobby's money and power still holds sway over Congress," May 1, 2013, Center for Public Integrity, http://www.publicintegrity.org/2013/05/01/12591/gun-lobbys-money-and-power-still-holds-sway-over-congress.

7. Bruce Drake, "5 Facts about the NRA and guns in America," Pew Research Center, April 24, 2014.

8. "Guns, Marriage, and the Constitution," Open Society Foundations (quoting David Keene).

9. Cox, interview.

10. For Wayne LaPierre quotation discussing the Brady Bill, see Winkler, *Gunfight*, 70; for LaPierre's remarks on Sandy Hook, see "CPAC NRAL Wayne LaPierre's full speech," dailycaller.com, March 15, 2013, http://dailycaller.com/2013/03/15/cpac-nra-wayne-lapierres-full-speech/.

11. Dan Baum, *Gun Guys: A Road Trip* (New York: Alfred A. Knopf, 2013), 270.

12. Kayne Robinson (former President and Executive Director, NRA), interview with author, 2013; Jim Baker (Executive Director, NRA-ILA), interview with author, 2013. Joel Achenbach, Scott Higham, and Sari Horwitz, "How NRA's True Believers Converted a Marksmanship Group into a Mighty Gun Lobby," *Washington Post*, January 12, 2013.

13. Robinson interview and Cox interview; Chuck Cunningham (Director of Political Affairs, NRA-ILA), interview with author, 2013.

14. "Guns, Marriage, and the Constitution," Open Society Foundations panel (quoting David Keene).

15. "CPAC NRA–Wayne LaPierre's full speech," dailycaller.com, March 15, 2013, at http://dailycaller.com/2013/03/15/cpac-nra-wayne-lapierres-full -speech/; Scott Higham and Sari Horwitz, "NRA Tactics: Take No Prisoners," *Washington Post*, May 18, 2013.

PART THREE: HUMAN RIGHTS IN THE WAR ON TERROR

1. William Rehnquist, *All the Laws but One: Civil Liberties in Wartime* (New York: Knopf, 1998), 221.

2. See generally Geoffrey Stone, *Perilous Times: Free Speech in Wartime* (New York: W. W. Norton, 2005); Rehnquist, *All the Laws but One.*

3. See, e.g., *Youngstown Sheet & Tube Co. v. Sawyer*, 343 U.S. 579 (1952); *Ex parte Milligan*, 71 U.S. 2 (1866); *Ex parte Mitsuye Endo*, 323 U.S. 283 (1944); *New York Times Co. v. United States*, 403 U.S. 713 (1971); *United States v. Robel*, 389 U.S. 258 (1967); *Scales v. United States*, 367 U.S. 203 (1961); see generally David Cole, "Judging the Next Emergency: Judicial Review and Individual Rights in Times of Crisis," *Michigan Law Review* 101 (2003): 2565.

4. One group, the Bill of Rights Defense Committee, did pursue a state strategy. It ran a remarkably successful campaign to convince municipal and state governing bodies to adopt resolutions objecting to the excesses of the war on terror. By 2004, more than 340 towns and cities across the country, including New York, Los Angeles, Chicago, Dallas, Philadelphia, and Washington, DC, had adopted such resolutions, as had four state legislatures—in Vermont, Alaska, Maine, and Hawaii. The measures were almost entirely symbolic, but each one provided an opportunity for public engagement, debate, and education. David Cole, "Uncle Sam Is Watching You," *New York Review of Books*, November 18, 2004.

CHAPTER 12: "COMPLETELY HOPELESS"

1. *Haitian Ctrs. Council v. McNary*, 969 F.2d 1326 (2d Cir. 1992); Michael Ratner, "How We Closed the Guantanamo HIV Camp: The Intersection of Politics and Litigation," *Harvard Human Rights Journal* 11 (1998): 187; Michael Ratner (President Emeritus, CCR), interview with author, 2013.

2. William Safire, "Seizing Dictatorial Power," *New York Times*, November 15, 2001; William Safire, "Essay: Kangaroo Court," *New York Times*, November 26, 2001.

3. *Johnson v. Eisentrager*, 339 U.S. 763, 768, 779 (1950).

4. *Rasul v. Bush*, 215 F. Supp.2d 55, 73 (D.D.C. 2002), *aff'd, Al Odah v. United States*, 321 F.3d 1134 (D.C. Cir. 2003).

5. *Hamdi v. Rumsfeld*, 542 U.S. 507, 532–33 (2004).

6. *Hamdan v. Rumsfeld*, 548 U.S. 557, 628–35 (2006). The Supreme Court's decision in *Rasul*, extending statutory habeas jurisdiction to Guantánamo prisoners, was superseded by the Detainee Treatment Act of 2005. Pub. L. No. 109–148, § 1003, 119 Stat. 2680, 2739–40 (codified at 42 U.S.C. § 2000dd (2006)), which sought to repeal habeas corpus for Guantánamo detainees. The Court's decision in *Hamdan*, which interpreted the Detainee Treatment Act as not applicable to pending cases, was in turn superseded by the Military Commissions Act of 2006, Pub. L. No. 109–336, 120 Stat. 2600 (2006), which repealed habeas corpus for Guantánamo detainees for all cases. The Court then declared that repeal unconstitutional in *Boumediene v. Bush*, 553 U.S. 723 (2008).

7. Military Commissions Act of 2006, P.L. 109–366, 120 Stat. 2600 (codified at 10 U.S.C. §§948–50).

8. Stephen Gillers, "The Torture Memo," *Nation*, April 9, 2008; S. Select Comm. on Intelligence, Study of the CIA's Detention and Interrogation Program, S.Rep. No. 113–7 (1st sess. 2013); David Cole, "Torture: No One Said No," *New York Review of Books* Blog, March 5, 2015; Alberto Gonzales, "Martial Justice, Full and Fair," *New York Times*, November 30, 2001; "President Bush's Speech on Terrorism," transcript, *New York Times*, September 6, 2006; Eur. Parl. Ass., Comm. on Legal Affairs and Human Rights, *Alleged Secret Detentions and Unlawful Inter-State Transfers Involving Council of Europe Member States*, 17th sitting, Doc. 10977 (2006). Extraordinary renditions to torture were employed most aggressively in the first few years of the Bush administration, and there are far fewer reports thereafter. Jane Mayer, *The Dark Side: The Inside Story of How The War on Terror Turned into a War on American Ideals* (New York: Knopf Doubleday, 2009), 101–138 (describing extraordinary renditions); Letter from Alberto R. Gonzales, Attorney General, to Patrick Leahy, Chairman, Senate Judiciary Committee, and Arlen Specter, Ranking Minority Member, Senate Judiciary Committee (January 17, 2007) (describing the end of unilateral electronic surveillance program and issuance of a judicial order authorizing surveillance); Foreign Intelligence Surveillance Act, Pub. L. No. 95–511, 92 Stat. 1782 (codified as amended at 50 U.S.C. §§ 1801–1862 (2006)). See also Protect America Act of 2007, Pub. L. No. 110–55, § 105B(g), 121 Stat. 552, 553–554 (2007) (legislative authorization for electronic surveillance program).

9. Joe Nocera, "The Detainees' Dilemma," *New York Times*, April 29, 2013 (Bush released more than five hundred from Guantánamo).

10. George W. Bush, *Decision Points* (New York: Crown, 2010), 169–170; Dick Cheney and Liz Cheney, *In My Time: A Personal and Political Memoir* (New York: Threshold, 2011), 360.

11. See, e.g., *Zadvydas v. Davis*, 533 U.S. 678, 693 (2001) (citing *Eisentrager* for proposition that "it is well established that certain constitutional protections available to persons inside the United States are unavailable to aliens outside of our geographic borders"); *United States v. Verdugo-Urquidez*, 494 U.S. 250, 269 (1990); *Ex Parte Quirin*, 317 U.S. 1 (1942). Jack Goldsmith and Cass R. Sunstein, "Military Tribunals and Legal Culture: What a Difference Sixty Years Makes" (John M. Olin Law and Economics Working Paper No. 153, 2d series, University of Chicago, Chicago, 2002). Still another indication that doctrine did not compel the results is that in two of the cases, *Hamdan* and *Boumediene*, the legal standards that proved decisive were extremely open-ended, and could not be said to "dictate" any particular result. Both decisions turned on questions of "practicability," a pragmatic assessment that hardly provides a judicial line in the sand. In *Hamdan*, the Court ruled that the Uniform Code of Military Justice, a federal statute, required that military commissions conform to the procedures the military uses to try its own troops unless those procedures would be "impracticable," *Hamdan*, 548 U.S. at 622. In *Boumediene*, the Court ruled that habeas corpus would extend to Guantánamo only if it were neither "impracticable" nor "anomalous" to do so, *Boumediene*, 553 U.S. at 770. Had the Court wanted to defer to the executive, the legal standards in these two cases plainly would have permitted it to do so.

12. *Braden v. 30th Judicial Circuit Court of Kentucky*, 410 U.S. 484 (1973). The case is cited only in two footnotes in *Rasul*'s opening brief in the Supreme Court, without development of the argument Justice Stevens eventually adopted to distinguish *Eisentrager*. Petitioners' Brief, *Rasul v. Bush*, 542 U.S. 466 (2004) (Nos. 03–334, 03–343) at 12 n.8, 38 n.41.

13. *Hamdan*, 548 U.S. at 559, 626–27; See Brief for Petitioner, *Hamdan v. Rumsfeld*, 548 U.S. 557 (2006) (No. 05–184) at 48–50. The "non-international armed conflict" argument was advanced in an amicus brief submitted on behalf of three law professors—Ryan Goodman, Derek Jinks, and Anne-Marie Slaughter. See Amicus Brief of Professors Ryan Goodman et al., *Hamdan v Rumsfeld*, 548 U.S. 557 (2006) (No. 05-184) at 18–23.

CHAPTER 13: KOREMATSU'S LEGACY

1. Peter Irons, *Justice at War* (Oxford: Oxford University Press, 1983), 85.

2. *Korematsu v. United States*, 333 U.S. 214, 233 (1944) (Murphy, dissenting).

3. John Christgau, "Collins versus the World: The Fight to Restore Citizenship to Japanese American Renunciants of World War II," in vol. 3 of *The Mass Internment of Japanese Americans and the Quest for Legal Redress*, ed. Charles McClain, (New York: Routledge, 1994).

4. For a detailed analysis of the 1967–1971 campaign to repeal the Emergency Detention Act, see Raymond Okamura, "Campaign to Repeal the Emergency Detention Act: Background and History," *Amerasia Journal* 2 (1974): 72–94.

5. Mitchell T. Maki, Harry H. Kitano, and S. Megan Berthold, *Achieving the Impossible Dream: How Japanese Americans Obtained Redress* (Champaign, IL: University of Illinois Press, 1999), 65, 82–91; "Paying a Debt to Interned Japanese," *New York Times*, November 12, 1979, A21.

6. See, e.g., *Korematsu v. United States*, 584 F.Supp 1406 (N.D. Cal. 1984) (vacating Korematsu's conviction).

7. Statement of the Congress, 50 App. U.S.C. § 1989a; Civil Liberties Act of 1988, 50 App. U.S.C. § 1989b et seq.; "About Fred Korematsu," Fred T. Korematsu Institute, http://korematsuinstitute.org/institute/aboutfred/.

8. See David Cole, *Enemy Aliens: Double Standards and Constitutional Freedoms in the War on Terrorism* (New York: New Press, 2004), 99, 261 n.42 (citing cases and articles by the justices criticizing *Korematsu*). The only justice who had not condemned Korematsu was Justice David Souter, who had not had the opportunity to address the issue. Justice Scalia compared *Korematsu* to *Dred Scott*. *Stenberg v. Carhart*, 530 U.S. 914, 953 (2000) (Scalia, dissenting).

CHAPTER 14: AT HOME ABROAD

1. *Hamdi v. Rumsfeld*, 542 U.S. 466, 514 (2004).

2. Elizabeth Bumiller and Steven Lee Myers, "Senior Administration Officials Defend Military Tribunals for Terrorist Suspects," *New York Times*, November 15, 2001, B6.

3. William Lietzau (former Deputy Assistant Secretary of Defense for Rule of Law and Detainee Policy), interview with author, 2013; email from William Lietzau to author, September 17, 2015.

4. Tom Malinowski, "Extraordinary Rendition, Extraterritorial Detention, and Treatment of Detainees," *Human Rights Watch*, July 25, 2007.

5. USA Freedom Act, Pub. L. No. 114–23, 129 Stat 268.

6. Peter Baker, "Obama Apologizes After Drone Kills American and Italian Held by Al Qaeda," *New York Times*, April 23, 2015.

7. "An Incursion of Briefs at Guantanamo," *Washington Post*, October 2, 2007; Lauren Collins, "Underwear Diplomacy," *New Yorker*, Oct. 29, 2007.

8. "Prison Camp Pictures Spark Protests," BBC News, January 20, 2002; Tom Baldwin, et al., "Straw Protests to U.S. Over al-Qaeda Prisoners," *Times* (London), January 15, 2002; Tom Baldwin, "Blair Backs Shackling of al-Qaeda Suspects," *Times* (London), January 17, 2002; David Charter and Sam Lister, "Camp X-Ray Threatens to Split Allies," *Times* (London), January 21, 2002; Tom Baldwin and Roland Watson, "Bagels and the Koran for Prisoners of Camp X-Ray," *Times* (London), January 22, 2002.

9. Michael Evans, et al., "Cuba Britons Barred from PoW Status," *Times* (London), January 28, 2002.

10. *Abbasi & Another v. Secretary of State for Foreign Affairs* [2002] EWCA Civ. 1598, at Par. 66; see also ibid. at 107.

11. Gareth Peirce (attorney and human rights activist), interview with author, 2013; Clive Stafford Smith (Director, Reprieve), interview with author, 2013; Daniel McGrory, "Taleban Tourists on Their Way Home," *Times* (London), February 20, 2004 (reporting that charging Abbasi and Begg in military court was turning point); Clare Dyer, "Law Lord Castigates U.S. Justice: Guantanamo Bay Detainees Facing Trial by Kangaroo Court," *Guardian*, November 26, 2003; Peter Riddell, "Guantanamo Bay gives rough justice a bad name," *Times* (London), July 10, 2003; Rosemary Bennett and Helen Rumblelow, "Blair calls for British terror suspects to be tried at home," *Times* (London), July 11, 2003; Michael Evans and Greg Hurst, "Britons Detained in Cuba Face Long Wait for a Hearing," *Times* (London), July 12, 2003.

12. Tim Reid, "Bush Agrees to Suspend Legal Action on Detained Britons," *Times* (London), July 19, 2003; Tim Reid, "No Death Penalty for Terror Suspects," *Times* (London), July 23, 2003; "Britons Detained at Guantanamo Bay," *Times* (London), November 18, 2003; "Fair Trial Plea," *Times* (London), November 19, 2003.

13. "Verbatim," *Times* (London), November 27, 2003; Dyer, "Law Lord Castigates U.S. Justice"; "British Detainees at Guantanamo Bay," *Times* (London), December 2, 2003; Brief of 175 Members of Both Houses of Parliament as Amici Curiae in Support of Petitioners, *Rasul v. Bush*, 542 U.S. 466 (2004) (Nos. 03–334, 03–434).

14. "Guantanamo Britons Home Next Week," *Times* (London), March 4, 2004; Tom Baldwin and James Bone, "Remaining Four Face Trial in America," *Times* (London), March 10, 2004; Andrew Clennell, "Freed Briton Tells of Camp X-Ray Ordeal," *Times* (London), March 12, 2004; Laura Peek and Steve Bird, "Beatings Not as Bad as Psychological Torture, Says Freed Briton," *Times* (London), March 13, 2004; David Rose, "How We Survived Jail Hell," *Guardian*, March 13, 2004; David Rose, "How We Survived Jail Hell, Part Two," *Guardian*, March 13, 2004.

15. Suzanne Goldenberg, et al., "Guantanamo Abuse Same as Abu Ghraib, Say Britons," *Guardian*, May 13, 2004.

16. David Charter, "Get Real on Fight for Trial, Says Hoon," *Times* (London), June 26, 2004; Tania Branigan, "Guantanamo Bay Prisoner's Letter Claims He Was Witness to Murders," *Guardian*, October 1, 2004.

17. Richard Beeston, "Britain Attacks U.S. Abuses in Iraq and Guantanamo Bay," *Times* (London), November 11, 2004; "Red Cross Finds Detainee Abuse in Guantanamo," *New York Times*, November 30, 2004.

18. David Rose, "Guantanamo Briton 'In Handcuff Torture,'" *Observer*, January 1, 2005.

19. Roland Watson, "Guantanamo May Close," *Times* (London), June 10, 2005 (archived article available at http://www.thetimes.co.uk/tto/news/world /article1980264.ece); Tom Baldwin, "Guantanamo Should Shut Says Bush," *Times* (London), June 15, 2006; Bronwen Maddox, "Pressure Grows on Guantanamo," *Times* (London), May 11, 2006; Sean O'Neill, et al, "Release of Inmates from Guantanamo Leaves Britain Facing a Security Headache," *Times* (London), August 8, 2007.

20. See, e.g., Sean O'Neill, "MI5 Knew About Torture, Says Guantanamo Briton Binyam Mohamed," *Times* (London), May 7, 2008; Clive Stafford Smith, "Why Has the Government Forsaken Binyam Mohamed?" *Independent*, May 30, 2008; Anil Dawar, "Guantanamo Bay: Death Row Inmate in Plea to PM," *Guardian*, May 30, 2008; "Briton in U.S. Terror Jail Facing Charges," *Yorkshire Post*, May 31, 2008; Benedict Moore-Bridger, "Guantanamo 'Londoner' in Plea to No 10," *Evening Standard*, May 30, 2008.

21. *R. (Binyam Mohamed) v. Secretary of State for Foreign Commonwealth Affairs*, 2008 EWHC 2048 (Admin) 23.

22. *R. (Binyam Mohamed) v. Secretary of State for Foreign Commonwealth Affairs*, 2008 EWHC 2100 (Admin) 22.

23. William Glaberson, "U.S. Drops Charges for 5 Guantanamo Detainees," *New York Times*, October 21, 2008; *R. (Binyam Mohamed) v. Secretary of State for Foreign Commonwealth Affairs*, 2008 EWHC 2519, at 29–30, 40–53 (Admin).

24. William Glaberson, "Questioning 'Dirty Bomb' Plot, Judge Orders U.S. to Yield Papers on Detainee," *New York Times*, October 31, 2008.

25. *Al Habashi v. Bush*, 591 F. Supp. 2d 1 (Mem) (D.D.C. 2008).

26. The former attorney general, Lord Goldsmith, appeared on BBC Radio 4 on January 2, 2009, urging the United Kingdom to take more Guantanamo prisoners in order to speed up closure of the camp, which he called a "symbol of injustice." The Foreign Office commented that its "priority has been to get Binyam Mohamed back to the U.K." Deborah Summers and Patrick Wintour, "U.K. Should Take in More Guantanamo Prisoners to Help Close

Camp, Says Goldsmith," *Guardian*, January 2, 2009; *R. (Binyam Mohamed) v. Secretary of State for Foreign Commonwealth Affairs*, 2008 EWHC 2048 (Admin) 23, at Par. 107. In September 2015, the United States announced that it would release Shaker Aamer, the last of the British residents held at Guantánamo. Charlie Savage, "Pentagon Says High-Profile Guantánamo Detainee Will Be Sent to Britain," *New York Times*, September 25, 2015.

27. For a list of investigations and reports on renditions and "black sites" by the Council of Europe, the European Parliament, Italy, Spain, Canada, Germany, Poland, Sweden, and others, see "Investigations into CIA Renditions," Open Society Foundations, November, 2013, http://www .opensocietyfoundations.org/fact-sheets/investigations-cia-renditions. For the European Court of Human Rights decisions finding complicity on the part of Poland and Macedonia, see *Al-Nashiri v. Poland*, App. No. 28761/11 Eur. Ct. H.R. (2014), http://hudoc.echr.coe.int/eng?i=001–146044; *El-Masri v. Macedonia*, App. No. 393630/09 Eur. Ct. H.R. (2012), http:// hudoc.echr.coe.int/eng?i=001–115621; "Globalizing Torture: CIA Secret Detention and Extraordinary Rendition" Open Society Justice Initiative, February, 2013, http://www.opensocietyfoundations.org/reports/globalizing -torture-cia-secret-detention-and-extraordinary-rendition; "CIA 'Extraor-dinary Rendition' Flights, Torture, and Accountability: A European Ap-proach," European Center for Constitutional and Human Rights, March, 2008, http://www.ecchr.eu/en/documents/publications/ecchr-publications /articles/publications.html (reviewing universal jurisdiction concept and sta-tus of investigations and prosecutions).

28. Matthew Waxman (former deputy assistant secretary of defense for detainee affairs), interview with author, 2012.

29. Daniel Fried (Special Envoy for Closure of the Guantánamo Defense Facility, United States Department of State), interview with author, 2012.

30. Fried, interview; Richard Fontaine (former foreign policy advisor to Senator John McCain), interview with author, 2012.

CHAPTER 15: MESSAGES AND MESSENGERS

1. For examples of early civil society critiques, see, e.g., "Presumption of Guilt: Human Rights Abuses of Post-September 11 Detainees," Human Rights Watch, August 15, 2002; "Amnesty International's Concerns Regarding Post September 11 Detentions in the U.S.A," Amnesty International, March 14, 2002, http://www.refworld.org/docid/3c9082a14.html. For representative news accounts picking up on these themes, see, e.g., Christopher Drew and Judith Miller, "A Nation Challenged: The Detainees; Though Not Linked to

Terrorism, Many Detainees Cannot Go Home," *New York Times*, February 18, 2002, A1; Dan Eggen, "U.S. Holds 6 of 765 Detained in 9/11 Sweep," *Washington Post*, December 12, 2002, A20; William Glaberson, "A Nation Challenged: Secret Trials; Closed Immigration Hearings Criticized as Prejudicial," *New York Times*, December 7, 2001, B7; William Glaberson, "A Nation Challenged: U.S. Asks to Use Secret Evidence in Many Cases of Deportation," *New York Times*, December 9, 2001, 1B.

2. Johan Steyn, "Guantanamo Bay: The legal black hole," *International & Comparative Law Quarterly* 53 (January 2004): 1 (delivered as 27th F. A. Mann Lecture, November 25, 2003); *Abbasi v. Secretary of State* [2002] EWCA (Civ) 1598, 2002 All ER (D) (UK); see Brief of Diego C. Asencio, et al., as Amici Curiae in Support of the Petitioners, *Rasul v. Bush*, 542 U.S. 466 (2004) (Nos. 03–334, 03–343) at 8–9.

3. Jack Goldsmith, *Power and Constraint: The Accountable President After 9/11* (New York: W. W. Norton, 2012), 168.

4. For reports or press statements from advocacy organizations, see, e.g., "The Law of War in the War on Terror," Human Rights Watch, https://www .hrw.org/news/2003/12/22/law-war-war-terror ("War rules should be used in such cases only when no law-enforcement system exists, and the other conditions of war are present, not when the rule of law happens to produce inconvenient results."); see also Fiona Doherty and Deborah Pearlstein, eds., "Assessing the New Normal: Liberty and Security for the Post-September 11 United States," Lawyers Committee for Human Rights, 2003 ("But the new normal is also defined by dramatic changes in the relationship between the U.S. government and the people it serves—changes that have meant the loss of particular freedoms for some, and worse, a detachment from the rule of law as a whole. As this report details, the United States has become unbound from the principles that have long held it to the mast."). For press commentary adopting a similar frame, see, e.g., "The Rule of Law at Gitmo," *New York Times*, November 10, 2004; "Reaffirming the Rule of Law," *New York Times*, June 29, 2004; Steve Hymon, "Rights a Victim of Terror War, U.S. Judge Says," *Los Angeles Times*, November 7, 2004; David Ignatius, "The Balance of Justice Amid a War," *Washington Post*, July 2, 2004.

The supporting amicus briefs in the enemy combatant cases show that the civil society frame was put forward consistently and forcefully. The American Bar Association's amicus brief in *Boumediene* insisted, in its Summary of Argument, that "the writ of habeas corpus is the cornerstone of the rule of law and should not be weakened by exceptions of the kind relied on by the Court of Appeals. . . . Exceptions to the writ, even in times of emergency, are inconsistent with the rule of law and threaten to produce tyranny." Brief for American Bar Association as Amicus Curiae Supporting Petitioners, *Boumediene v. Bush*, 553 U.S. 723 (2008) (Nos. 06–1195, 06–1196), at 5, 6. The United Nations High Commissioner for Human Rights, Louise Arbour, filed an amicus brief in *Boumediene*, arguing that the United States was obliged by the International Covenant on Civil and Political Rights to provide judicial review, and maintaining that "a State's compliance with its obligations under the Covenant and other human rights treaties reflects its basic commitment to the rule of law." Brief for United Nations High Commissioner for Human Rights as Amicus Curiae Supporting Petitioners, *Boumediene v. Bush*, 553 U.S. 723 (2008) (Nos. 06–1195, 06–1196), at 3. Meanwhile in the *Rasul* case, three former American prisoners of war filed a brief emphasizing the importance of enforceable international law for our own soldiers when they are taken prisoners of war. Brief of Former American Prisoners of War as Amici Curiae in Support of Petitioners, *Rasul v. Bush*, 542 U.S. 466 (2004) (Nos. 03–334, 03–343); See also Brief for Coalition of Non-Governmental Organizations as Amici Curiae Supporting Petitioners, *Boumediene v. Bush*, 553 U.S. 723 (2008) (Nos. 06–1195, 06–1196), at 12; Brief for 383 United Kingdom and European Parliamentarians Supporting Petitioners, *Boumediene v. Bush*, 553 U.S. 723 (2008) (Nos. 06–1196 and 06–1195), at 13.

5. Howard Bashman, "Coverage of Today's Third Circuit Oral Argument in Case Challenging the INS's Blanket Closure of Terror-Related Deportation Proceedings," How Appealing Blog, Sept. 17, 2002, http://howappealing.abovethelaw.com/2002_09_01_appellateblog_archive.html. I was co-counsel for North Jersey Media Group in this case.

6. *Hamdi v. Rumsfeld*, 542 U.S. at 536; *Boumediene*, 553 U.S. at 797; *Rasul*, 542 U.S. at 483–84; *Hamdan*, 548 U.S. at 631.

7. *Rumsfeld v. Padilla*, 542 U.S. 426 (2004); *Ashcroft v. Iqbal*, 556 U.S. 662, 678–682 (2009); *Holder v. Humanitarian Law Project*, 561 U.S. 1 (2010); *Ashcroft v. al-Kidd*, 563 U.S. 731 (2011); *Clapper v. Amnesty Int'l-U.S.A.*, 133 S. Ct. 1138 (2013). In some cases, especially the "material support" case, the deference is dramatic; there, the Court held that Congress could make it a crime to advocate for peace and human rights if one did so with a designated "terrorist organization," because even if the advocacy led only to peaceful conduct, it might burnish the organization's image and thereby allow it to garner more support for terrorist ends. I represented the Humanitarian Law Project in this case.

8. Leif Hendrickson (retired Marine Corps brigadier general), David Irvine (retired US Army strategic intelligence officer and former Utah state legislator); John D. Hutson (retired rear admiral and dean of University of New Hampshire Law School), Charles Otstott (retired US Army lieutenant

general), and John Adams (retired US Army brigadier general), joint interview with author, 2013.

9. In their first letter, for example, to President Bush in 2005, seven former generals and an admiral argued that torture was wrong for multiple reasons: "Experience and common sense have shown that information gathered through physical torture or dehumanizing humiliation is notoriously unreliable. It has a demoralizing, dehumanizing effect not only on those subject to violations, but also on our own troops—those who may be directly involved, and those unfairly tarred with the same brush. Violation of basic rules of international law by those acting under U.S. control also puts U.S. forces at greater risk. It jeopardizes the United States' moral and practical authority to promote democracy and human rights abroad. And it seriously undermines the United States' ability to 'win the hearts and minds' of the global community—a goal essential to defeating terrorism over the long term." Letter from David Brahms et al. to President Bush (September 7, 2004), http://www.humanrightsfirst.org/wp-content/uploads/pdf/090108-ETN -sept7-mil-ldrs-ltr.pdf.

10. "Transcript: Mike Huckabee on 'FOX News Sunday,'" Fox News, January 6, 2008, http://www.foxnews.com/story/2008/01/07/transcript-mike -huckabee-on-fox-news-sunday/.

11. "The Democratic Presidential Debate on MSNBC," *New York Times*, September 26, 2007.

12. Charles Krulak and Joseph Hoar, "It's Our Cage, Too," *Washington Post*, May 17, 2007.

13. John McCain, "Statement of Senator John McCain on the Detainee Amendments to the Defense Authorization Bill: (1) The Army Field Manual and (2) Cruel, Inhumane, and Degrading Treatment," http://www .mccain.senate.gov/public/index.cfm/speeches?ID=73cf492c-0b17-44c7 -b824-7dd7d09ff972; Elisa Massimino (President, Human Rights First), interview with author, 2012 (recounting story of McCain meeting with Cheney).

14. Richard Fontaine (former foreign policy advisor to Senator John McCain), interview with author, 2012.

15. Eric Schmitt, "Exception Sought in Detainee Abuse Ban," *New York Times*, October 25, 2005.

16. See Senate Select Committee on Intelligence, *Study of the CIA's Detention and Interrogation Program*, S.Rep. No. 113–7 (1st sess. 2013), at Findings and Conclusions, 15.

17. For cases dismissing challenges to torture and rendition, see *Arar v. Ashcroft*, 585 F.3d 559 (2d Cir. 2009); *Mohamed v. Jeppesen DataPlan, Inc.*, 579 F.3d 943 (9th Cir. 2009); *Rasul*, 542 U.S. 466. For the Justice Department

memos finding that coercive CIA interrogation tactics were not barred by the Torture Convention or the Geneva Conventions, see David Cole, *The Torture Memos: Rationalizing the Unthinkable* (New York: New Press, 2009) (reproducing and analyzing the memos).

CHAPTER 16: TRANSFORMATIVE TRANSPARENCY

1. Scott Shane, "A.C.L.U Lawyers Mine Documents for Truth," *New York Times*, August 29, 2009; Jameel Jaffer (Deputy Legal Director, ACLU), interview with author, 2015; *ACLU v. Dep't of Defense*, 339 F. Supp. 2d 501, 503–04 (S.D.N.Y. 2004).

2. Neil A. Lewis, "F.B.I. Memos Criticized Practices at Guantánamo," *New York Times*, December 7, 2004; Kate Zernike, "Newly Released Reports Show Early Concern on Prison Abuse," *New York Times*, January 6, 2005; Barton Gellman and R. Jeffrey Smith, "Report to Defense Alleged Abuse By Prison Interrogation Teams," *Washington Post*, December 8, 2004; Eric Lichtblau, "Justice Dept. Opens Inquiry Into Abuse of U.S. Detainees," *New York Times*, January 14, 2005; Eric Lichtblau and Scott Shane, "Report Details Dissent on Guantánamo Tactics," *New York Times*, May 21, 2008; Randall Mark Schmidt and John T. Furlow, "Army Regulation 15–6: Final Report. Investigation into FBI Allegations of Detainee Abuse at Guantanamo Bay, Cuba Detention Facility," United States Department of Defense, April 1, 2005 (declassified report available through the Torture Database, maintained by the ACLU, https://www.thetorturedatabase.org /files/foia_subsite/pdfs/schmidt_furlow_report.pdf).

3. David Johnston, "C.I.A. Tells of Bush's Directive on the Handling of Detainees," *New York Times*, November 15, 2006; Conor Friedersdorf, "The Ongoing Disgrace of Gitmo," *Atlantic*, April 25, 2011; Neil A. Lewis, "Documents Say Detainees Cited Koran Abuse," *New York Times*, May 26, 2005; Neil A. Lewis and David Johnston, "New F.B.I. Files Describe Abuse of Iraq Inmates," *New York Times*, December 21, 2004; Gail Gibson, "FBI Agents Complained of Prisoner Abuse," *Baltimore Sun*, December 21, 2004.

4. See, e.g., Mark Mazzetti and Scott Shane, "Interrogation Memos Detail Harsh Tactics by the C.I.A.," *New York Times*, April 16, 2009; Mark Mazzetti, "Report Provides New Details on C.I.A. Prisoner Abuse," *New York Times*, August 22, 2009.

5. Jameel Jaffer and Amrit Singh, *Administration of Torture* (New York: Columbia University Press, 2007).

6. See Larry Siems, *The Torture Report: What the Documents Say about America's Post 9/11 Torture Program* (New York: OR Books, 2011).

7. I participated in the readings in New York and Washington. See David Cole, "Reading American Torture," *New York Review of Books* Blog, October 15, 2009, http://www.nybooks.com/blogs/nyrblog/2009/oct/15/reading-american-torture/.

8. For court refusals to review challenges to torture and rendition, see, e.g., *Arar v. Ashcroft*, 585 F.3d 559 (2d Cir. 2009) (en banc) (dismissing constitutional and Torture Victim Protection Act suit for rendition of Maher Arar, a Canadian, to Syria to be tortured there); *El-Masri v. United States*, 479 F.3d 296 (4th Cir. 2007) (dismissing on "state secrets" grounds a constitutional challenge to the rendition and torture of Khaled El-Masri, who the U.S. concedes, was picked up in a case of mistaken identity).

9. Letter from James Madison to W. T. Barry, August 4, 1822, reprinted in *The Founders' Constitution*, vol. 1, eds., Philip B. Kurland and Ralph Lerner (Chicago: University of Chicago Press, 1987), 690.

10. See generally, Daniel Patrick Moynihan, *Secrecy: The American Experience* (New Haven, CT: Yale University Press, 1999); Scott Horton, *Lords of Secrecy: The National Security Elite and America's Stealth Warfare* (New York: Nation Books, 2015); Jack Goldsmith, "My Speech at ODNI Legal Conference: 'Toward Greater Transparency of National Security Legal Work,'" Lawfare Blog, May 12, 2015, http://www.lawfareblog.com/my-speech-at-odni-legal-conference-toward-greater-transparency-of-national-security-legal-work/ (arguing that national security officials too often jeopardize their credibility "through exaggerated claims about the national security harms of disclosure"). On the role of leaks, see Rahul Sagar, *Secrets and Leaks: The Dilemma of State Secrecy* (Princeton, NJ: Princeton University Press, 2013); Jack Goldsmith, *Power and Constraint: The Accountable Presidency After 9/11* (New York: W. W. Norton, 2012).

University of Pennsylvania law professor Seth Kreimer has shown that civil liberties and human rights groups employed a "strategy of transparency" not only in connection with the abuse of detainees overseas, but more broadly. Seth F. Kreimer, "Rays of Sunlight in a Shadow 'War': FOIA, the Abuses of Anti-Terrorism, and the Strategy of Transparency," *Lewis & Clark Law Review* 11 (2007): 1168–1185; see also Seth F. Kreimer, "The Freedom of Information Act and the Ecology of Transparency," *University of Pennsylvania Journal of Constitutional Law* 10 (2008): 1011. When the Bush administration used immigration authority to lock up thousands of Arabs and Muslims in the United States in the first two years after 9/11, civil liberties groups used FOIA and related litigation to challenge the secrecy surrounding the practice. Suits challenging immigration proceedings closed to the public succeeded in three district courts and one court of appeals, and the Bush administration then ended the practice before the Supreme Court could weigh in. *Detroit Free Press v. Ashcroft*, 195 F. Supp. 2d 937 (E.D. Mich. 2002), aff'd, 303 F.3d 681 (6th Cir. 2002); *Haddad v. Ashcroft*, 221 F. Supp. 2d 799 (E.D. Mich. 2002), appeal dismissed as moot, 76 Fed. App'x 672 (6th Cir. 2003); *North Jersey Media Group, Inc. v. Ashcroft*, 205 F. Supp. 2d 288 (D.N.J. 2002), rev'd, 308 F.3d 198 (3d Cir. 2002). A suit seeking the identity of those detained as "of interest" to the 9/11 investigation did not obtain the detainees' names but did divulge official records regarding the numbers of persons detained, how long they were in jail, and under what authority. *Center for National Security Studies v. U.S. Dep't of Justice*, 215 F. Supp. 2d 94 (D.D.C. 2002), aff'd in part and rev'd, 331 F.3d 918 (D.C. Cir. 2003). Other FOIA requests forced the government to provide records on its enforcement of controversial investigative authorities established in the USA Patriot Act.

11. See, e.g. "Tipton three complain of beatings," BBC News, March 14, 2004, http://news.bbc.co.uk/2/hi/uk_news/3509750.stm; Andrew Clennell, "Camp Delta Briton: We Were Chained and Beaten," *Times* (London), March 12, 2004 (archived article available at http://www.thetimes.co.uk/tto/news /article1892892.ece); David Rose, "How We Survived Jail Hell," *Guardian*, March 13, 2004; Transcript of Oral Argument, April 28, 2004, *Hamdi v. Rumsfeld*, 542 U.S. 507 (2004), at 48–50, http://www.supremecourt.gov/oral _arguments/argument_transcript/03-6696.pdf; Transcript of Oral Argument, April 28, 2004, *Rumsfeld v. Padilla*, 542 U.S. 426 (2004) (No. 03–1027), at 22– 23, http://www.supremecourt.gov/oral_arguments/argument_transcript/03 -1027.pdf.

12. Seymour M. Hersh, "Torture at Abu Ghraib," *New Yorker*, May 10, 2004.

13. Mark Denbeaux et al., "Report on Guantanamo Detainees: A Profile of 517 Detainees through Analysis of Department of Defense Data," Seton Hall University School of Law, Center for Policy and Research, February 8, 2006. This report and others written by the Denbeaux brothers have been cited by, among others, CBS, ABC, NBC, MSNBC, CNN, NPR, PBS, BBC, Fox News, the *New York Times*, the *Wall Street Journal*, the *Washington Post*, and many other news outlets. See Guantánamo Reports, http://law.shu .edu/policy-research/guantanamo-reports.cfm.

14. Mark Denbeaux et al., "No-Hearing Hearings: An Analysis of the Proceedings of the Combatant Status Review Tribunals at Guantanamo," *Seton Hall Law Review* 41 (2011): 1231. For news reports, see, e.g., Andrew Cohen, "Gitmo Justice Is a Joke," *Washington Post*, November 30, 2006; Ben Fox, "Report: Gitmo Detainees Denied Witnesses," *Washington Post*, November 16, 2006. Brief for the Boumediene Petitioners, *Boumediene v. Bush*, 553 U.S. 723 (2007) (Nos. 06–1195, 06–1196) at 20, 30, 32.

15. Brief Amicus Curiae of the American Civil Liberties Union in Support of Petitioner, *Hamdan v. Rumsfeld*, 548 U.S. 557 (2006) (No. 05–184); Brief of Amicus Curiae Human Rights First in Support of Petitioner, *Hamdan v. Rumsfeld*, 548 U.S. 557 (2006) (No. 05–184); Charles Babington and Michael Abramowitz, "U.S. Shifts Policy on Geneva Conventions," *Washington Post*, July 12, 2006; Mark Mazzetti and Kate Zernike, "White House Says Terror Detainees Hold Basic Rights," *New York Times*, July 12, 2006; George W. Bush, "President Discusses Creation of Military Commission to Try Suspected Terrorists" (remarks in East Room, the White House, September 6, 2006).

CHAPTER 17: THE OBAMA DIFFERENCE

1. Press Release, The White House, "Remarks by the President on National Security," May 21, 2009; "President Obama's Statement on the Memos," *New York Times*, April 16, 2009.

2. *Al-Bihani v. Obama*, 590 F.3d 866 (D.C. Cir. 2010), reh'g en banc denied, 619 F.3d 1 (D.C. Cir. 2010) (en banc court declares the panel opinion's statements about international law to be nonbinding dicta).

3. Kenneth Roth, "Obama and Counterterrorism: The Ignored Record," *New York Review of Books*, February 5, 2015.

4. Catherine Ho, "ACLU Lays Off 7 Percent of National Staff," *Washington Post*, April 2, 2015; Stephen Shapiro (Legal Director, ACLU), interview with author, 2015; Carolyn Chambers (Associate Executive Director, CCR), e-mail to author, July 16, 2015.

5. See Ryan Goodman, "Advancing Human Rights from Within: The Footsteps of Harold Koh," *Just Security*, April 10, 2015; Press Release, Human Rights First, "United States Clarifies Position on Extraterritorial Application of Torture Convention," November 12, 2014.

6. Margo Schlanger, "Intelligence Legalism and the National Security Agency's Civil Liberties Gap," *Harvard National Security Journal* 6 (2015): 112; Harold Koh (former legal advisor, United States Department of State), interview with author, 2014.

7. Koh, interview; John Bellinger (former legal advisor, United States Department of State), interview with author, 2013. Matthew Waxman, who worked with Bellinger in the Bush administration, expressed similar views. Matthew Waxman (former deputy assistant secretary of defense for detainee affairs), interview with author, 2012.

8. See, e.g., "'Will I Be Next?' U.S. Drone Strikes in Pakistan," Amnesty International, October 23, 2013; "Living Under Drones: Death, Injury, and Trauma to Civilians from US Drone Practices in Pakistan," International

Human Rights and Conflict Resolution Clinic at Stanford Law School and Global Justice Clinic at NYU School of Law, September, 2012; "Death by Drone: Civilian Harm Caused by U.S. Targeted Killings in Yemen," Open Society Justice Initiative, April, 2015; "A Wedding That Became a Funeral," Human Rights Watch, February 19, 2014; "Between a Drone and Al-Qaeda: The Civilian Cost of U.S. Targeted Killings in Yemen," Human Rights Watch, October 22, 2013; see also "Drone Strikes: America's Deadly Drones Programme," Reprieve, http://www.reprieve.org.uk/case-study/drone-strikes/; Peter Bergen and Katherine Tiedemann, "The Year of the Drone: An Analysis of U.S. Drone Strikes in Pakistan, 2004–2010," New America Foundation, February 24, 2010; Dana Milbank, "A Human Face for Drone Victims," *Washington Post*, October 29, 2013; Rachel Stohl, "Recommendations and Report of the Stimson Task Force on U.S. Drone Policy," Stimson Center, June 30, 2014.

9. "UN Expert Criticizes 'Illegal' Targeted Killing Policies and Calls on the US to Halt CIA Drone Killings," United Nations Office of the High Commissioner for Human Rights, June 2, 2010 (discussing report by Philip Alston, A/HRC/14/24/Add.6); Ben Emmerson (Special Rapporteur), "Annual Report of the Special Rapporteur to the Human Rights Council," United Nations General Assembly, A/HRC/25/59, March 11, 2014.

10. Jo Becker and Scott Shane, "Secret 'Kill List' Proves a Test of Obama's Principles and Will," *New York Times*, May 29, 2012; Daniel Klaidman, *Kill or Capture: The War on Terror and the Soul of the Obama Presidency* (Boston, MA: Houghton Mifflin Harcourt, 2012).

11. For negative foreign commentary, see, e.g., Steve Boxer, "War Really Has Now Become a Videogame," *Guardian*, July 16, 2008; Owen Bowcott, "Robot Warfare: Campaigners Call for Tighter Controls of Deadly Drones," *Guardian*, September 16, 2010; "We Don't Need No Stinking Authority," *Economist*, January 14, 2010; Klaus Brinkbäumer and John Goetz, "Obama's Shadowy Drone War: Taking Out the Terrorists by Remote Control," *Der Spiegel*, October 12, 2010. Mary Dobbing, Amy Hailwood, and Chris Cole, *Convenient Killing: Armed Drones and the 'PlayStation' Mentality* (Oxford, England: Fellowship of Reconciliation, 2010). Dennis C. Blair, "Drones Alone Are Not the Answer," *New York Times*, August 14, 2011 (advising abandonment of drone killing in Pakistan).

12. *Al-Aulaqi v. Obama*, 727 F. Supp. 2d 1 (D.D.C. 2010). For representative press coverage, see Glenn Greenwald, "Lawsuit Challenges Obama's Power to Kill Citizens without Due Process," *Salon*, August 30, 2010; Mark Tran, "Legal Challenge to US Assassination Policy Divides Rights Groups," *Guardian*, November 15, 2010; Nick Baumann, "Judge Dismisses Anwar

al-Awlaki Targeted Killing Lawsuit," *Mother Jones*, December 7, 2010; Charlie Savage, "Suit over Targeted Killings Is Thrown Out," *New York Times*, December 7, 2010.

13. Aaron Blake, "Poll Shows Huge Support for Rand Paul's Filibuster Stance on Drone Attacks," *Washington Post*, March 25, 2013.

14. Harold Koh, "The Obama Administration and International Law" (speech, Annual Meeting of the American Society of International Law, Washington, DC, May 25, 2010); Koh, interview.

15. See, e.g., John O. Brennan, "The Efficacy and Ethics of U.S. Counterterrorism Strategy" (speech, Woodrow Wilson International Center for Scholars, Washington, DC, April 30, 2012); Eric Holder (speech, Northwestern University School of Law, Chicago, IL, March 5, 2012); Stephen Preston, "The Legal Framework for the United States' Use of Military Force Since 9/11" (speech, Annual Meeting of the American Society of International Law, Washington, DC, April 10, 2015).

16. Press Release, The White House, "Remarks by the President at the National Defense University," May 23, 2013.

17. *New York Times Co. v. U.S. Dep't of Justice*, 752 F.3d 123, 138 (2d Cir. 2014) opinion revised and superseded, 756 F.3d 100 (2d Cir. 2014) opinion amended on denial of reh'g, 758 F.3d 436 (2d Cir. 2014) supplemented, 762 F.3d 233 (2d Cir. 2014) and reh'g denied, 762 F.3d 233 (2d Cir. 2014) and reh'g granted, 756 F.3d 97 (2d Cir. 2014); See also Benjamin Weiser, "U.S. Ordered to Release Memo in Awlaki Killing," *New York Times*, April 21, 2014.

18. "All Estimated Casualties in Pakistan by Year (correct as of 17/7/14)," Bureau of Investigative Journalism, https://www.thebureauinvestigates.com /wp-content/uploads/2012/07/All-Totals-Dash54.jpg; see also Bill Roggio, "Charting the Data for US Airstrikes in Pakistan, 2004–15," *Long War Journal*, http://www.longwarjournal.org/pakistan-strikes. For similar trends in Yemen, see "Charting the Data for US Airstrikes in Yemen, 2002–15," *Long War Journal*, http://www.longwarjournal.org/yemen-strikes/.

19. See Ali Gharib, "Human Rights Groups to Obama: Investigate All Civilian Victims of Drone Strikes," *Nation*, May 13, 2015.

CONCLUSION

1. Don E. Ferenbacher, ed., *Lincoln: Speeches and Writings: 1832–1858* (Des Moines, IA: Library of America, 1989), 524–525 (from a debate at Ottawa, IL, on August 21, 1858).

2. Advocates of constitutional changes who seek to cut back on rights will often have a tougher challenge than those seeking to expand rights. Given the

Notes

importance of finding alternative forums to press one's claims, efforts to cut back on an existing constitutional protection are likely to be more difficult than efforts to expand constitutional protections. When, as with abortion, the Court has declared that the Constitution protects a right, that declaration forecloses many of the forums that are available where one seeks to expand rather than to contract a constitutional right. When the US Constitution did not recognize same-sex marriage, it remained open to states to do so. But when the Constitution forbids prohibitions of abortion, the states are bound to respect that prohibition, and there are fewer available channels for reform.

3. Gareth Peirce (attorney and human rights activist), interview with author, 2013.

4. Roberto Mangabeira Unger and Cornel West, *The Future of American Progressivism: An Initiative for Political and Economic Reform* (Boston: Beacon Press, 1998).

Index

Sam Hollenshead

DAVID COLE is the national legal director of the ACLU and the Hon. George J. Mitchell Professor in Law and Public Policy at Georgetown University Law Center. A regular contributor to the *New York Review of Books* and the legal affairs correspondent for the *Nation*, he has also written for the *New York Times*, *Washington Post*, *New Republic*, *New Yorker*, *Atlantic*, *Wall Street Journal*, and *Los Angeles Times*, among others. He is the author of numerous books, including *Enemy Aliens* and *No Equal Justice*, and received the inaugural Norman Dorsen Presidential Prize from the ACLU for lifetime commitment to civil liberties. Cole lives in Washington, DC.